One Nation, Indivisible?

A Study of Secession and the Constitution

by

Robert F. Hawes Jr.

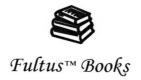

Fultus™ Books

One Nation, Indivisible?

A Study of Secession and the Constitution

Robert F. Hawes Jr.

ISBN 1-59682-091-8

Published by Fultus Corporation

Corporate Web Site: *http://www.fultus.com*
Fultus eLibrary: *http://elibrary.fultus.com*
Online Book Superstore: *http://store.fultus.com*
Writer Web Site *http://writers.fultus.com/hawes/*

Table of Contents

This book is dedicated to those incomparable men and women throughout history who refused to surrender their dignity, bow the knee to empires, or go gently into the night.

Acknowledgments

Writing a book of this size and depth is no simple task. It helps to have good friends and supporters along the way, and I believe that I have been blessed with the best. For that reason, I would like to extend my sincerest thanks to the following individuals, without whom this book might never have come about:

Paul Bonneau, Joseph A. Swyers, Dr. Ben F. Irvin, the late Phyllis A. Schatz, Betty W. Hawes, Robert F. and Connie J. Hawes Sr., Sean T. Kelly, Rocky Frisco, Paul C. Shearer, Eric D. Bostwick, Matthew W. Hawes, Adrian L. and Betty J. Knight, and Michael Stedman, co-owner Leopard Print & Mail.

Introduction

"One nation, indivisible..."

Like most Americans, I grew up reciting the Pledge of Allegiance at the beginning of every school day, and at a variety of other activities as well, from church services to sporting events. I gave very little conscious thought to this ritual; I simply considered it a part of everyday life and my patriotic duty as an American. I didn't entirely understand what those words "one nation, indivisible" meant, and wouldn't understand them for a number of years, but it was enough for me as a child to follow along because I saw everyone else doing it. Besides that, it just sounded so good.

In time, I learned that the words "one nation, indivisible," meant that the fifty United States cannot be separated from one another, that the entity we call the "Union" is a permanent institution. As much as modern Americans seemed to take that idea for granted, however, I soon learned that this had not always been the case. Indeed, it seemed that up until the 1860s there was quite a lot of disagreement concerning the nature of the American Union, whether it was a nation or a confederation, whether the states were bound to one another in perpetuity or could "secede," if they so chose. Eventually, I learned that our sixteenth president, Abraham Lincoln, had supposedly put these issues to rest by militarily opposing the secessions of eleven discontented states, including my own home state of Virginia, in a war that became the bloodiest conflict ever fought by Americans. Lincoln saw the United States of America as "a nation proper," a permanent institution from which no state could be permitted to separate of its own accord. Those who contended otherwise were traitors, threatening us with the prospect that "government of the people, by the people, and for the people" might very well "perish from the earth".

My discovery that Virginia had been once involved in a shooting war with other states of the Union, that Americans had fought so bitterly against other Americans, and that landmarks I passed frequently in

Northern Virginia had once been bloody battlegrounds in that war, quite frankly, appalled me. I could not comprehend any reason why Americans might fight other Americans, nor could I fathom why anyone would choose to fight against Mr. Lincoln. Everything I'd been taught about him indicated that he might very well be one of the greatest men the world had ever produced. As I understood matters, Lincoln had fought for our country's very right to exist; and, if this were not enough, why, he was also a great humanitarian. Had he not freed the slaves? I was proud of the Lincoln legacy, proud to visit places where he once stood, and especially proud that the date of my birth had fortuitously fallen on his. In my young mind, he was ever Abraham Lincoln: Patriot and Humanitarian – an American for the Ages and the standard by which true political greatness must invariably be measured in this country, perhaps in the world, for all time.

Imagine my consternation then to learn that one of my own ancestors had sided with the traitorous secessionist states, fighting under the command of a man named Mosby in the Confederate Army of Northern Virginia. Imagine also my confusion at hearing even my teachers at school praising the virtues and nobility of a Confederate general named Robert E. Lee. But how could anyone who was supposed to be virtuous and noble, whether from my own lineage or not, have sided against a man such as Lincoln and a cause such as the Union?

These were the initial questions that drove my search for answers concerning this conflict, the persons involved, and the reasons for which they fought. In conducting this search, I soon found myself in the hitherto unimaginable position of questioning the integrity and legacy of Abraham Lincoln; and in doing so, I inevitably had to question the words "one nation, indivisible". The facts I eventually uncovered in this search astonished me, and my view of the United States of America and its history will never be the same.

This is a timely discussion. The 200th anniversary of Lincoln's birth (2009) is fast approaching, and much will undoubtedly be said in the coming months and years concerning his legacy. Much is being said already. For example, former New York governor Mario Cuomo recently released a book entitled: *Why Lincoln Matters: Today More than Ever*, a work that concentrates on applying the Lincoln legacy to our modern political climate. In an interview with *Newsweek* prior to the book's release, Cuomo remarked that Lincoln's "superior intelligence" has always impressed him. "There has never been an equal," Cuomo stated. "Not Jefferson, not John F. Kennedy. He had the finest mind in American political history – certainly among presidents."[1]

At one time, I would have wholeheartedly agreed with Cuomo's statement; and many, perhaps even most Americans agree with it now. Such has been the enduring power of Abraham Lincoln's legacy. For this reason alone, I feel that it's altogether fitting and proper for us to re-examine Lincoln's life and deeds. However, even if we were not faced with the imminent bicentennial anniversary of Lincoln's birth, we would still find ourselves confronting his legacy, particularly that of "one nation, indivisible".

Search for the word "secession" on the Internet sometime and you may be surprised by what you find. Secession movements are cropping up at an increasing rate worldwide, most famously to date in the Canadian province of Quebec. Quebec has not yet voted to secede, however, the Canadian Supreme Court has ruled that the province does have the right to do so, and the issue may return to the ballot again in the future, although it may be a disgruntled Alberta that takes up the torch next time. In another interesting example, Scotland now seems to be seriously re-evaluating its relationship with the United Kingdom for the first time since the 1700s, and is steadily acquiring more political clout. In 1999, the Scottish parliament convened for the first time in nearly three hundred years. Where Scotland may go from here remains to be seen, but its present path certainly could lead to secession and independence. Nor is the United States of America immune to the secessionist bug, despite its past history. At present, there are small but numerous secessionist movements underway within this country. Prominent examples include: Vermont, California, Alaska, the states of the old Southern Confederacy – most notably, South Carolina – the New England states, and Hawaii.

Now some who read this, or who have otherwise come across references to modern American secession movements in other sources, surely must be asking, "Why?" Why are secession movements arising here, of all places? Why would anyone not want to be a part of this country? For what possible reason would anyone consider giving up the title of 'American citizen'? How would a state or region even go about leaving the Union? Didn't we settle this issue with Lee's surrender? Are we not truly "one nation, indivisible"?

Typically, there are three principle elements that drive a secession movement: fears concerning a loss of cultural, religious, or ideological distinctiveness; fears concerning a loss of individual liberty; and conflicting loyalties – such as between one's state or region and the country as a whole. All these elements can be found at work in our society today, and their impact is slowly but inexorably intensifying. We are now being forced to confront the fact that there are serious, fundamental divisions among those of us living here in these United States. Whether we would prefer to admit it or not, we can no longer claim to be one people. The 2000 and 2004 general elections served to exemplify this growing political-ideological division in our midst in no uncertain terms, bringing about the first serious, open discussion of secession outside of fringe politics in over a century. Hearkening back to the infamous "red and blue state" electoral maps of Elections 2000 and 2004, it appears that some in the "blue states" may want out of the Union, and some in the "red states" may be glad to see them go.

In a November 9, 2004, article entitled, "Blue States Buzz over Secession," the *Washington Times* reported that the Internet had "exploded with talk of a blue-state confederacy," which would separate various left-leaning portions of the country from what some termed the "rednecks in Oklahoma" and "homophobic knuckle-draggers in Wyoming." The article quotes an anonymous Internet user who had this to say to red-state conservatives: "We hold our noses as we fly over you. We are sickened by the way you treat people that are different from you. The rest of the world despises America, and we don't want to be lumped in with you anymore."[2] In an article entitled "The Case for Blue State Secession: Why Prolong this Marriage?" an Internet commentator simply named "Rene G." described the United States as a "marriage" beset by domestic strife, and suggested that divorce is preferable to both sides getting together every 4th of July and putting on a false front for a global neighborhood that "knows our marriage is a sham".[3] One resident of Arlington, Massachusetts wrote a letter to red-state newspaper readers, calling for a "no-fault" divorce:

> So let's settle this amicably. We'll let you visit the Pacific Ocean and the Smithsonian without a passport if you'll let us visit the Grand Canyon and Orlando. Your Democratic voters are welcome to move to our new, Scandinavian-style nation.[4]

And here are some examples from "right-wing" secession movements that predate the post Election 2004 secession buzz:

From a letter by Dr. Michael Hill, President of the League of the South [displayed on Dixienet.org]:

> The people of the South must come to understand that they indeed are a "nation" in the organic, historical sense of the word. As individuals and communities, we must secede culturally from a world that is waging cultural genocide against our traditions, our heritage and our values.

From the "Lowell Declaration" on Vermont Sovereignty.com:

> The U.S. government has grown too large, is too out of touch with the people of the nation and is too expensive too maintain.

> The U.S. government has often usurped the Constitutional limits set by the 10th amendment.

A California independence website calling itself "Free the Bear" cites several grievances against the US federal government, including the following:

> For erecting a multitude of new bureaucracies and sending swarms of their agents to harass our people and to tax our people out of their substance.

> For abolishing our most valuable laws by unconstitutional edicts by the federal judiciary.

> For the federal legislature's usurping of power from our own legislature by issuing unconstitutional edicts to legislate for our supposed benefit.

ChristianExodus.org, an organization calling for Christians to move to South Carolina and secede, cites recent gay marriage rulings and other issues as causes for secession on its website:

> The efforts of Christian activism have proven futile over the past five decades and, whereas desperate times require desperate measures, we are now in the most desperate of times...Christians must now draw a line in the sand and unite in a sovereign state to dissolve our bond with the current union comprised as the United States of America.

These are not new concerns. For as long as nations have existed, men have longed for governments made in their own image, and Americans are no exception, as the following two examples from our history illustrate:

From the Declaration of Independence, 1776:

> Prudence, indeed, will dictate that Governments long established should not be changed for light and transient causes; and accordingly all experience hath shewn, that mankind are more disposed to suffer, while evils are sufferable, than to right themselves by abolishing the forms to which they are accustomed. But when a long train of abuses and usurpations, pursuing invariably the same Object evinces a design to reduce them under absolute Despotism, it is their right, it is their duty, to throw off such Government, and to provide new Guards for their future security.

From South Carolina's address to the Southern states, 1860:

> The Southern States now stand exactly in the same position toward the Northern States that our ancestors in the colonies did toward Great Britain. The Northern States, having the majority in Congress, claim the same power of omnipotence in legislation as the British Parliament. "The general welfare" is the only limit to the legislation of either...Thus the Government of the United States has become a consolidated Government, and the people of the Southern States are compelled to meet the very despotism their fathers threw off in the Revolution of 1776.

The question of what ails our country politically, and whether secession is a suitable cure for the disease, will be addressed, to some extent, in the final section of this book; however, it is not the primary consideration I would like to draw the reader's attention to here. Instead, I would rather focus on a more fundamental question: is secession even possible in the American Republic? For if we truly are "one nation, indivisible," then it's useless to talk of secession in any other than a purely academic fashion.

Inevitably, some will ask, "Didn't we already settle this issue of secession at Appomattox?" For many, the answer is yes. As far as they are concerned, right or wrong, Lee's surrender was the death-knell of secession, and it is there that the matter should forever rest. We fought a long, bloody, devastating war over the issue more than a century ago, so why should we not simply allow the results of that contest to stand?

The reader will have to evaluate this question for his or her own self, but I feel that we can ill afford to end our discussion of secession on the basis of who won a historical military conflict. After all, war is the exercise of force, not right; and those who defend the idea that Northern triumph rightfully decided the issue of secession would probably not want that same logic extended to other areas of life and experience. For instance, if a man draws a gun on you and takes your wallet, is it now rightfully his because he had the power to take it? If a woman is unable to fend off an attacker and is raped, should her assailant walk free because he won a contest of brute strength?

I dare say few of us would be willing to defend the idea that "might makes right" – which is really nothing more than back-alley bully logic – should serve as the cornerstone of legitimate government in any country that prides itself on being "the land of the free". Yet it amazes me how few of us find fault with the idea that the destinies of eleven Southern states, and even the entire issue of secession itself, was "rightfully" decided because the North was able to militarily subjugate the South. Surely an intellectually sophisticated people can manage a better justification for their political convictions than a glorified big-stick policy! And surely any President who is praised for his superior intellect must have had nobler reasons for his deeds than to act as wielder of such a policy. If the United States of America truly is "one nation, indivisible," we should see evidence of this aside from the notion of "he-who-beats-up-the-other-guy-wins". The facts of history, and logic itself, should stand united with Lincoln on the unassailable heights of the political-intellectual battlefield, supremely triumphant against all comers.

The purpose of this book will be to see whether the facts of history and logic do stand with Lincoln, what if anything was decided at Appomattox, and how these considerations should affect our reception to the idea of secession today. Abraham Lincoln, particularly his words and deeds during the secession crisis of the 1860s, will be brought to trial within these pages. Daniel Webster, Senator from Massachusetts, respected orator, and a man often considered the foremost constitutional scholar of his day, will be brought as co-defendant. The positions advocated by these two famous political figures formed the core of anti-secession scholarship in the 19th Century, and are still invoked by their admirers today. Any discussion of secession, whether it has to do with the Southern states in the 1860s, or with modern American political movements, must necessarily come to terms with these men; and, therefore, so must we.

In part one, we will examine the arguments brought primarily by Webster concerning the idea of secession in light of the founding and composition of the Union. In part two, we will examine arguments, primarily Lincoln's, directed against the secession of the Southern states in 1860 and 1861. In part three, we will examine anti-secession arguments that are mostly modern in nature and bear on both the Southern Confederacy and the general matter of secession. Finally, in part four, we will briefly discuss the implications of what we have examined in light of our country's current political climate and contemporary secession movements. By the end of this discussion, I hope that you the reader will have gleaned something definitive, or at least benefited in some small way from the research that I have conducted on this subject over the years. We will be making a serious effort to determine whether the United States of America really is "one nation, indivisible". We will test and see how strong the ties that bind our political fabric truly are.

That said, before beginning I believe I should take a moment to reveal a bit about my perspective in presenting this material.

Most Americans know the War of 1861-1865 as "the Civil War". However, since I'm already choosing to quibble with a number of commonly accepted notions, many of which I held to myself for some time, I hope that the reader will not begrudge me one additional deviation from the norm. For that reason, I ask your indulgence in referring to this war as the "War of Secession," as opposed to "the Civil War".

"Okay," sighs the reader who is already wondering what he or she has gotten into, "Why the name change? Is nothing sacred?"

I believe the term "Civil War" is a misnomer for this conflict. A civil war is a conflict between opposing factions of the same country, and is waged for control of the whole. Historical examples of this would include such infamous power struggles as took place in Rome, England, and France, and where the goal was domination of the entire nation or empire through control of the central government. However, this was not the case in our own so-called "Civil War". Southern secessionists in 1861 were not seeking to conquer Washington or the Northern states and rule the entire American Union; they were fighting for their independence. In the South, the war was, and is sometimes still referred to as, "the War for Southern Independence". In the North, the war was known as "the War of the Rebellion" or "the War for the Union". Any of these titles for the conflict would be applicable from the position of the particular side they represent; however, since control of the central government was never an issue in the conflict, I do not believe that the term "civil war" is at all applicable.

Nor is the term "War Between the States" an entirely accurate description of this conflict. The states were directly involved in the fight because they provided the troops that both sides fielded; however, the war was directed, not by individual states, but by two central governments: the United States and the Confederate States. Thus there were two primary factions in conflict here, not a jumble of separate states in conflict with one another, as the title "War Between the States" suggests.

"War of Secession" is, I feel, the best term for this conflict because it unites the disparate interests of both sides in one truly common theme. Without the fact of secession, there would have been no war, certainly not as we know it today. The opposing forces took to the battlefield under the color of different ideological and political banners, but it was the single question of secession that brought them there, regardless of their opinion on that question.

Now having provided a bit of background and purpose, I ask that you allow the information you find in these pages to speak for itself. Let reason stand as your guiding light in evaluating the evidence and analysis offered. For the purpose of this trial, let traditional heroes briefly descend from the cloud-tops and traditional villains rise up from perdition. Let us, with Benjamin Franklin, doubt a little of our own infallibility. Let us turn back time and endeavor, like the ancient Bereans who so impressed the Apostle Paul, to see whether the things we have been taught are so.

Robert F. Hawes Jr.

Lexington, SC – May 2006

"Having lived long, I have experienced many instances of being obliged, by better information or fuller consideration, to change opinions even on important subjects, which I once thought right, but found to be otherwise."

– Benjamin Franklin

"For the great enemy of truth is very often not the lie – deliberate, contrived and dishonest – but the myth – persistent, persuasive, and unrealistic. Too often we hold fast to the clichés of our forebears. We subject all facts to a prefabricated set of interpretations. We enjoy the comfort of opinion without the discomfort of thought."

– John F. Kennedy

"Woe unto the defeated, whom history treads into the dust."

– Arthur Koestler, *Darkness at Noon*

"The reputation of individuals is of minor importance compared to the opinion posterity may form of the motives which governed the South in their late struggle for the maintenance of the principles of the Constitution. I hope, therefore, that a true history will be written, and justice done them."

– Robert E. Lee

Part One:

The Compact Theory versus
the Nationalist Theory of the Union

"All of us need to be reminded that the federal government did not create the states. The states created the federal government."

– Ronald Reagan

"If, Sir, this be our political condition, it is time the people of the United States understood it."

– Daniel Webster

Worldviews Apart

The central point of contention in American history and political discourse, where the subject of secession is concerned, has to do with competing theories as to the origin and composition of that entity we call the "Union". Those who believe that secession is possible rest the justification of their position in what is usually referred to as the "Compact Theory". Compact adherents – arguably the political heirs of Thomas Jefferson and James Madison – believe that the Constitution of the United States is a compact: an agreement or covenant, between the states that comprise the Union, and that the United States of America is not a consolidated nation-state, but rather, more of a confederated republic. Accordingly, they see the states as sovereign, independent entities voluntarily united for certain purposes by a federal government that acts as the agent of their Union along strictly limited, constitutional lines.

Those on the opposite side of the ideological fence, whom I will call "nationalists" – the political heirs of Abraham Lincoln – believe that the United States of America is a true nation-state, operating under a supreme, consolidated central government. Not surprisingly, they reject the Compact Theory's emphasis on the states, holding instead to the idea that the people of the United States as a whole created the Union, and that the states exist as little more than administrative subdivisions of the American nation, much like counties are subdivisions of states. Adherents to this consolidated nation-state school elevate the federal government to absolute supremacy in all matters, and reduce the Constitution to a guidebook instead of a strict plan of government. Nationalists are more likely to refer to the United States as a democracy than a republic.

Thus we see that the core of the secession debate is grounded in one question: is the Union a consolidated nation-state, or a confederation of states? I hope to answer this question in the coming pages, and I will attempt to do so by examining the arguments of the foremost proponents of the Nationalist Theory. I will begin with Daniel Webster and his celebrated Senate speech of February 16, 1833, interspersed with supporting quotations from Abraham Lincoln. In Part

Two, I will concentrate more heavily on Lincoln and the arguments he brought against the seceded Southern states in 1861.

In examining these issues, I believe it's supremely important that we let the persons in question explain themselves as completely as possible, wherever possible, in order to ensure that their views are accurately assessed. For that reason, I have chosen lengthy expository excerpts from speeches given by Lincoln and Webster in regard to their views on the Union. Those excerpts are too lengthy to be incorporated into the main body of the book, so I have relegated them to the appendices (D and E) where they may be easily referenced. I would strongly advise the reader to peruse these excerpts before continuing, as I will make repeated references to the arguments contained in them. I do provide occasional recaps and summaries, but the speech excerpts are much more complete, and will offer a more fluid and whole view of the positions held by Webster and Lincoln.

The Webster-Lincoln Case
Against
the Compact Theory

Position One:
The Union is older than the States

Daniel Webster - In 1789, and before this constitution was adopted, the United States had already been in a union, more or less close, for fifteen years. At least as far back as the meeting of the first Congress, in 1774, they had been, in some measure, and to some national purposes, united together.

Abraham Lincoln - The Union is much older than the Constitution. It was formed in fact, by the Articles of Association in 1774. It was matured and continued by the Declaration of Independence in 1776. It was further matured and the faith of the then thirteen States expressly plighted and engaged that it should be perpetual, by the Articles of Confederation in 1778. And finally, in 1787, one of the declared objects for ordaining and establishing the Constitution, was "to form a more perfect union."

The Origin and Evolution of the Union

Daniel Webster and Abraham Lincoln believed that the American Union began with the Articles of Association in 1774, and was, to use Lincoln's terminology, "matured and continued" by the Declaration of Independence, the Articles of Confederation and, finally, by the Constitution. To determine whether or not they were correct in this view, we should start by asking the question: just what is a "union"?

Merriam-Webster defines a "union" as follows:

> 1 a: an act or instance of uniting or joining two or more things into one: as (1): the formation of a single political unit from two or more separate and independent units.

From this definition, it is obvious that a "union" can be many things, not all of them equal in composition or importance by any means.

There are civil unions, such as marriages. There are private unions, such as sports teams. There are labor unions, such as the Teamsters. There are economic unions, such as OPEC. And then there are political unions, which can take the form of defensive alliances, such as NATO; representative bodies, such as the United Nations; and countries united under one national banner, such as Canada. To state it succinctly, a union is virtually any condition that combines individual entities under some collective identity.

For this reason, the Webster-Lincoln view of the age of the Union is extremely broad and flexible. As long as the states were joined together for any purpose whatsoever, that joining could reasonably be termed a "union" of sorts. Nevertheless, Webster and Lincoln were incorrect in the conclusions they attempted to draw from that point forward. There was not one Union that was "matured and continued" over time in early American history, but rather, several unions, each with specific beginning and ending points, each somehow fundamentally different from its predecessor.

Colonial Unity and the Articles of Association

It is true, as far as it goes, that the British colonies in North America did unite for mutual benefit at various times prior to the emergence of the "United States". For example, the New England colonies officially confederated with one another in May of 1643 to defend themselves against an alarming increase in Indian attacks. At that time, England had busied herself with affairs abroad and was unable to provide her colonies with, in their words, "those comfortable fruits of protection, which at other times we might well expect". The New Englanders titled their agreement: The Articles of Confederation of the United Colonies of New England.

Other temporary associations, or unions, amongst the colonies followed, including the Articles of Association, as referenced by Webster and Lincoln. Effective October 20, 1774, the Articles of Association were adopted as a means of protesting various acts of the British Parliament, and consisted of a general agreement to restrict imports, exports, and the consumption of certain goods. Consider the following statement of purpose found in the Articles:

> We, his majesty's most loyal subjects, the delegates of [the 13 colonies are then listed]...avowing our allegiance to his majesty,

our affection and regard for our fellow-subjects in Great-Britain and elsewhere…find, that the present unhappy situation of our affairs is occasioned by a ruinous system of colony administration, adopted by the British ministry about the year 1763, evidently calculated for enslaving these colonies, and, with them, the British Empire…

To obtain redress of these grievances, which threaten destruction to the lives, liberty, and property of his majesty's subjects, in North-America, we are of the opinion, that a non-importation, non-consumption, and non-exportation agreement, faithfully adhered to, will prove the most speedy, effectual, and peaceable measure…

The Articles of Association are certainly noteworthy as being the first time Britain's thirteen American colonies acted in concert to assert themselves, but it should be noted that they were just an association and only an association. The Articles did not form a government, laid no claim to sovereignty, and existed only at the agreement of the participating colonies and only for specified purposes. In all other aspects, save for their allegiance to the British crown, and in spite of Webster's insistence that they acted together "to some national purposes," the colonies were quite independent of one another. They made no more pretense of nationhood at that time than the Allied powers did during World War II or the NATO member countries do today.

In fact, based on the short excerpt that we reviewed from the text of the Articles, it is clear that the colonists thought of themselves at that time as British subjects appealing for their rights under British law. Note that they referred to themselves as "We, his majesty's most loyal subjects". Given the use of such subordinating language, it would certainly be a stretch to refer to colonial unity at that time as being somehow "national" in character, unless one is referring to British nationalism. There is simply no evidence of American nationalism in the Articles of Association. Taken at face value, the Articles were really little more than a group protest.

Writing in his *Commentaries on the Constitution of the United States*, Joseph Story, one time Associate Justice of the Supreme Court – and an advocate of the nationalist school of political thought – testified as to the state of colonial unity in those pre-independence days:

Though the colonies had a common origin, and owed a common allegiance, and the inhabitants of each were British subjects, they had no direct political connexion with each other. Each was independent of the others; each, in a limited sense, was sovereign within its own territory. There was neither allegiance nor confederacy between them…They made several efforts to procure the establishment of some general superintending government over them all: but their own differences of opinion, as well as the jealousy of the crown, made these efforts abortive.[1]

The Declaration of Independence

Lincoln – The "United Colonies" were declared to be "free and independent States;" but, even then, the object plainly was not to declare their independence from one another, or of the Union, but directly the contrary…

Our States have neither more nor less power than that reserved to them in the Union by the Constitution—no one of them ever having been a State out of the Union. The original ones passed into the Union even before they cast off their British colonial dependence.

Having formed their first mutual association, the colonies continued to assert themselves and their claims to traditional rights under English law, while, at the same time, still professing their loyalty to King George III. However, by 1776, it was clear that the king was not interested in hearing their pleas, and a call for independence – once unthinkable – quickly rose up from one end of British North America to the other. Nevertheless, despite their common grievances with the crown, the thirteen colonial governments were not entirely united on the question of whether actual independence was a wise move at that time, or even how delegates at the Continental Congress should address the matter. Thomas Jefferson, writing in his *Autobiography*, recorded some delegates as pointing out the following difficulties with the process:

Some of them [the colonies] had expressly forbidden their delegates to consent to such a declaration, and others had given no instructions, and consequently no powers to give such consent:

If the delegates of any particular colony had no power to declare such colony independent, certain they were the others could not declare it for them; the colonies being as yet perfectly independent of each other...2

It is significant to note here that the colonies were described as being "perfectly independent" of each other, and as being unable to make decisions for one another. Certainly, this challenges the assertion that the colonies were "in Union" at this time to any "national" purposes. Indeed, at first it seemed as if only certain colonies would opt for independence, given that others, mostly the smaller colonies, were not satisfied that an independence effort could succeed. Thomas Jefferson also recorded this aspect of the debate in his *Autobiography*, noting that pro-independence delegates were undeterred by the prospect of a less than unanimous declaration. These delegates argued that, "The history of the Dutch Revolution, of whom three states only confederated at first proved that a secession of some colonies would not be so dangerous as some apprehended".3

Thus, if a Union did exist among the colonies at this time, it was apparently of no overriding importance to them; for while they preferred a unanimous action, they recognized no authority higher than themselves, and were prepared to act independently of one another. Overall though, the desire to move for autonomy was strong enough with most of the colonies that the Continental Congress created a committee to draft a declaration of independence. Once completed, it was presented to Congress and voted upon in the affirmative on July 4, although New York's delegates abstained until receiving approval from their state, which came on July 9.4 The unanimous declaration was then formally signed on August 2, 1776.

Thus we reach another milestone in the evolution of the Union, according to the view espoused by Webster and Lincoln. In their view, the colonies created the Union, and, upon the signing of the Declaration of Independence, the Union made the colonies states, giving birth to the United States of America as a sovereign, independent nation in 1776. Inventive as this theory is, however, there are some significant logical and historical problems with it.

First, Lincoln's objection that the colonies did not "declare their independence from one another, or of the Union" in the Declaration is misdirected. The Declaration was intended to address only the relationship between the colonies and the British government, not the relationship between the colonies themselves, a relationship that underwent no formal change at the time and is nowhere mentioned in the document. There is simply no compelling reason to think that the Declaration made the colonies anything more with respect to one another than what they had always been: independent entities.

This is not to say that there was no hope of their becoming something more, far from it. Many of the convention delegates assembled in Philadelphia hoped their actions would spell the beginning of a new American Republic. Benjamin Rush, a prominent convention delegate from Pennsylvania, exemplified this attitude when he declared: "We have been too free with the word independence. We are dependent on each other – not totally independent states…When I entered that door, I considered myself a citizen of America."[5] As Rush indicated, the colonies realized there were many points upon which they were mutually dependent for their general well being, particularly in regard to the then inevitable war with England. The idea was: "We must all hang together, or most assuredly we shall hang separately," as Benjamin Franklin is reported to have said.

Nevertheless, as important as it was for the colonies to act together at that time, and as much as they desired some common bond between them, we should not exaggerate the true nature of their affiliation. Of the two statements offered by Rush and Franklin, Franklin's statement concerning unity of necessity more accurately reflects the true state of America at the time of the Declaration. There was unity of purpose among the colonies and, to some degree action, but little more at that time. In fact, even their first true Union under the Articles of Confederation in 1781 would prove to be a half-hearted affair, as illustrated by James Wilson, delegate to the Constitutional Convention in 1787:

> He admitted that the large states did accede, as had been stated, to the Confederation in its present form [under the Articles]; but it was of the effect of necessity, not of choice.[6]

Now consider the following observation, as recorded by Thomas Jefferson in his *Autobiography*. On the subject of the future unity of the colonies following the Declaration of Independence, Jefferson recorded:

The larger colonies had threatened they would not confederate at all if their weight in congress should not be equal to the numbers of people they added to the confederacy; while the smaller ones declared against a union if they did not retain an equal vote for the protection of their rights.

All men admit that a confederacy is necessary. Should the idea get abroad that there is likely to be no union among us, it will damp the minds of the people, diminish our struggle, and lessen its importance; because it will open to our view future prospects of war and dissension among ourselves.[7]

But if the Union already existed at that time, how could Jefferson – quoting the Reverend John Witherspoon, delegate to Congress from New Jersey – speculate on a situation in which "there is likely to be no union among us"? How could the larger states threaten not to confederate "at all"? Obviously, there was no formal Union at this time, Lincoln and Webster not withstanding, else the states would not have been discussing whether they should establish one. Consider also the words of David McCullough in his Pulitzer Prize winning biography *John Adams*:

"With independence proclaimed, confederation – a working union of the colonies – had become the focus of "spirit" animating the delegates. Union was as essential as independence, nearly all contended, more important in the view of many – and the issues to be resolved were formidable."[8]

The second problem with this Webster-Lincoln notion that the Union pre-dated, and in fact created, the states via the Declaration of Independence, is that the colonies already had reasons to think of themselves as states even before the Declaration was adopted. This fact is illustrated in the following quotation from Jefferson's recollections of certain arguments expounded at the Independence Congress. Pro-independence delegates contended:

That the question was not whether, by a declaration of independence, we should make ourselves what we are not; but whether we should declare a fact *which already exists*:

That as to the King, we had been bound to him by allegiance, but that this bond was now dissolved by his assent to the late act of parliament, by which he declares us out of his protection, and by his levying war upon us, a fact which had long ago proved us out of his protection; it being a certain position in law that allegiance and protection are reciprocal, the one ceasing when the other is withdrawn. [9] [Emphasis mine]

Thus taken in light of the debates on the Declaration of Independence, it becomes apparent that at least some of the American colonies felt the Declaration did not assert some new truth, but rather, underscored an existing state of affairs. Jefferson's reference to the reciprocal relationship of allegiance and protection indicates that King George III effectively forced statehood upon the colonies by declaring them to be out of his protection. Since they found themselves deserted by the only power they had recognized as sovereign, they were forced to appropriate that mantel for themselves in determining their own destinies. Consequently, they were already free and independent states by the time the Declaration was adopted; and so their mutual declaration was not an act of conveying statehood through the auspices of some central, sovereign unifying power. How could it be when no such power existed?

Indeed, by Lincoln's own definition, although contrary to his designs, the American colonies became sovereign entities – states – at this time by their own hand. Lincoln, in his address to Congress in special session, July 4, 1861, defined a sovereign entity as "a political community without a superior"; and, clearly, the colonies recognized no entity superior to themselves. There was no general government over them to restrain them or obligate them to any certain course of action. The Continental Congress did not qualify as a general government because it had no legitimate, overriding authority; it could issue only resolutions representative of the view of a majority of its delegates, not laws. The colonies were not obligated by anything more than good faith and their own self-interest to cooperate with Congress and with one another.

It should also be noted that some of the states took action to declare independence from England and establish their own governments prior to the general Declaration of Independence on July 4, 1776, a fact that flies in the face of Lincoln's assertion that no state ever had a constitution outside of the Union. Virginia was one such state. On May 15, 1776, a state convention in Virginia resolved, "that the delegates appointed to represent this colony in General Congress be instructed to propose to that respectable body to declare the United Colonies free and independent states..." Once this resolution was adopted, Virginia declared its independence from England and adopted its own constitution in June, just prior to the adoption of the Declaration of Independence on behalf of all thirteen colonies. The intent of the Virginia lawmakers was unmistakable, as they clearly titled their work:

> THE CONSTITUTION OR FORM OF GOVERNMENT, AGREED TO AND RESOLVED UPON BY THE DELEGATES AND REPRE-SENTATIVES OF THE SEVERAL COUNTIES AND CORPORA-TIONS OF VIRGINIA.

Within the body of this document, the State of Virginia enumerated its grievances against the King of England and very clearly declared its independence, as demonstrated by the following excerpts:

> Whereas George the third, King of Great Britain and Ireland, and elector of Hanover, heretofore intrusted with the exercise of the kingly office in this government, hath endeavoured to pervert the same into a detestable and insupportable tyranny...the govern-ment of this country, as formerly exercised under the crown of Great Britain, is TOTALLY DISSOLVED.

Thus Virginia chose to inaugurate her independence from Great Brit-ain and establish a state government prior to the July 4th declaration on behalf of all the colonies. Although Daniel Webster and Abraham Lincoln maintained that Virginia was part of a Union at this time, the state's actions make it evident that she was acting for herself. In fact, Thomas Jefferson later referred to Virginia as a "nation" among na-tions at this time in her history, as found in the following excerpt from his letter to Major John Cartwright, dated June 5, 1824:

> Virginia, of which I am myself a native and resident, was not only the first of the States, but, I believe I may say, the first of the na-tions of the earth, which assembled its wise men together to form a fundamental constitution, to commit it to writing, and place it among their archives, where every one should be free to appeal to its text.[10]

Still, in spite of the clear intent of the Virginia lawmakers, some, such as Joseph Story, have taken issue with the significance of their actions.

Story acknowledged Virginia's move, and also made mention of similar actions by other colonies; however, he was of the opinion that any governments the states formed for themselves were merely "done in compliance with the recommendations of Congress."[11] "No state had presumed of itself to form a new government," Story claimed, "or to provide for the exigencies of the times, without consulting Congress on the subject; and when they acted, it was in pursuance of the recommendation of Congress. It was, therefore, the achievement of the whole for the benefit of the whole."[12]

Story's argument makes the fatal error of forgetting the fact that, as we have seen, the states declined to make decisions for one another in either their individual or corporate capacities. Congress claimed no authority to act as a sovereign entity and only made suggestions to the states at that time. Given the inauguration of hostilities with England, it was only natural that the individual colonies consult with Congress, as Virginia did; but we should not confuse an act of consultation with an assumption of subservience. If the Continental Congress itself *did* represent a sovereign entity with authority over all of the states, why did it merely *recommend* that Virginia draft its own constitution? Why did it not *command* Virginia to do so? Or, even better, why did it not simply draft a general constitution for the new nation at that time and make it applicable to all of the states? Why handle things piecemeal when you have a sovereign Union to do them corporately?

A third problem with the idea that the Declaration of Independence established a nation-state is that its language clearly indicates otherwise. Note the following:

> We, therefore, the Representatives of the United States of America, in General Congress, Assembled, appealing to the Supreme Judge of the world for the rectitude of our intentions, do, in the Name, and by the authority of the good People of these Colonies, solemnly publish and declare.

> That these United Colonies are, and of Right ought to be Free and Independent States; that they are Absolved from all Allegiance to the British Crown, and that all political connection between them and the State of Great Britain is and ought to be totally dissolved; and that as Free and Independent States, they have full Power to

levy War, conclude Peace, contract Alliances, establish Commerce, and to do all other Acts and Things which Independent States may of right do.

Note that the colonies declared their right to be "free and independent *states*," not a "free an independent nation". They very clearly titled their declaration: "The unanimous Declaration of the thirteen united States of America". In it, they proclaimed their individual status with the force of their collective will as thirteen allied powers, not consolidated nationhood through the auspices of some central sovereignty. As we have seen already, they acknowledged no central sovereignty, and they immediately undertook the very telling action of attempting to create a plan for unifying the states. If they were creating a new nation via the Declaration of Independence, why did they not simply indicate this? Why use language identifying themselves as "free and independent states," unless, of course, that is precisely what they meant?

Webster and Lincoln argued that the Declaration "matured" and "furthered" the Union, but this hardly seems feasible. The Declaration united the colonies only on the basis that they were mutually declaring their independence from England. As a form of "union," it was actually a substantial step backward from what had existed under the Articles of Association; for, it effectively dissolved the only formal connection that had ever existed between the colonies up to that time: their status as fellow British subjects. Realistically speaking, immediately following the Declaration of Independence, the colonies had never been more loosely affiliated since their establishment. Some years later during the Constitutional Convention, delegate Luther Martin stated this fact outright when he remarked that:

> At the separation from the British empire, the people of America preferred the establishment of themselves into thirteen separate sovereignties, instead of incorporating themselves into one.[13]

The Articles of Confederation

Despite the assertions of men like Lincoln and Webster, the fact of history is that the United States of America did not come into existence as a real political Union until March 1, 1781, when Maryland became the last state to ratify the Articles of Confederation. Quoting Jefferson once again from his *Autobiography*:

These articles reported July 12, 76 were debated from day to day, & time to time for two years, were ratified July 9, '78, by 10 states, by N. Jersey on the 26th of Nov. of the same year, and by Delaware on the 23rd. of Feb. following. Maryland alone held off 2 years more, acceding to them Mar 1, 81. and thus closing the obligation.[14]

The Articles of Confederation were stipulated for all thirteen states and did not go into effect until all thirteen approved them. Delaware, New Jersey and Maryland were not held to any obligation by the other ten states; each state decided the matter for itself as a sovereign entity. The states were still united in their bid for independence, but there was no true Union among them until Maryland provided its approval on March 1, 1781; and then, *and only then*, was the "obligation closed" and the states formally united.

Thus far, the Webster-Lincoln story of the genesis of the Union has proven untenable at best. Now, pressing forward with an examination of the language of the Articles of Confederation, we will see it meet with total disaster.

In the fourth paragraph of the Articles, we find the following phrase:

> *Each state retains its sovereignty, freedom, and independence*, and every power, jurisdiction, and right, which is not by this Confederation expressly delegated to the United States, in Congress assembled. [Emphasis mine]

What's this? How can it be said that each state "retains its sovereignty, freedom, and independence" if the states never possessed those qualities in the first place? And instead of the Union assigning various rights and privileges to the states, we actually find the states delegating powers to the Union, a Union that could not have existed had the states not agreed to it. Surely this flies in the face of the Webster-Lincoln view! Nor did the formation of this first true American Union under the Articles supplant the states. They remained the new country's most defining political characteristic. The quote from Article Four illustrates that quite nicely for us above, but there is further evidence available for this conclusion as well.

In the Treaty of Paris, signed on September 3, 1783, King George III recognized the independence of his former American colonies with the following statement:

His Brittanic Majesty acknowledges the said United States, viz., New Hampshire, Massachusetts Bay, Rhode Island and Providence Plantations, Connecticut, New York, New Jersey, Pennsylvania, Maryland, Virginia, North Carolina, South Carolina and Georgia, to be free sovereign and independent states, that he treats with them as such, and for himself, his heirs, and successors, relinquishes all claims to the government, propriety, and territorial rights of the same and every part thereof.

Note that King George recognized the "said United States," and then proceeded to name the states individually, concluding that they were "free sovereign and independent states," and that "he treats them as such". The language used here is very important. Even though the states had been united under the Articles of Confederation since March of 1781, the King did not grant recognition to a new nation. Instead, he granted recognition to each state individually, and in the same manner as they are listed in the fourth paragraph of the Articles of Confederation. He also referred to the United States as "them".

This use of the plural for "United States" extends throughout the Treaty of Paris and is echoed repeatedly throughout American history until after the War of Secession, and even then it occasionally appears. Here is another example from the Treaty of Paris:

And that all disputes which might arise in future on the subject of the boundaries of the said United States may be prevented, it is hereby agreed and declared, that the following are and shall be their boundaries...

Note that the King did not refer to "its" boundaries, but rather, "their" boundaries. If the United States recognized themselves as being a single, sovereign nation, why did they sign off on a document that clearly regarded them as separate, independent entities? This treaty came about as a result of negotiation with the crown. Why would the United States have not negotiated the proper wording to reference their new political status? Could anything have been more important to them at this time? Now here is an example from the Articles of Confederation in which the same terminology was used:

The said states hereby severally enter into a firm league of friendship with each other, for their common defence, the security of their Liberties, and their mutual and general welfare, binding themselves to assist each other, against all force offered to, or attacks made upon them, or any of them, on account of religion, sovereignty, trade, or any other pretence whatsoever.

Note the use of the plurals again, and also note the agreement to defend each state from attack on account of any pretense whatever, including *sovereignty*. There is that troublesome word once again being uttered in reference to the states themselves instead of the Union.

In noting the use of the plural terminology, even when referring to the United States in general, one can readily see that the stress was placed upon the *states*. The British government did not acknowledge the independence of a nation, but of thirteen separate, sovereign *states*, and therein lies the heart of the issue. The thirteen American states may have won their independence while working together in a united front, but, contrary to the Webster-Lincoln school, the Union did not give them their independence. Their independence was asserted, and later recognized, on the basis that they comprised separate, sovereign communities, a basis that the states themselves upheld in their own Articles of Confederation.

Position Two:
The Constitution is a Union of the "People"

Webster - The powers conferred upon the new Government were perfectly well understood to be conferred, not by any State, or the people of any State, but by the people of the United States.

Lincoln - Our adversaries...have adopted a temporary national constitution, in the preamble of which...they omit "We, the People," and substitute "We, the deputies of the sovereign and independent States." Why? Why this deliberate pressing out of view the rights of men and the authority of the people?

What exactly is a "People"?

The underlying reason why Webster, Lincoln and other members of what I term the nationalist school of American history and government felt the Union could be older than the states, in spite of the contrary evidence and reasoning we have seen, is because they believed that the Union was a creation of the American people as a whole. By this way of thinking, the states did not make the Union; therefore, they have no say as to their continuing status within it. Thus, secession is impossible. The only way a state can leave the Union is by overthrowing the work of the "people" and instigating a revolution. Americans are one "people" and their government is the government of one "people".

Joseph Story was an early influence in promoting this notion. Like Webster and Lincoln, Story advocated the idea that Americans had been "one people" since at least 1774:

> The colonies were fellow-subjects, and for many purposes, *one people*. Every colonist had a right to inhabit, if he pleased, in any other colony; and as a British subject, he was capable of inheriting lands by descent in every other colony.[1]

In response to Story, consider the following thought from Albert Taylor Bledsoe, author of *Is Davis a Traitor?*

> In many respects, indeed, the whole human race may be said to be one. They have a common origin, a common psychology, a common physiology, and they are all subjects of the same great Ruler of the world. But this does not make all men "one people" in the political sense of the words.[2]

Just as there are many types of "union," so there are many different ways in which groups of individuals may be referred to as "a people," but this does not necessarily mean that they are subject to a supreme central government. Did the Allied powers in either world war comprise "one people" even though they were thoroughly engaged as a united front in global warfare? Do the NATO or OPEC member nations today comprise "one people" even though they possess a form of unity? Do they pledge their allegiance to a central authority, salute one flag, or make one body of laws for the whole? Bledsoe's phrase "in the political sense of the words" is fundamental here. The reader may already have noted similar qualifications in the words of Story and Webster, who referred to the "oneness" of the American people as applying "for many purposes," "in a variety of respects," "in some measure," and "to some national purposes". As emphatic as they were that the American colonies represented one people in a continuous Union, even they could not escape the fact that, realistically speaking, there was no such thing as an American nation at that time.

Nevertheless, they tried their best to work around this problem. Daniel Webster in particular went to considerable pains in his speech to the Senate in 1833 to show that the states were, if anything, of secondary importance in the formation of the Union, particularly after the adoption of the Constitution. In so doing, he offered many different evidences for his Union of the people, evidences that I would now like to examine on a point-by-point basis. In so doing, we will add discussion of the Constitution and its adoption to our on-going examination of the colonial period, the Declaration of Independence, and the Articles of Confederation.

Summarizing Webster's Key Arguments against the Compact Theory

In 1833, the State of South Carolina and the United States government hovered on the brink of a violent confrontation over South Carolina's decision to nullify a federal tariff law on the basis that it was unconstitutional and, therefore, not binding on the state (see Part Three, Position Three "Lincoln Fought to End Slavery" for details). The situation created a constitutional crisis in that it cast doubt upon the authority of the federal government versus that of the states. Senator John C. Calhoun of South Carolina, in a speech on January 22, introduced three resolutions concerning the nature of the Union; resolutions in which he argued for the Compact Theory of the Constitution and South Carolina's right to nullify an unconstitutional law. The first and most important of Calhoun's resolutions read as follows:

> *Resolved*, That the people of the several States, composing these United States are united as parties to a constitutional compact, to which the people of each State acceded as a separate sovereign community, each binding itself by its own particular ratification; and that the union, of which the said compact is the bond, is a union between the States ratifying the same.

Massachusetts senator Daniel Webster disagreed with Calhoun's interpretation of the Constitution; and, on February 16, attacked Calhoun and the Compact Theory with all his oratorical might. See Appendix D for the full text of Calhoun's resolutions, and lengthy excerpts from Webster's rebuttal.

The following are summaries and examinations of Webster's key arguments against the Compact Theory of the United States Constitution:

1. The Constitution is not a compact between states because the states did not "accede" to the Constitution. The people "ratified" it.

Webster – "*The people of the United States...do not say that they accede to a league, but they declare that they ordain and establish a constitution...*"

Merriam-Webster defines the word "accede" as meaning: "to become a party (as to an agreement)...to express approval or give consent: give in to a request or demand..." As for the word "ratify," *Merriam-Webster* defines it as meaning: "to approve and sanction formally: CONFIRM".

As you can see, these words *accede* and *ratify* are very close in meaning, both conveying the idea of approval or sanction, and either word could likely be used as a synonym for the other by today's typical usage standards. Nevertheless, the word *accede* embodies more of a connotation with regard to 'joining' or, as per the definition, 'to become a party (as to an agreement)'. As Webster stated: "Accession, as a word applied to political associations, implies coming into a league, treaty, or confederacy, by one hitherto a stranger to it." For this reason, Webster reacted strongly to Calhoun's use of the word *accede* in his 1833 resolutions, claiming that the states did not accede to – or join – some new Union under the Constitution; the people merely ratified – or sanctioned – a change to an existing Union of which the states were already members. Here are his words on that subject:

> Having thus used the terms, *ratify* and *confirm*, even in regard to the old confederation, it would have been strange, indeed, if the people of the United States, after its formation, and when they came to establish the present constitution, had spoken of the States, or of the people of the States, as acceding to this constitution. Such language would have been ill-suited to the occasion. It would have implied an existing separation or disunion among the States, such as never existed since 1774. No such language, therefore, was used. The language actually employed is "adopt," "ratify," "ordain," "establish."

As Webster himself admitted in his speech, "the natural converse of accession is secession"; thus if the states did actually accede to the Constitution, they might very well be within their rights to secede from it. The question then is: did they accede? Having seen what Webster had to say on the subject, let's look at what the founders themselves said about it. [Emphasis in the following quotations is mine unless otherwise indicated]:

George Washington:

From a letter to Bushrod Washington, November 10, 1787: "Let the opponents of the proposed Constitution in this State be asked – and it is a question they certainly ought to have asked themselves – what line of conduct they would advise it to adopt, if nine other States, of which I think there is little doubt, should *accede* to the Constitution?"[3]

From a letter to James Madison, January 10, 1788: "But of all the arguments that may be used at the Convention which is to be held, the most prevailing one I expect will be that nine States at least will have *acceded* to it."[4]

Writing to Charles Pinckney on June 28, 1788: Washington referred to news received to the effect that: "The Convention of New Hampshire had, on the 21st instant, *acceded* to the new Confederacy by a majority of eleven voices..."[5]

In an address to Congress in joint session, January 8, 1790: "I embrace with great satisfaction the opportunity which now presents itself on congratulating you on the present favorable prospects of our public affairs. The recent *accession* of the important State of North Carolina to the constitution of the United States (of which official information has been received)..."[6] **The Senate then drafted a response** to the President's address, which read, in part: "The accession of the State of North Carolina to the Constitution of the United States gives us much pleasure: and we offer you our congratulations on that event..."[7]

In an address to the United States Congress, June 1, 1790: "Having received official information of the accession of the State of Rhode Island and Providence Plantations to the constitution of the United States, I take the earliest opportunity of communicating the same to you, with my congratulations on this happy event, which unites, under the General Government, all of the States which were originally confederated..."[8]

Benjamin Franklin: "Our new Constitution is now established with eleven States, and the *accession* of a twelfth is soon expected."[9]

James Wilson of Pennsylvania, during the Constitutional convention, stated that he hoped: "The provision for ratifying would be put on such a footing as to admit of such a partial union, with a door open for the *accession* of the rest..."[10]

Elbridge Gerry of Massachusetts, speaking during the Constitutional convention, stated that he was opposed to: "a partial confederacy, leaving other States to *accede* or not to *accede*, as has been intimated."[11]

John Randolph of Virginia, on Virginia's decision to join the new Union said: "The *accession* of eight States reduced our deliberations to the single question of Union or no Union."[12]

Patrick Henry of Virginia, speaking of the Constitution: "If it be amended, every State will *accede* to it."[13]

These quotations should be sufficient to establish that the word *accede* was, in fact, used by the founders in reference to the Constitution. Witness even the response of the United States Senate to President Washington's letter announcing the accession of North Carolina. Here we have the Senate itself employing the very word that Daniel Webster would later denounce as not a "constitutional mode of expression" before the very same body in 1833! Interestingly enough, Justice Story also used the word *accede* in reference to Rhode Island's ratification of the Constitution when he stated that, "Rhode Island did not accede to it, until more than a year after it had been in operation…"[14]

So much for the idea that the states did not accede to the Constitution!

2.   The Constitution did not represent a new Union, merely a perfecting of the old Union that had first been formed via the Articles of Association in 1774.

Webster – "*It would have been strange, indeed, if the people of the United States, after its formation, and when they came to establish the present constitution, had spoken of the States, or of the people of the States, as acceding to this constitution. Such language would have been ill-suited to the occasion. It would have implied an existing separation or disunion among the States, such as never existed since 1774.*"

We have already seen evidence demonstrating that there was no formal American Union until the Articles of Confederation were adopted in 1781, contrary to Daniel Webster's assertions. But in spite of this, could it be that Webster was at least partially right? Did the Constitution represent a continuation of the old Union established at the time of the Articles, as opposed to the formation of an entirely new Union?

The Articles of Confederation were established as follows from its introductory paragraph, as seen previously:

Articles of Confederation and perpetual Union between the states of New Hampshire, Massachusetts-bay Rhode Island and Providence Plantations, Connecticut, New York, New Jersey, Pennsylvania, Delaware, Maryland, Virginia, North Carolina, South Carolina and Georgia.

These words established the Union and enumerated its member states. Now, let's review Article Seven of the Constitution, which states:

> The Ratification of the Conventions of nine States, shall be sufficient for the Establishment of this Constitution between the States so ratifying the Same.

Pursuant to the above provision, the ratification of nine states was sufficient to activate the Constitution, and this creates a serious problem for those who believe that the Constitution merely represented a continuation or perfection of the old Union:

Both the Articles and the Constitution provide for a form of central government, but they are radically different forms of government, thus both could not have been in effect over the same states at the same time. For the Constitution to go into effect, the Articles of Confederation had to come to an end; and since the states were united by the Articles, if that document ceased to have effect, the Union it represented also had to come to an end. When the ninth state – New Hampshire – ratified the Constitution on June 21, 1788, the new government became binding only upon the nine ratifying states. Since the Articles of Confederation expressly applied to all thirteen states, the Union they represented was effectively dissolved. Nine of the stipulated thirteen member states no longer acknowledged their obligations under that compact; they had seceded and formed their own Union. The remaining four states were no longer united with them. In fact, they lacked unity even amongst themselves at that point, and were effectively restored to the condition they had enjoyed immediately following the Declaration of Independence: complete autonomy.

The only way in which the Union could have been maintained unbroken through this transition period would have been for all thirteen states to have simultaneously ratified the Constitution, or else for the Constitution to have gone into effect only after eventually being ratified by all thirteen (as had been done with the Articles). But as seen above, the Constitution was permitted to go into effect without either a simultaneous or unanimous ratification by the states. Indeed, the dissolution of the old Union upon ratification of the Constitution by only nine states was acknowledged in the Constitutional Convention, and gave a number of the delegates serious cause for alarm. They fully understood the nature of what was being proposed, and warned against "The indecency and pernicious tendency of dissolving, in so slight a manner, the solemn obligations of the Articles of Confederation."[15]

James Madison was more to the point, acknowledging the end of the old Union and the formation of a new one while writing to Alexander Hamilton on July 20, 1788. In his letter, he referred to a conditional ratification of the Constitution by the State of New York, and objected to it by arguing: "That it does not make New York a member of the New Union, and consequently that she could not be received on that plan."[16] Speaking to Congress on June 8, 1789, Madison again used language clearly indicating that the old Union had been dissolved and a new Union had been created. Commenting in reference to North Carolina and Rhode Island, neither of which had ratified the Constitution by that time, Madison said:

> I allude in a particular manner to those two states who have not thought fit to throw themselves into the bosom of the confederacy: it is a desirable thing, on our part as well as theirs, that a re-union should take place as soon as possible.[17]

Now why should Madison refer to a "re-union" between North Carolina, Rhode Island and the other states, to say nothing of a "New Union," if all the states were still members of the same old Union? With these statements, Madison provided undeniable evidence that the old Union was gone and a new one had been instituted.

3. The Constitution could not possibly be a confederation or compact between the states because it is doing "strange violence" to language to refer to a confederation or compact as a government. In fact, the founders rejected the idea of compacts and confederations altogether, and chose a new form of government.

Webster – "Is it not doing strange violence to language to call a league or a compact between sovereign Powers a Government? ... They [the founders] were asked to continue the existing compact between States; they rejected it. They rejected compact, league, and confederation, and set themselves about framing the constitution of a National Government; and they accomplished what they undertook..."

Interestingly enough, if it be "strange violence" to call a league or confederation a 'government,' the founders were guilty of it, for this is how they referred to the old Articles of Confederation, even using the term "constitution" as well. Consider the following examples. Emphasis, where it appears, is mine:

James Madison:

> **From a letter to James Monroe, dated August 7, 1785**, in which Madison discussed the regulation of trade in regard to the "separate capacities" of the states: "They can no more exercise this power separately, than they could separately carry on war, or separately form treaties of alliance or Commerce. The nature of the thing therefore proves the former power, no less than the latter, to be within the reason of *the federal Constitution.*"[18]

> **From a letter to George Washington, dated December 9, 1785**: "Nothing but the peculiarity of our circumstances could ever have produced those sacrifices of sovereignty on which the *federal Government* now rests."[19]

> **From a document entitled *Vices of the Political System of the United States*** in which Madison enumerates issues arising under the Articles of Confederation and reasons for reforming the Articles. One of Madison's headings reads: "Failure of the States to comply with the *Constitutional* requisitions."[20]

> **From a letter to George Washington, dated Sept. 30, 1787**, in which Madison referred to objections on revising the Articles as a "Constitutional" issue: "It was first urged that as the new Constitution was more than an Alteration of the Articles of Confederation under which Congress acted, and even subverted these articles altogether, there was a *Constitutional impropriety* in their taking any positive agency in the work."[21]

Message of Congress to the States, April 18, 1783: "Some departure, therefore, in the recommendation of Congress, from the *Federal Constitution*, was unavoidable…"[22]

The Annapolis Convention, September, 1786: The convention determined that the Articles of Confederation should be revised and made a recommendation to the states on the "Appointment of commissioners to take into consideration the situation of the United States, to devise such further provisions as shall appear to them necessary to render the *constitution of the federal government* adequate to the exigencies of the union..."[23]

Resolution of Congress, February, 1787: "Resolved, That in the opinion of congress, it is expedient, that...a convention of delegates...be held at Philadelphia, for the sole and express purpose of revising the articles of confederation, and reporting to congress and the several legislatures, such alterations and provisions therein, as shall, when agreed to in congress, and confirmed by the states, *render the federal constitution adequate to the exigencies of the government* and the preservation of the union."[24]

Thomas Jefferson:

> **In his *Autobiography*,** Jefferson referred to the Confederation as a "government": "As the Confederation had made no provision for a visible head of the *government* during vacations of Congress," and again, later, "Among the debilities of the *government* of the Confederation..."[25]
>
> **From a letter to James Monroe, dated June 17, 1785**, in which Jefferson spoke of placing the power to regulate commerce into the hands of Congress: "So far as the imperfect provisions of our *constitution* will admit, and until the states shall by new compact make them more perfect."[26]

Tench Coxe, delegate from Pennsylvania to the Constitutional Convention: "We framed a *Federal Constitution* now universally admitted to be inadequate...the object of our wishes is to amend and supply the evident and allowed errors and defects of the *Federal Government.*"[27]

Richard Henry Lee to George Mason, October 1, 1787: "Upon due consideration of the *Constitution under which we now Act*, some of us were clearly of opinion that the 13th article of the Confederation precluded us from giving an opinion concerning a plan subversive of the present system and eventually forming a new Confederacy of Nine instead of 13 States."[28]

Patrick Henry, in Virginia's Ratifying Convention, June 4, 1788: On the new Constitution: "This proposal of altering our *Federal Government* is of a most alarming nature..."[29]

Many more quotes could be provided to the contrary of Webster's statement that a league or confederacy cannot properly be called a "government" or a "constitution," as least as far as the founders were concerned. We have clearly seen that they spoke of the old confederation quite easily in terms of a "government," a "Federal government," and a "Constitution," just as they did of the new Union. The founders also tended to speak of the government of the Confederation as "the United States in Congress assembled," or simply "Congress," due to the fact that Congress was the only branch of government under the Articles.

As for the founders "rejecting confederation," we have already seen a number of noteworthy examples where they referred to the Union under the Constitution as a "confederation," and we will see more in the future. For the moment though, consider the comments of James Wilson, made in the midst of the Constitutional Convention on June 5, 1787, as recorded in *Elliott's Debates*. Wilson was afraid that disagreements on proposed methods of ratifying the Constitution would doom the entire process by allowing the attempt "to confederate anew on better principles," to be defeated by the inconsiderate or selfish opposition of a few states. He hoped the provision for ratifying would be put "on such a footing as to admit of such a partial union, with a door open for the accession of the rest."[30]

The phrase "to confederate anew upon better principles" sounds remarkably similar to the words "to form a more perfect Union," and, indeed, I believe they are entirely compatible. The Constitution is certainly different than the Articles of Confederation, but this does not mean that it cannot also be a form of confederation. All confederations need not be the same.

4. The Constitution is not a compact between the states because it never calls itself a compact.

Webster – *"What the constitution says of itself, therefore, is as conclusive as what it says on any other point. Does it call itself a compact? Certainly not. It uses the word "compact" but once, and that is when it declares that the States shall enter into no Compact. Does it call itself a league, a confederacy, a subsisting Treaty between the States? Certainly not. There is not a particle of such language in all its pages."*

Webster was correct when he stated that the Constitution does not call itself a compact between states; however, the Constitution never calls itself a "national government" either. Thus, if we force Webster to turn the rigorous demands of his logic upon his own arguments, we could also conclude that the Constitution is not a "national government" because it never uses that term in regard to itself. Webster's own logic proves to be his ultimate undoing here. Arguing that the Constitution cannot be a compact simply because it does not call itself a compact is rather like arguing that a door is not a door unless it is clearly labeled DOOR. A thing does not necessarily have to be labeled in any certain way in order to be what it is. Furthermore, even though the Constitution does not actually call itself a compact between states, it does employ other terminology to that end. Consider:

We have seen proof throughout our discussion that the old confederation was a compact between the states, a fact that is made clear in the opening paragraphs of the Articles of Confederation, where we see who the parties to that Union were to be:

> Articles of Confederation and perpetual Union *between the states* of New Hampshire, Massachusetts-bay Rhode Island and Providence Plantations, Connecticut, New York, New Jersey, Pennsylvania, Delaware, Maryland, Virginia, North Carolina, South Carolina and Georgia.

This language, conclusive in and of itself, was also transferred to the Constitution, where it appears in Article Seven:

> The Ratification of the Conventions of nine States, shall be sufficient for the Establishment of this Constitution *between the States* so ratifying the Same.

Can the words, the very *same* words, "between the states," words that were so clear in the Articles of Confederation, have lost their meaning when transferred to the Constitution? On the contrary, the language employed by the Constitution is also clear, and it devastates Webster's argument. The Constitution may not call itself a *compact*, but the language of Article Seven clearly tells us that the states are the parties to the Union, just as they were under the Articles of Confederation.

5. Instead of establishing a new compact between the states, the founders actually created a consolidated national government.

Webster – *"They rejected compact, league, and confederation, and set themselves about framing the constitution of a National Government..."*

We have seen already that if Webster's logic concerning the omission of the word *compact* from the Constitution is applied to his own arguments, then the Constitution could not be a national government either. But even more significant here is the fact that the founders did not simply fail to include the word *national* in the Constitution; they specifically *excluded* this word. Consider:

Edmund Randolph of Virginia essentially opened the Constitutional Convention by introducing a series of resolutions, the most important of which read: "Resolved, That a national government ought to be established, consisting of a supreme legislative, judiciary, and executive."[31] The committee adopted this resolution, as Daniel Webster also mentioned in his celebrated speech of 1833; however, after more delegates arrived at the convention, Randolph's resolution was brought to the floor again. Oliver Ellsworth of Connecticut moved to alter Randolph's resolution as follows in the record of *Elliott's Debates*:

> Mr. ELLSWORTH, seconded by Mr. GORHAM, moves to alter it, so as to run "that the government of the United States ought to consist of a supreme legislative, executive, and judiciary." This alteration, he said, would drop the word national and retain the proper title "the United States"...

> The motion of Mr. Ellsworth was acquiesced in, *nem. Con.* [without dissent]

> The second resolution, "That the national legislature ought to consist: of two branches," being taken up, the word "national" struck out, as of course.[32]

The word *national* was subsequently removed from each resolution presented to the convention, and it must be admitted that the deliberate exclusion of a word is certainly of greater significance than the alleged incidental omission of a word. The convention delegates deliberately removed the word *national* from the language of the Constitution. Webster actually acknowledged this fact in his speech, but dismissed its significance by stating that: "The substance of this resolution was retained, and was at the head of that list of resolutions which was afterwards sent to the Committee who were to frame the instrument." But this is a strange statement indeed coming from a man who otherwise insisted upon rigorous semantic standards. When faced with facts that denied his conclusions, Webster seemed prepared to relax those standards somewhat.

And while they used the terms *ratify* and *accede* interchangeably, the founders debated loud and long upon the issue of whether the government they sought to frame was a *national* or a *federal* government. The debates in the Constitutional Convention, as well as the various state conventions, are replete with examples of this. But what is the difference between a *national* and a *federal* government? Here are some comments from the Constitutional Convention that serve to explain the founders' perception of the differences between those terms:

William Patterson of New Jersey:

> The commissions under which we acted were not only the measure of our power, they denoted also the sentiments of the states on the subject of our deliberation. The idea of a national government, as contradistinguished from a federal one, never entered into the mind of any of them; and to the public mind we must accommodate ourselves. We have no power to go beyond the federal scheme…A confederacy supposes sovereignty in the members composing it, and sovereignty supposes equality. If we are to be considered as a nation, all state distinctions must be abolished…[33]

Alexander Hamilton of New York [an ardent nationalist]:

> A federal government he conceived to mean an association of independent communities into one. Different confederacies have different powers, and exercise them in different ways. In some instances, the powers are exercised over collective bodies; in others, over individuals, as in the German Diet, and among ourselves, in cases of piracy. Great latitude, therefore, must be given to the signification of the term.[34]

James Madison:

> One characteristic was, that, in a federal government, the power was exercised not on the people individually, but on the people collectively, on the states. Yet in some instances, as in piracies, captures, etc., the existing Confederacy… must operate immediately on individuals. The other characteristic was, that a federal

government derived its appointments not immediately from the people, but from the states which they respectively composed. Here, too, were facts on the other side. In two of the states, Connecticut and Rhode Island, the delegates to Congress were chosen, not by the legislatures, but by the people at large...[35]

These quotes are a sampling of the general debates that took place on the question of whether a *national* or a *federal* government would be instituted by the Constitution. From what we have seen, the founders generally regarded a *national* government as a government composed "of the people" and acting directly on individuals, while a *federal* government was composed of "independent communities" and acted on those communities. At the same time though, they used the terms *national* and *federal* in regard to the old confederation, and their discussions indicate that they regarded the confederation as a federal Union of states that also embodied certain 'national' qualities. The states of the confederation were separate, independent entities in regard to one another; yet, in matters such as treaties and declarations of war, they operated as one entity. Thus the government under the Articles, although certainly a compact between states, was something of a mixed nature when it came to the issue of *national* versus *federal*.

The basis of the Union under the Articles was clearly federal in that it was certainly a Union of States; however, as Hamilton stated, "different confederacies have different powers, and exercise them in different ways," including some powers exercised directly upon individuals and not states. Hamilton then provided the example of provisions regarding piracy as being indicative of a national power, yet he clearly considered the United States of America as being a confederation at the time, another evidence that flies in the face of Webster's assertion that a confederation cannot be regarded as a "government proper".

There were certainly those in the Constitutional Convention who wished to see to it that the new system was a consolidated nation-state, with some even advocating the total destruction of state governments, but this viewpoint did not prevail. The Constitution that finally emerged from the lengthy Philadelphia convention was clearly a federal document, establishing a federal Union. That government was then, and still is today, referred to as a *federal* government. The advocates of the Constitution were known as *Federalists*. Those who opposed the Constitution were known as *Anti-federalists*. The foremost body of thought offered by Constitution advocates was collected into what we now call *The Federalist Papers*. This emphasis on the term *federal* cannot simply be overlooked, and certainly not deliberately replaced with the word *national*, not when the delegates to the Constitutional Convention purposefully struck out that word from the document they were preparing.

Our country's founders did sometimes use the term *national* in regard to the government of the Union; however, it is important to understand that they perceived a very real difference between the formal and informal uses of this term, as I believe I have just illustrated. In informal usage the term "nation" can serve as a synonym for words like "country," "confederation," or "union," and the founders did occasionally use it like this, just as we sometimes use it today. In fact, the term "nation" is not altogether inappropriate where matters of foreign policy are concerned because, in instances where we have dealings with other countries, the United States speak with one voice, just as a consolidated nation-state would behave. There is no harm in this informal usage as long as we remember that, in terms of its formal, legal, constitutional relations to the states, the government of the United States of America is properly described as *federal*, not *national*.

6. The preamble to the Constitution clearly indicates that it is a government of whole people, and not a compact between the states.

Webster – *"How can any man get over the words of the constitution itself? 'We, the people of the United States, do ordain and establish this constitution.' These words must cease to be a part of the constitution, they must be obliterated from the parchment on which they are written, before any human ingenuity or human argument can remove the popular basis on which that constitution rests, and turn the instrument into a mere compact between sovereign States!"*

The preamble to the United States Constitution comprises some of history's most famous and easily recognized lines of prose. Certainly, in regard to all that we have just seen about how the founding fathers viewed the Constitution as a compact between the states, it seems only fitting to examine the preamble and ask why they chose to word it as they did.

The Constitution underwent many revisions before it eventually took the familiar shape we recognize today, and this revision process included the wording of the preamble. The first version of the preamble, as reported by a committee of five delegates on August 6, 1787, read as follows:

> We, the people of the states of New Hampshire, Massachusetts, Rhode Island and Providence Plantations, Connecticut, New York, New Jersey, Pennsylvania, Delaware, Maryland, Virginia, North Carolina, South Carolina, and Georgia, do ordain, declare, and establish, the following Constitution for the government of ourselves and our posterity...[36]

The final preamble reads:

> We, the People of the United States, in Order to form a more perfect Union, establish Justice, insure domestic Tranquility, provide for the common defence, promote the general Welfare, and secure the Blessings of Liberty to ourselves and our Posterity, do ordain and establish this Constitution for the United States of America.

This issue of the preamble's wording caused some noteworthy controversy during the ratification process. One of the most famous exchanges involving the issue took place during Virginia's ratifying convention, where Anti-federalist Patrick Henry argued that the Constitution's preamble proved that it was a wholly consolidated national government:

> And here I would make this enquiry of those worthy characters who composed a part of the late Federal Convention. I am sure they were fully impressed with the necessity of forming a great consolidated Government, instead of a confederation. That this is a consolidated Government is demonstrably clear, and the danger of such a Government, is, to my mind, very striking. I have the highest veneration for those Gentlemen – but, Sir, give me leave to demand, what right they had to say, We, the People. My political curiosity, exclusive of my anxious solicitude for the public welfare, leads me to ask, who authorized them to speak the language of, We, the People, instead of We, the States? States are the characteristics, and the soul of a confederation. If the States be not the agents of this compact, it must be one great consolidated National Government of the people of all the States.[37]

This quote from Henry has been used many times over the years by members of the nationalist school of government to advocate the same idea that Daniel Webster and Abraham Lincoln supported; namely the idea that the Constitution was created as an act of the people, and is, therefore, not a compact between the states. However, it should be well noted that Henry's charge did not go unanswered. James Madison, among others, answered and refuted the argument, a fact glossed over by the advocates of consolidation (whom I cannot regard as simply being ignorant of Madison's response to Henry).

Consider Madison's reply in the Virginia ratifying convention:

> I can say, notwithstanding what the Honorable Gentleman has alleged, that this Government is not completely consolidated – nor is it entirely federal. *Who are the parties to it? The people – but not the people as composing one great body – but the people as composing thirteen sovereignties:* Were it as the Gentleman asserts, a consolidated Government, the assent of the majority of the people would be sufficient for its establishment, and as a majority have adopted it already, the remaining States would be bound by the act of the majority, even if they unanimously reprobated it: Were it such a Government as it is suggested, it would be now binding upon the people of this State, without having had the privilege of deliberating upon it: But, Sir, no State is bound by it, as it is, without its own consent. *Should all the States adopt it, it will be then a Government established by the thirteen States of America, not through the intervention of the legislatures, but by the people at large.*[38]
> [Emphasis mine]

Richard Henry Lee, also speaking in the Virginia ratifying convention, rebuked Henry's accusation along the same lines as Madison:

> If this were a Consolidated Government, ought it not to be ratified by a majority of the people as individuals, and not as States? Suppose Virginia, Connecticut, Massachusetts, and Pennsylvania had ratified it; these four States being a majority of the people of America, would, by their adoption, have made it binding on all the States, had this been a Consolidated Government. But it is only the Government of the seven States who have adopted it. If the Honorable Gentleman will attend to this, we shall hear no more of consolidation.[39]

James Madison also remarked in detail upon this subject in *The Federalist Papers*. The following is an excerpt from Federalist 39:

"In its foundation it is federal, not national..."

> It appears on one hand that the constitution is to be founded on the assent and ratification of the people of America, given by deputies elected for the special purpose; but on the other that this assent and ratification is to be given by the people, not as individuals comprising one entire nation; but as composing the distinct and independent states to which they respectively belong. It is to be the assent and ratification of the several states derived from the supreme authority in each state, the authority of the people themselves. The act therefore establishing the constitution, will not be a national but a federal act...

> Were the people regarded in this transaction as forming one nation, the will of the majority of the whole people of the United States, would bind the minority; in the same manner as the majority in each state must bind the minority...Each state in ratifying the constitution, is considered as a sovereign body independent of all others, and only to be bound by its own voluntary act. In this relation then the new constitution will, if established, be a federal and not a national constitution. [Emphasis mine]

Such was the opinion of James Madison, a man who was prominently involved in the Constitutional Convention, favored a stronger government than was actually created, and later became known as the "Father of the Constitution". Madison's response to Henry's arguments also serves to answer those of Abraham Lincoln and Daniel Webster. The Constitution was not ratified by the "people" of the United States in any aggregate or national capacity, but rather, as "composing thirteen sovereignties".[40] Madison supported the idea that the Constitution was a compact between states, a confederation of thirteen peoples. And there are many more examples to this effect [Unless otherwise indicated, emphasis in the following quotations is mine]:

James Madison

> **Summary of a speech to the Constitutional Convention on May 31, 1787,** in regard to the use of force by the federal government

against states as tantamount to a dissolution of the Union, as cited in Elliott's Debates: "Mr. MADISON observed that...*A union of states* containing such an ingredient seemed to provide for its own destruction. The use of force against a state would look more like a declaration of war than an infliction of punishment, and would probably be considered by the party attacked as a dissolution of all previous *compacts by which it might be bound.*"[41]

From a letter to Thomas Jefferson, dated October 24, 1787, in which Madison described the Constitutional Convention to Jefferson: "It appeared to be the sincere and unanimous wish of the Convention to *cherish and preserve the Union of the States.*"[42]

From a letter to Thomas Jefferson, dated September 29, 1798: "Have you ever considered thoroughly the distinction between the power of the State, and that of the Legislature, on questions relating to *the federal pact?*"[43]

From the *Virginia Resolutions Against the Alien and Sedition Acts of 1798*, as drafted by Madison: "RESOLVED...That this Assembly most solemnly declares a warm attachment to *the Union of the States*...That this Assembly doth explicitly and peremptorily declare, that it views the powers of the federal government, as resulting from *the compact to which the states are parties*; as limited by the plain sense and intention of *the instrument constituting that compact...*"[44]

From Madison's report on the *Virginia Resolutions Against the Alien and Sedition Acts*, January 7, 1800: "The resolution declares, first, that 'it views the powers of the Federal Government, as resulting from *the compact to which the states are parties*,' in other words, that the federal powers are derived from the Constitution, and that *the Constitution is a compact to which the states are parties*.

"*Clear as this position must seem*, that the federal powers are derived from the Constitution, and from that alone, the committee are not unapprised of a late doctrine which opens another source of federal powers, not less extensive and important, than it is new and unexpected...

"The next position is, that the General Assembly views the powers of the Federal Government, "as limited by the plain sense and intention of *the instrument constituting that compact*," and "as no farther valid than they are authorized by the grants therein enumerated." *It does not seem possible that any just objection can lie against either of these clauses...*

"It does not follow, however, that because *the states as sovereign parties to their constitutional compact,* must ultimately decide whether it has been violated, that such a decision ought to be interposed in a hasty manner, or on doubtful and inferior occasions."[45]

Thomas Jefferson

From the Kentucky Resolutions on the Alien and Sedition Acts of 1798, as drafted by Jefferson: "RESOLVED: That *the several States composing the United States of America, are* not *united* on the principle of unlimited submission to their General Government; but that, *by a compact under the style and title of a Constitution for the United States...*that *to this compact each State acceded as a State...*that *the government created by this compact* was not made the exclusive or final judge of the extent of the powers delegated to itself..."[46]

From Draft Declaration and Protest of the Commonwealth of Virginia, on the Principles of the Constitution of the United States of America, and on the Violations of them, dated December 1825: "We, the General Assembly of Virginia, on behalf, and in the name of the people thereof, do declare as follows: The States in North America which confederated to establish their independence of the government of Great Britain, of which Virginia was one, became, on that acquisition, free and independent States, and as such, authorized to constitute governments, each for itself, such form as it thought best.

"They entered into a compact, (which is called the Constitution of the United States of America)...they do not mean to raise the banner of disaffection, or separation from their sister States, co-parties with themselves to this compact...

"And as a further pledge of the sincere and cordial attachment of this commonwealth to the union of the whole, so far as has been consented to by *the compact called "The Constitution of the United States of America,* "(constructed according to the plain and ordinary meaning of its language, to the common intendment of the time, and of those who framed it)..."[47]

Robert Livingston, a Federalist during New York's ratification debates: "My argument was, that *a Republic might very properly be formed by a league of States*, but that the laws of the general Legislature must act, and be enforced upon individuals. *I am contending for this species of Government.*"[48]

Alexander Hamilton [capitalization in the original]:

From New York's ratification debates, speaking of the Constitution: "Thus it appears that the very structure of the *Confederacy* affords the surest preventions from error, and the most powerful checks to misconduct."[49]

From Federalist 9, comparing confederate systems from the writings of Montesquieu: "So far are the suggestions of Montesquieu from standing in opposition to the general Union of the States that he explicitly treats of a CONFEDERATE REPUBLIC as the expedient for extending the sphere of popular government and reconciling the advantages of monarchy with those of republicanism..." And later..."I have thought it proper to quote at length from these interesting passages, because they contain a luminous abridgment of the principle arguments in favor of the Union..."

From Federalist 27, speaking of the Constitution's 'Supremacy clause': "It merits particular attention in this place, that *the laws of the Confederacy* as to the enumerated and legitimate objects of its jurisdiction will become the SUPREME LAW of the land..."

From Federalist 85, speaking against arguments that the Constitution is imperfect: "The *compacts which are to embrace thirteen distinct States* in a common bond of amity and Union must as necessarily be a compromise of as many dissimilar interests and inclinations. How can perfection spring from such materials..." And later... "Hence the necessity of moulding and arranging all the particulars which are to compose the whole in such a manner as to satisfy *all the parties to the compact.*"

James Wilson of Pennsylvania, speaking during Pennsylvania's ratification debates: "...it is natural to assume that Providence has designed us for a united people, under *one great political compact*. If this is a just and reasonable conclusion, supported by the wishes of the people, the Convention did right in proposing a single *confederated Republic.*"[50]

Nathaniel Dane of New York writing to Melancton Smith on July 3, 1788; a letter in which he encourages ratification of the Constitution: "It is not to be pretended that *the ratifying States* will have any Just cause to make war upon any non ratifying State, merely because she does not *accede* to a *national compact*, where she has a right to act according to her discretion."[51]

Ratification of the Constitution by the State of Massachusetts: "The Convention having impartially discussed, and fully considered, the Constitution for the United States of America...and acknowledging, with grateful hearts, the goodness of the Supreme Ruler of the Universe in affording the people of the United States, in the course of his providence, an opportunity, deliberately and peaceably, without fraud or surprise, *of entering into an explicit and solemn compact with each other, by assenting to and ratifying a new Constitution...*"[52]

Thus we see Webster's arguments for a consolidated nation-state continue to collapse under a punishing barrage of quotations from the founding fathers and the rigorous demands of logic as well. In creating the Constitution, the founders truly sought to "confederate anew on better principles". They established a new compact, which the states, as distinct entities, entered into. Each state convened a convention of persons appointed by the people of that state, conventions that ratified the Constitution for each state in its separate, sovereign capacity. There was never any vote of the people of the United States in some supposed aggregate capacity. In fact, we have seen that the founders even argued against that very claim. Thus, in considering the question of the Constitution's preamble, we must be careful to keep the phrase "people of the United States," in its proper context.

But then, if the founders meant that the Constitution was to form another Union of States, why did they not simply say "we the states," as Patrick Henry had suggested, and thereby avoid the confusion that occurred at the time among Anti-federalists like Henry, and later, among men like Webster and Lincoln?

There are three things to keep in mind here:

1. It would not have been practical to have included the names of the states in the Constitution at that time because it was not known which states would join the new Union. The Constitution did not require the ratifications of all thirteen states to go into effect, nor was it binding

on any non-ratifying states. Thus the names of specific states were rightly omitted from the document.

2. Although nationalists always use the term "the United States" to refer to the entire country, the Union, we have also seen that it can be – and was – used in reference to the states themselves at the time of the founding. Witness in particular how the phrase was used in the Declaration of Independence, when there was no formal American Union at all.

Now, considering that we have seen ample evidence of the fact that the people of the states – acting as separate states – formed the Union under the Constitution, it seems entirely reasonable to read "We the People of the United States" as a reference to the people of the individual states, and not the Union itself. This seems especially plausible when we read, just forty words later, that the "People of the United States" are ordaining and establishing this Constitution *for the United States of America*". Notice the differences in phraseology here. The "People of the United States" are establishing a government "for the United States of America," *not* for "the United States". "The United States" needed no constitution because each already had its own individual charter of government. On the other hand, "the United States of America," the Union, did need a constitution.

Some may argue that "the United States" and "the United States of America" both refer to the Union itself, but this seems highly unlikely. If both mean the same thing, then why did the founders use two different terms, separated by only forty words? Why does the preamble not read, "We the People of the United States of America...do ordain and establish this Constitution"? The use of such phraseology would seem far more obviously nationalistic than how the preamble actually reads.

3. Their experience with the Articles of Confederation caused the founders to put a great deal of emphasis upon the people of the individual states as forming the consensual basis for the Constitution's authority. The reasons for this are summarized well by James Madison's comments during the Constitutional Convention when the method of ratification was being discussed.

> [Madison] thought this provision [popular ratification] essential. The Articles of Confederation themselves were defective in this

respect, resting, in many states, on the legislative sanction only... He suggested also that, as far as the Articles of Union were to be considered as a treaty only, of a particular sort, among the governments of independent states, the doctrine might be set up that a breach of any one article, by any of the parties, absolved the other parties from the whole obligation. For these reasons, as well as others, he thought it indispensable that the new Constitution should be ratified in the most unexceptionable form, and by the Supreme authority of the people themselves.[53]

By appealing to the people of each state, the framers of the Constitution were appealing to the ultimate, sovereign authority of the states, that authority to which the individual state governments also had to bow: the people of each state. Thus the powers and maintenance of the Union would be taken from the hands of the individual state governments and delivered up to the ultimate sovereignty of the people of each state. The result would be a Union that derived its foundation from the people, but from the people as "composing thirteen sovereignties".

In addition to these practical aspects of the preamble's wording, there are those who point out that it was authored by Gouverneur Morris: delegate to the convention from Pennsylvania and an ardent nationalist. The preamble, they claim, was Morris' way of emphasizing the consolidated, nationalistic nature of the new government. In essence, they argue that it was a subtle nationalistic 'coup' on the part of Morris.

Gouverneur Morris did indeed pen the preamble, along with most of the rest of the Constitution. He did so as head of the Committee on Style, and after an initial draft of the Constitution had already been completed by the convention delegates. Once completed, Morris' consolidated draft was submitted to the delegates, who approved it but added some last minute changes. As for whether it was a nationalistic 'coup,' I believe we should consider three things:

1. James Madison was also a member of the Committee on Style, and we have already seen his reply to the notion that the Constitution's preamble identifies it as a consolidated, nationalistic government. Madison flatly disagreed with that interpretation, and offered definitive proof against it.

2. Morris' draft did not stand on his will alone. It was voted upon and approved by the convention delegates, who, as we have seen, deliberately struck the word *national* from the Constitution.

3. Morris was not happy with the finished Constitution; it was not at all the type of government that he thought it should be. In fact, Morris is recorded in *Elliott's Debates* as remarking, toward the close of the Constitutional Convention, that he "had long wished for another Convention, that will have the firmness to provide a vigorous government, which we are afraid to do."[54] Indeed, Morris himself accepted the Compact Theory as fact, stating that:

> The Constitution was a compact, not between individuals, but between political societies, the people, not of America, but of the United States, each enjoying sovereign power and of course equal rights.[55]

No, it seems abundantly clear that the people of the individual states established the Constitution in order "to form a more perfect Union," or, in the words of James Wilson, "to confederate anew upon better principles". View the term *United States* as a plural reference to the individual states, as the founders – including Gouverneur Morris himself – did, instead of as a singular term for the entire Union, and the mystery of the preamble's wording vanishes. The Constitution even speaks of "the United States" in an obviously plural fashion in its text. Consider Article Three, Section Three:

> Treason against the United States, shall consist only in levying War against *them*, or in adhering to *their* enemies…

Thus the preamble and general language of the Constitution pose no resistance to the idea that the document is a compact between the states instead of a consolidated national government. The idea that the founders were preserving the Union of States in their work on the Constitution is also testified to by the manner in which the Convention's proceedings were brought to an end. *Elliott's Debates* records that an amended Constitution was submitted to the Convention on September 15, 1787, and notes the following [capitals are in the original]:

> On the question to agree to the Constitution as amended, it passed in the affirmative – ALL THE STATES CONCURRING.[56]

When the final form of the Constitution was complete, the following notation was made prior to its signing by the delegates:

> DONE in Convention *by the Unanimous Consent of the States present* the Seventeenth Day of September in the Year of our Lord one thousand seven hundred and Eighty seven and the Independence of the United States of America the Twelfth In Witness whereof We have hereunto subscribed our Names…

The delegates then signed their names *by state*. But if the Constitution was to represent a consolidated national government of the people as a whole, thus emphasizing the people over the states, then why do we find these prominent and continuous references to the action and consent of the states? It is strange indeed that the founders would muddy the waters with such repeated references to the states instead of the people if their act was designed to create one great nation, and particularly if they wished their descendents to understand this clearly. Why, instead, did they not simply sign the document as individual citizens and omit these prominent references to the states in their proceedings?

7. The Constitution could not be a compact between the states because it uses the language of "injunction and prohibition" to the states. Webster said that this is because, in the Constitution, "it is the people who speak," and not the states.

Webster – *"The people ordain the constitution, and therein address themselves to the States, and to the Legislatures of the States, in the language of injunction and prohibition."*

With this objection, Webster seemed to have forgotten that the Articles of Confederation, certainly representative of a compact between states, also used the language of "injunction" and "prohibition" toward the states, just as the Constitution does. In fact, many of the same prohibitions found in the Constitution were transferred from the Articles of Confederation. The following partial excerpts are from Article Six of the Articles of Confederation:

> No state without the Consent of the united states in congress assembled, shall send any embassy to, or receive any embassy from, or enter into any conference, agreement, alliance or treaty with any King prince or state…

No two or more states shall enter into any treaty, confederation or alliance between them...

No state shall lay any imposts or duties...

No vessels of war shall be kept up in time of peace by any state...

No state shall engage in any war without the consent of the united states in congress assembled, unless such state be actually invaded...

The fact that the Constitution speaks the language of "injunction and prohibition" to the states certainly does not mean that the states themselves could not be parties to that Constitution. Persons engaging in contractual relations with one another today often agree to abide by various stipulations that amount to "injunctions and prohibitions" toward themselves; the contract simply binds them to their agreement within the scope of its provisions. In ratifying the Articles of Confederation, the states merely agreed to refrain from the exercise of certain powers in favor of having those powers exercised by the entire Union.

It was no different under the Constitution. As parties to the new compact of Union, the states once more agreed to refrain from exercising various powers individually in favor of having those powers exercised corporately via the Union. In ratifying the Constitution, each state was bound only by its own voluntary act. Once again, there was no overriding determination made by the people of the United States as a whole to impose anything upon any state. The people of the United States "spoke" only via their status as members of the separate and distinct political entities to which they belonged.

8. Under the Articles of Confederation, the states entered into agreements with one another, but no such language is found in the Constitution. If the Constitution is truly a compact between the states, we should see such agreements in it, just as with the Articles.

Webster – "*If the States be parties, as States; what are their rights, and what [are] their respective covenants, and stipulations expressed? The States engage for nothing, they promise nothing. In the articles of confederation, they did make promises, and did enter into engagements, and did plight the faith of each State for their fulfillment; but in the constitution there is nothing of that kind.*"

First, it should be understood that, as we have seen already, the Articles of Confederation and the Constitution rested on different foundations. They were both compacts to which the states were parties, but under the Articles it was the state governments that formed the Union, while, under the Constitution, it was the people of each state, as indicated in the preamble: "We the People of the United States...ordain and establish this Constitution for the United States of America". Thus we should not be surprised to find that the language of the Constitution differs from the Articles in terms of who is pledging to do what and how.

Second, as a compact, the Constitution itself is a mass of stipulations. It describes how the government is to be structured, what the government may or may not do, and what the states may or may not do. The states, in the act of acceding to the Constitution, put those stipulations into effect amongst themselves, as we are clearly shown in Article VII by the words "between the states". Indeed, as we saw, the word *accede* means "to become a party (as to an agreement)," and the evidence is abundant that the founders did consider state ratifications of the Constitution as *accessions*. The Constitution, as a compact, was – and remains – an agreement between the states as to the basis of their Union.

Webster was rather obviously reaching with this argument. There is absolutely no reason why the Constitution, simply because it does not read exactly as the Articles of Confederation did, cannot be a compact, an agreement to which the states engaged, promised, and plighted their faith in the act of accession.

9. The Constitution could not be a confederation or compact between the states because it empowers the government to work directly upon individuals instead of just the states themselves. Webster declared that only a national government operates against individuals directly.

Webster – "*The Constitution of the United States creates direct relations between this Government and individuals. This Government may punish individuals for treason, and all other crimes in the code, when committed against the United States. It has power, also, to tax individuals, in any mode, and to any extent; and it possesses the further power of demanding from individuals military service. Nothing certainly, can more clearly distinguish a*

Government from a confederation of States than the possession of these powers."

In reviewing this objection to the compactual nature of the Union, we can point to some evidence that we have already seen to demonstrate that, just because the Constitution does operate on individuals in some of its provisions, this does not mean that it cannot be a confederation or compact between the states. Alexander Hamilton, while commenting on the nature of a federal government during the Constitutional Convention, made the statement that a federal government can operate upon both states and individuals. The following excerpt is taken from a speech made by Hamilton during the Convention, as quoted at greater length during our previous discussion of *national* vs. *federal*. Hamilton was recorded as saying:

> Different confederacies have different powers, and exercise them in different ways. In some instances, the powers are exercised over collective bodies; in others, over individuals... Great latitude, therefore, must be given to the signification of the term.

We also reviewed a speech that James Madison made during the Convention in which he commented on the nature of a federal government and stated:

> One characteristic was, that, in a federal government, the power was exercised not on the people individually, but on the people collectively, on the states. Yet in some instances, as in piracies, captures, etc., the existing Confederacy...must operate immediately on individuals.

In that same speech, Madison also showed that the powers of a federal government can come directly from the people as represented by their individual states due to the fact that, under the Articles of Confederation, the states of Connecticut and Rhode Island allowed their people to elect delegates to Congress, whereas the other states sent delegates by legislative appointment. Therefore, as far as at least those two states were concerned, there was definitely a strong relationship between the people of the state and the federal government where they were represented. Madison's speech makes it clear that he viewed the idea that the federal government can have direct relations with individuals as being no new thing. The proposed Constitution would simply take the matter further than the Articles of Confederation had.

It should also be pointed out that all governments, no matter what form they take, ultimately include and impact individuals. Consider the words of Rufus King concerning the Articles of Confederation in light of the government's federal nature. These comments were made during the Constitutional Convention:

> If the union of states comprises the idea of a confederation, it comprises also that of consolidation. A union of states is a union of the men composing them, from whence a national character results to the whole. Congress can act alone without the states...If they declare war, war is de jure declared; captures made in pursuance of it are lawful; no acts of the states can vary the situation, or prevent the judicial consequences.[57]

King correctly expressed the concept that even a confederated Union of States, such as certainly existed under the Articles of Confederation, is ultimately a Union incorporating those who inhabit the member states. And, as we have seen, the provisions of the Articles of Confederation did operate directly upon individuals in certain circumstances. We have also seen that, in spite of the fact that they were granting expanded powers for the government to act upon individuals under the Constitution, the founders were quite clear that they were establishing another federal government, sometimes even calling it a "confederate republic". The fact that this new government was to operate on individuals as well as states did not diminish the fact that the states themselves were the contracting parties to the Constitution.

Therefore, it is quite feasible to say that the Constitution could prescribe a federal government possessing certain "national" functions, just as the Articles of Confederation had. As King noted, when Congress declared war under the Articles, the United States effectively functioned as one "people" in that every state, and thus all of their inhabitants, was obliged to abide by that declaration. The same principle applied to treaties, alliances, and other matters dealing with foreign powers in particular. In those times, the United States spoke with one voice even though they were separate entities in most other aspects.

The key to this concept was expressed in a speech made by John Adams of Virginia during the formation of the Articles of Confederation:

> The question is not what we are now, but what we ought to be when our bargain shall be made. The confederacy is to make us one individual only; it is to form us, like separate parcels of metal, into one common mass. We shall no longer retain our separate individuality, but become a single individual, as to all questions submitted to the confederacy.[58]

The operative phrase here is: "as to all questions submitted to the confederacy". Adams clearly understood that the Articles of Confederation represented a compact and federal Union of States. Nevertheless, he was able to speak of the Articles as making the people of the United States "one individual" in relation to all questions that concerned the confederacy as a whole. The situation was to be the same under the new Constitution.

10. The Constitution cannot be a compact between states because a "constitution" is, by definition, a fundamental law. A compact is not a fundamental law, but merely an agreement.

Webster – *"What is a constitution? Certainly not a league, compact, or confederacy, but a fundamental law... This then, sir, is declared to be a constitution. A constitution is the fundamental law of the State; and this is expressly declared to be the supreme law. "*

The first and most obvious problem with Webster's declaration is that we have already seen examples where the founders referred to the old Articles of Confederation as a "constitution". This fact alone invalidates Webster's claim that a confederation cannot be formed by a constitution. The founders obviously found no contradiction in the idea.

But let's go a step further and take a look at the definitions of some key words. *Merriam-Webster* defines a "constitution" as "an established law or custom: ORDINANCE," and as "the basic principles and laws of a nation, state, or social group that determine the powers and duties of the government and guarantee certain rights to the people in it...a written instrument embodying the rules of a political or social organization". The word "fundamental" is defined as "serving as an original or generating source: PRIMARY," and "serving as a basis supporting existence or determining essential structure or function: BASIC".

As the central unifying agent of the United States, the Constitution is the fundamental – primary or basic – aspect of the Union. It is the core, the hub, the nucleus of the Republic. Its provisions are supreme. It is the law of the land. It must be so; if it were not, it would amount to nothing more than a mere figurehead document, without any real power or influence, incapable of unifying anything. But what is it about any of this that prevents the Constitution from being a compact, or acting as the unifying agent of a collection of states? If the Constitution is indeed a compact between states, does that fact make it any less fundamental to the Union than if it represented a consolidated nation-state? Is it not still the underlying aspect, the primary or basic means by which we find our identity, just as the Articles of Confederation were to the first American Union? Do its provisions not have the force of law? Further, are those provisions not, in fact, the "supreme law" of the land?

Regardless of the fact that they were enacted as compacts between individual, sovereign states, the Articles and the Constitution were both fundamental to their respective Unions, and both carried the force of law. As a result, even as compacts, both were fundamental laws; and, to this day, the Constitution remains both a compact and a fundamental law.

One Last Note on Daniel Webster

At the end of this first part in our discussion of the Constitution and secession, I feel the reader may be interested to know that Daniel Webster eventually re-evaluated some of his claims concerning the Constitution and the nature of the Union.

Speaking before the United States Supreme Court in 1839, during the case of *The Bank of Augusta vs. Earle,* Webster stated:

> I am not prepared to say that the states have no national sovereignty. The laws of some of the states - Maryland and Virginia, for instance - provide punishment for treason. The power thus exercised is certainly not municipal. Virginia has a law of alienage: that is, a power exercised against a foreign nation. Does not the question necessarily arise, when a power is exercised concerning an alien enemy- enemy to whom? The law of escheat, which exists in all the states, is also the exercise of a great sovereign power...[1]

In deciding this case, the Supreme Court [Roger Taney speaking for the majority] sided with Webster's view and stated, in part:

> We think it is well settled, that by the law of comity [friendly relations, or courtesy] among nations, a corporation created by one sovereignty is permitted to make contracts in another, and to sue in its Courts; and that the same law of comity prevails among the several sovereignties of this Union.[2]

Another example of Webster's altered thinking can be found in a speech that he made in Capon Springs, Virginia, on June 28, 1851. The following two quotations are excerpts from that speech:

> How absurd it is to suppose that when different parties enter into a compact for certain purposes, either can disregard any one provision, and expect, nevertheless, the other to observe the rest!

> I have not hesitated to say, and I repeat, that if the northern States refuse, willfully and deliberately, to carry into effect that part of the constitution which respects the restoration of fugitive slaves, and Congress provide no remedy, the South would no longer be bound to observe the compact. A bargain cannot be broken on one side and still bind the other side.[3]

Here, in these quotes, we have nothing less than Senator Webster doing a complete about-face from his propositions of 1833, adopting the view that states possess sovereignty and that the Constitution is a compact! It would be a disservice to Mr. Webster's memory to omit these statements showing his developing view of the Constitution. Nevertheless, his earlier views on the subject were given and refuted first because, even though Webster himself later neglected them, they were used by Lincoln and the Republicans in 1861, and they are still used by nationalists today under the authority of Webster's name.

Part Two:

Lincoln's Case Against Southern Secession

"What I do...I do because I believe it helps to save the Union."

– Abraham Lincoln

"Those who make peaceful revolution impossible will make violent revolution inevitable."

– John F. Kennedy

Lincoln Takes on the South

Our previous discussion on the nature of the Union and the government established by the Constitution can now serve as a basis for answering specific arguments made against the Southern states in 1861, primarily by Abraham Lincoln. We have touched on some of these arguments already, but Lincoln employed a particular approach that will allow us to further refine our previous observations while branching off into some new issues as well.

As I did for Webster in Part One, I have summarized Lincoln's arguments and included some brief excerpts from his speeches in this section. The interested reader can find lengthier excerpts from Lincoln in Appendix E.

Position One:
The Union belongs to the "People"

Speaking against the seceded states in his message to Congress in special session on July 4, 1861, Lincoln chided them for abandoning the wording and meaning of the Declaration of Independence and the Constitution:

> Our adversaries have adopted some declarations of independence, in which, unlike the good old one, penned by Jefferson, they omit the words "all men are created equal." Why? They have adopted a temporary national constitution, in the preamble of which, unlike our good old one, signed by Washington, they omit "We, the People," and substitute "We, the deputies of the sovereign and independent States." Why? Why this deliberate pressing out of view the rights of men and the authority of the people?

Lincoln accused the Southern states of improperly emphasizing the role of the states over that of the people in the act of creating the Union. Yet we have already seen abundant evidence that Lincoln's view of the Union as a creation of the American people in some aggregate sense was erroneous. The Constitution is a compact, the Union a confederated republic. In referring to the "deputies of the sovereign and independent States," the authors of the Confederate Constitution committed no wrong. They merely felt they were clarifying the truth that the founders meant to convey in the Constitution of the United States, a truth that, over time, was masked by the designs of ambitious men who stood to gain from consolidating power in Washington.

Thus, by denying the basis upon which the government of the United States truly rested, it was Lincoln himself who had deliberately "pressed the truth out of view". The principles of the seceded states were directly in line with the Declaration of Independence and the

Constitution of 1787. Lincoln's principles of forced unity and military coercion were more in line with King George's than those of Jefferson and Washington.

Position Two:
The Union is Perpetual

In his first inaugural address, Lincoln stated:

> I hold, that in contemplation of universal law, and of the Constitution, the Union of these States is perpetual. Perpetuity is implied, if not expressed, in the fundamental law of all national governments. It is safe to assert that no government proper, ever had a provision in its organic law for its own termination.

A Perpetual Union? The Moral Implications

Lincoln's statement that no government ever had a provision for its own termination is true as far as it goes; however, we have already seen an instance in our own history where the lack of provision for ending a form of government did not prevent it from happening. In fact, the Articles of Confederation had a provision specifically designed to prevent their termination:

> **Title paragraph:** Articles of Confederation and perpetual Union between the states of...

> **Following Article Thirteen:** The Articles thereof shall be inviolably observed by the States we respectively represent, *and...the Union shall be perpetual.*

How long did these "perpetual" Articles last before being terminated? Six years. Bearing this in mind, it is little wonder the founders failed to include a similar provision in the new Constitution. They well understood that no government could last forever.

Speaking to the Constitutional Convention, Benjamin Franklin underscored this fact:

> In these sentiments, sir, I agree to this Constitution with all its faults – if they are such – because I think a general government

necessary for us, and there is no form of government but what may be a blessing to the people if well administered; and I believe, further, that this is likely to be well administered for a course of years, and can only end in despotism, as other forms have done before it, when the people shall become so corrupted as to need despotic government, being incapable of any other.[1]

We have already reviewed James Madison's quotation in which he referred to the fact that fewer than all the states could dissolve the Articles of Confederation due, if for no other reason, "to the transcendent law of nature and of nature's God, which declares that the safety and happiness of society are the objects at which all political institutions aim and to which all such institutions must be sacrificed". We have seen that, in making this declaration, Madison did nothing more than hearken back to the words of the Declaration of Independence itself in which the "unalienable" right of the people to a government of their consent was advanced. It was that ideology that compelled the Founding Fathers to move forward and caused the states to declare their independence from Great Britain. Without this ideology, the United States of America could never have come into being.

Interestingly enough, although Abraham Lincoln opposed secession, he did claim to favor the right of revolution. "No man is good enough to govern another man, without that other's consent," Lincoln once stated. "I say this is the leading principle – the sheet anchor of American republicanism."[2] During his brief time as a United States congressman from Illinois, Lincoln addressed the House of Representatives on the subject, proclaiming:

> Any people anywhere, being inclined and having the power, have the right to rise up, and shake off the existing government, and form a new one that suits them better. Any portion of such people that can, may revolutionize, and make their own, of so much territory as they inhabit. This is a most valuable, – a most sacred right – a right, which we hope and believe, is to liberate the world. Nor is this right confined to cases in which the whole people of an existing government may choose to exercise it. Any portion of such people that can may revolutionize, and make their own of so much of the territory as they inhabit.[3]

Lincoln reaffirmed this principle again even while decrying secession during his inaugural address in 1861. "This country, with its institutions, belongs to the people who inhabit it," Lincoln told Americans. "Whenever they shall grow weary of the existing Government, they can exercise their constitutional right of amending it or their revolutionary right to dismember or overthrow it." These quotations may come as a shock to the reader, who might very well ask how it was that Lincoln could forcefully oppose Southern secession if he truly believed that the peoples' right to a government of their consent justified revolutionary measures. On the surface, that seems a rather hypocritical posture. Indeed, one observant British periodical asked how the United States government could oppose Southern secession when the United States of America itself "was founded on secession from the British Empire?"[4]

Lincoln did support the theoretical right to revolution, but his ideology concerning it was hopelessly convoluted, and it was indeed hypocritically applied to the Southern states, at least in part. Essentially, Lincoln had two requirements for what might be termed a 'legitimate' revolution: first, it must be a revolution of the "people," and second, it must be "'exercised for a morally justifiable cause.'"[5] Let's consider these requirements.

First, although Lincoln had stated that "any portion" of a country's population could revolutionize rather than just "the whole people," in his first inaugural address he claimed that anyone who rejected majority rule "does, of necessity, fly to anarchy or despotism". This is certainly problematic from both logical and practical standpoints. One cannot consistently speak of a right as "valuable" and "most sacred," with potential to "liberate the world," and yet accuse practitioners of that right as committing some terrible wrong by invoking it. Also, it was not known what the majority of Americans thought of the secession question. Prior to the outbreak of war, there was a sizeable "peaceable separation" movement afoot in the Northern states, backed by some well-known public figures. It is a very real possibility that a majority of Americans might have voted to let the Southern states go in peace, but Lincoln took no steps to ascertain the will of the majority on that matter. Instead, he actively scorned offers of negotiation and compromise that might have led to a peaceful adjustment of the crisis (see Position Nine: The South Started It).

Second, the idea that a revolution must be conducted for morally justifiable reasons automatically suggests the question: who determines what causes are morally justifiable? Lincoln felt that Southerners were in a state of revolution in 1861, but he did not see any justification for it. As he stated in his first inaugural, he could not see that any "clearly written provision of the Constitution has ever been denied" the South. Therefore, to his way of thinking, the Southern revolution was not justified, and so he was justified in opposing it. Lincoln, as the leader of the majority power, took it upon himself to determine whether the minority's revolution was justifiable. Was he right to do so? Is a right only a right if everyone agrees to its basis and its exercise, particularly the majority group from a minority wishes to separate? Compare the situation in 1861 to the American Revolution if you will. When the Founding Fathers declared their independence, did the British government find their reasons morally defensible? Probably not, given the fact that British leaders referred to America's Patriots as "rebels" and "traitors" and fought a lengthy war against them to suppress their revolution. Also, note that, although the founders thought they had morally defensible reasons for their revolution, they did not consult with the British before proceeding. If they had, they would have been the first revolutionaries in history to do so.

When the Southern states seceded in 1861, they emulated the pattern set forth by the founding fathers in both the Declaration of Independence and the formation of the Union under the Constitution. They appealed to that inherent, unalienable right of the people to a government of their consent. They held conventions in each state, with each state seceding of its own accord just as the original states of the Union had acceded of their own accord. Thus the Union between themselves and the other states was dissolved as it had been formed: as an act of the people of each state in their ultimate sovereign capacities.

Yet, despite his rumblings to the effect that no one was good enough to rule another without that person's consent, and that any portion of a population may revolutionize, Lincoln contended that his war to overturn the expressed will of the people of the Southern states was "essentially a people's contest," even referring to it in his famous Gettysburg Address as a struggle to see to it that "government of the people, by the people, for the people shall not perish from the earth". Social commentator H.L. Mencken once referred to Lincoln's Gettysburg Address as "the highest emotion reduced to a few poetical phrases...poetry, not logic; beauty, not sense":

Think of the argument in it. Put it into the cold words of every-day. The doctrine is simply this: that the Union soldiers who died at Gettysburg sacrificed their lives to the cause of self-determination – that government of the people, by the people, for the people, should not perish from the earth. It is difficult to imagine anything more untrue. The Union soldiers in the battle actually fought against self-determination; it was the Confederates who fought for the right of their people to govern themselves.[6]

Like most American young people, I was required to memorize the Gettysburg Address while in high school. And even then, before I had ever had an opportunity to study the matter in depth, this speech bothered me. It seemed eloquent enough, as speeches go, and I could see how it had become so well preserved over the years. Yet even then I knew that the Southern states had fought for their freedom and independence, and I could not, for the life of me, see how a President who fought against these things could attribute his actions to a glorious quest for the preservation of free government! Preserve freedom by denying it, by forcefully suppressing it? Can a more self-contradictory concept be imagined? It was the implications of the Gettysburg Address that actually created the first real cracks in Lincoln's armor for me.

"To preserve the Union." This is the high and noble cause we are told the Northern states contended for under the leadership of their great chieftain. Yet, the only way it can be said that Lincoln preserved the Union is that he held one geographical region in political connection with other geographical regions. In all other aspects, he overthrew the Union the founders created because he undermined its foundation and core ideology.

The following letter from Abraham Lincoln to a widow by the name of Mrs. Bixby, has been tearfully extolled over the years as being perhaps the most touching letter ever penned by a president, although scholars are not certain that Lincoln even wrote it.[7] If you've seen the movie *Saving Private Ryan*, you've heard this letter gravely read to a backdrop of stirring music:

Dear Madam,

I have just been shown in the files of the War Department a statement of the Adjutant General of Massachusetts, that you are the mother of five sons who have died gloriously on the field of battle.

I feel how weak and fruitless must be any word of mine which should attempt to beguile you from the grief of a loss so over-whelming. But I cannot refrain from tendering to you the consolation that may be found in the thanks of the Republic they died to save.

I pray that our Heavenly Father may assuage the anguish of your bereavement, and leave you only the cherished memory of the loved and lost, and the solemn pride that must be yours, to have laid so costly a sacrifice upon the altar of Freedom.

The greatest travesty of all here is not just that this letter has come to be a sacred relic of a hypocritical cause, but the fact that a great many more than just five men died for the furtherance of this affront to the principles of American liberty. More than half a million Northern and Southern soldiers perished in the war; many more were wounded and maimed, and there were countless civilian victims as well.

Lincoln's apocalyptic rhetoric aside, when the Southern states left the Union in 1861, they did not dissolve the entire Union, only the Union between themselves and the remaining states. If they had succeeded in their quest for independence, the Union would have continued to exist among those remaining Northern states. The period of the war itself supports this conclusion perfectly; for, despite the secessions of the Southern states, the United States not only continued to exist but thrived at that time. They added states, defined new territory, continued the functions and offices of government, held elections, and successfully fought a war without the participation of the Southern states. Southern secession did not affect the vitality of the United States of America in the least. The Republic needed no saving, not by Mrs. Bixby's sons or anyone else's.

A perpetual, compulsory Union? It is true that the founding fathers did all they could to ensure that the Constitution would provide for a lasting Union; however, as Franklin's speech clearly demonstrated, they were under no delusions to the effect that the Union would last for eternity. And are we to believe that these men, the same men who once stood and boldly proclaimed that all men have an inherent right to a government of their consent, would impose upon their own posterity a government that would deny them the very right they themselves had spared no expense of blood, sweat and tears to obtain?

Thomas Jefferson, in a letter to Major John Cartwright, dated June 5, 1824, said the following in regard to the right of self-determination in a people:

> Can one generation bind another, and all others, in succession forever? I think not. The Creator has made the earth for the living, not the dead...A generation may bind itself as long as its majority continues in life; when that has disappeared, another majority is in place, holds all the rights and powers their predecessors once held, and may change their laws and institutions to suit themselves. Nothing then is unchangeable but the inherent and unalienable rights of man.[8]

Clearly, in both word and deed, the founders felt that the people of a sovereign political community had the power and moral authority to institute governments of their consent. They drafted a declaration of independence without any promise that all of the states would agree to it; and later, they dissolved one Union in favor of experimenting with another, again with no promise that all the states would agree to it. What was of paramount concern to them was doing what they could to best provide for their own security and happiness. This is the essence of what we call American freedom. Not the maintenance of government or Union for its own sake, but for freedom's sake.

A Perpetual Union? The Legal Question

Another argument advanced against secession by Lincoln, and by modern nationalists as well, is that the Constitution does not give states the power to secede, therefore, they do not have it. The problem with that reasoning, though, is that the states do not derive their powers from the Constitution. State power pre-dates federal power, and is actually the source of federal power. The Constitution is clear that the states possess all powers that they have not specifically delegated to the federal government via the Constitution. Thus it is the federal government that relies on the Constitution as the basis of its authority, not the states.

"But the Constitution also forbids the states from exercising certain powers," the nationalists object, and that statement is accurate, as far as it goes. The states cannot declare war or make treaties, etc. These powers are shared by all the states and exercised via the Union. However, as the 10th Amendment declares, the states retain all powers not specifically delegated to the federal government or denied to them by the Constitution. As we have seen, Alexander Hamilton, ardent nationalist that he was, went so far as to say that this truth would have existed had it not even been expressly stated in the Constitution. Hamilton thought the matter was that obvious. It follows, logically, that if you create a government that has only certain specified areas of authority, all other areas of authority must be off-limits to it. Otherwise, why would you bother specifying any particular powers for it? What would be the point?

Based on this, there are two questions we should ask and answer: 1) Does the Constitution tell the states that they cannot secede; and 2) Did the states delegate to the federal government a power to use force to prevent states from seceding from the Union?

The answer to both questions is no; the Constitution does not prohibit states from withdrawing from the Union, nor does it give power to the federal government to force states to remain in the Union. As surprising as this may sound to some, secession, because its exercise has not been prohibited to the states, nor has the federal government been empowered to prevent it, is a valid, constitutionally reserved power of the states. The question of "Union or no Union" was put to the people of the states, and it is with those same people that the continuance of the Union lies, not with the federal government.

"The people of the states," is the phrase I use here because, again, the Constitution does not recognize the American people as existing in any aggregate or national fashion – remember that the word *national* was deliberately excluded from the document. It speaks only to the federal government and the states; the states as state governments and as the people composing the states, the latter being the source from which the Constitution and the Union were created and are thus empowered. Therefore, it cannot even be said that the American people as a whole have some constitutional say in the matter of secession.

But what of Lincoln's statement that secession presents the question of whether a government, "can or cannot maintain its territorial integrity against its own domestic foes?" Let's ask a clarifying question in reply: "Are the states that compose the Union to be considered the property or territory of the government?"

Consider the following excerpts from the Constitution in regard to state land and the federal government:

> Article II, Section 8. The Congress shall have Power...to exercise exclusive Legislation in all Cases whatsoever, over such District (not exceeding ten Miles square) as may, by Cession of particular States, and the Acceptance of Congress, become the Seat of the Government of the United States, and to exercise like Authority over all Places purchased by the Consent of the Legislature of the State in which the same shall be, for the Erection of Forts, Magazines, Arsenals, dock-Yards, and other needful Buildings...

> Article IV, Section 3. New States may be admitted by the Congress into this Union; but no new State shall be formed or erected within the Jurisdiction of any other State; nor any State be formed by the Junction of two or more States, or Parts of States, without the Consent of the Legislatures of the States concerned as well as of the Congress.

These portions of the Constitution make it clear that the federal government must obtain the consent of the states in order to acquire or alter their territory. Now if the states *were* the property of the federal government, why would it require their consent to obtain their lands? The fact is that the states are *not* the property of the federal government. The federal government was not created to manage their territory or control their internal affairs; it was created to manage their relationships among one another and among foreign powers. Washington has no legal right whatsoever to prevent any state from leaving the Union on the pretext that it is defending its "territory" against a "domestic foe". A state leaving the Union would be taking its own territory with it, not the federal government's.

Yet, in recent years, nationalists have made in-roads against the Constitution in this area. Now it seems that the federal government seizes whatever land it pleases no matter the requirements of the Constitution. For example: In 1996, President Bill Clinton issued an executive order effectively seizing several million acres of the State of Utah and turning it into a national park to prevent mining from taking place there. The President has no constitutional authority to requisition state land like a king apportioning sections of his fiefdom, yet this is what happened; and it proceeded directly from this dogma of sweeping federal authority set forth by Lincoln and his fellow nationalists so long ago. Indeed, with such things as civil forfeiture and the Draft (the latter of which is a clear violation of the 13th Amendment's prohibition against involuntary servitude), it seems the American people themselves have become the property, or subjects, of the federal government.

Having reviewed history and the language of the Constitution, it is clear that the federal government has no moral or legal right to force states to remain in the Union. The "implied perpetuity" of the Union under the Constitution speaks only to the intention of the founders that the Union should last as long as possible. It cannot be used as a basis for forcing states to remain in the Union against their will, not when the founders set so many precedents to the contrary. It should also be remembered that the Articles of Confederation did not merely imply perpetuity, they specifically stipulated it! And yet, they were dissolved within six years.

Secession is a reserved power of the states. They are not prohibited from engaging in it, nor is the federal government permitted to prevent it. There is, therefore, simply no moral or legal basis for arguing that the states are bound to one another in perpetuity under federal supervision.

Position Three:
States would require permission to leave the Union

Lincoln made this argument in his first inaugural address:

> If the United States be not a government proper, but an association of States in the nature of contract merely, can it, as a contract, be peaceably unmade by less than all the parties who made it? One party to a contract may violate it — break it, so to speak — but does it not require all to lawfully rescind it?

Like Webster, Lincoln also held to the notion that only a consolidated nation-state can truly be considered "a government proper," an idea that I believe has been successfully disproved, both via reason and the evidence of history. But even viewing the Constitution for the compact the founders clearly declared it was, does it necessarily follow that individual states can secede from it without the approval of all of the states? Did Lincoln at least have this part right?

As we saw previously, while the Constitutional Convention was underway in Philadelphia, the question arose concerning whether all of the states had to adopt the Constitution before it could go into effect. This was an issue because inaugurating the Constitution would necessarily dissolve the Articles of Confederation, a government that had been created for all of the states. Elbridge Gerry of Massachusetts argued against the idea that any fewer than all of the states could dissolve the Articles of Confederation:

> Mr. GERRY urged the indecency and pernicious tendency of dissolving, in so slight a manner, the solemn obligations of the Articles of Confederation. *If nine out of thirteen can dissolve the compact, six out of nine will be just as able to dissolve the new one hereafter.*[1] [Emphasis mine]

Gerry's comment is instructive for us in that it demonstrates what sort of government he believed would be instituted by the Constitution: yet another type of compact between the states. Obviously he would not have made such a comment had he thought that the Constitution would result in a Union from which no state could withdraw.

James Madison also weighed in on this issue of dissolving the Articles during the convention, directly challenging the idea that the consent of all of the states would be required:

> It has been alleged...that the Confederation, having been formed by unanimous consent, could be dissolved be unanimous consent only. Does this doctrine result from the nature of compacts? Does it arise from any particular stipulation in the Articles of Confederation?

> If we consider the Federal Union as analogous, not to the social compacts among individual men, but to the conventions among individual states, what is the doctrine resulting from these conventions? Clearly, according to the expositors of the law of nations, that a breach of any article, by any one party, leaves all the other parties at liberty to consider the whole convention as dissolved, unless they choose rather to compel the delinquent party to repair the breach.[2]

Madison also commented on this issue in Federalist 43, addressing two questions "of a very delicate nature"; the first of which was: "On what principle the Confederation, which stands in the solemn form of a Compact among the States, can be superseded without the unanimous consent of the parties to it". In answer to his own question, Madison went on to outline two particular justifications:

The first of Madison's reasons invoked "the great principle of self-preservation... the transcendent law of nature and of nature's God, which declares that the safety and happiness of society are the objects at which all political institutions aim and to which all such institutions must be sacrificed." Here, Madison referred to the principles articulated in the opening lines of the Declaration of Independence, namely that governments are properly based upon the consent of the governed, and may be abolished when they become destructive to the happiness and security of the people.

The second of Madison's reasons was in the form of an appeal to the "nature of compacts," advancing the argument that a violation of the terms of a compact by one or more parties might very well release all of the parties from their mutual obligations.

> A compact between independent sovereigns, founded on ordinary acts of legislative authority, can pretend to no higher validity than a league or treaty between the parties. It is an established doctrine on the subject of treaties that all the articles are mutually conditions of each other; that a breach of any one article is a breach of the whole treaty; and that a breach, committed by either of the parties, absolves the others, and authorizes them, if they please, to pronounce the compact violated and void.

Madison then went on to say that, if certain states should protest the withdrawal of other states from the Union, the seceding states could simply point out various violations of the Articles of Confederation to the embarrassment of the "complaining parties". Since, as Madison testified, the Articles of Confederation had been violated numerous times, the compact was essentially maintained by nothing more than the good will of the various member states who could have declared it void otherwise.

Some may object that, while "the nature of compacts" argument might have been applicable to the Articles of Confederation, it cannot be applied to the Constitution. After all, did Madison not say that the Articles, since they were "founded on ordinary acts of legislative authority, can pretend to no higher validity than a league or treaty between the parties"? The Constitution was not founded on "ordinary acts of legislative authority," but upon the sovereignty of the people of each state.

While this is true, it does not invalidate the "nature of compacts" argument when it comes to the Constitution; for the Constitution *is* a compact. And do the people not possess greater, more fundamental power than their legislative representatives? How feasible is it to argue that while the legislature may withdraw from a Union it has made, the people of the state – to whom the legislature is beholden – may not withdraw from one that *they* have made? Consequently, I would argue that Madison's "nature of compacts" approach could also be legitimately applied to the Union under the Constitution.

These comments lend themselves to our current question in several ways:

By allowing the dissolution of the Articles of Confederation without the unanimous consent of the states, our founders set the precedent that some members of the Union could withdraw without the approval of all of the members *even though this meant the dissolution of the entire Union.* In short, given the fact that the founders approved of the dissolution of an entire Union by less than all of its member states – from a Union that declared itself to be perpetual, no less – can we then look to them to condemn the actions of a minority of states whose secessions could be enacted while leaving the Union itself intact between the non-seceding states? Can we condemn the Southern states for seceding without asking the permission of the Northern states when the nine states that originally ratified the Constitution, and thus dissolved the entire Union at that time, did not look to the other four for permission to do so?

The precedent set by the men who laid the foundational framework for the United States of America denies Mr. Lincoln's assertions. For what Lincoln found so objectionable on the part of the Southern states in 1861 was far less extreme than the course the founders sanctioned in 1787. The truth is that as highly as the founders valued Union, they valued liberty and consensual government even more highly, else they should never have separated from England in the first place; and then, having formed their own Union, they should never have risked it by experimenting with a new Constitution. They also made it quite plain, time and time again, that they favored the establishment of the Union because it was necessary to the defense of liberty and justice. Union was, therefore, a means by which to achieve certain ends, not an end in and of itself.

Lincoln further developed his argument against the secession of one ore more states without the approval of all during his address to Congress in special session on July 4, 1861:

> If all the States, save one, should assert the power to drive that one out of the Union, it is presumed the whole class of seceder politicians would at once deny the power, and denounce the act as the greatest outrage upon State rights. But suppose that precisely the same act, instead of being called "driving the one out" should be

called "the seceding of the others from that one:" it would be exactly what the seceders claim to do; unless, indeed, they make the point that the one, because it is a minority, may rightfully do what the others, because they are a majority, may not rightfully do.

This aspect of Lincoln's argument also fails. First, secession and expulsion are not the same thing. The idea of expulsion is punitive, and involves states taking action against one another, while secession is defensive, and involves a state acting only for itself.

Second, Lincoln's comments rest on an unfounded assumption, namely that states defending the right of secession would automatically reject the idea of expulsion. Perhaps not. In fact, depending on how it was handled, expulsion could be entirely consistent with the central tenet of States Rights: the idea that states have the freedom to act for themselves as long as they do not violate the stipulations of any voluntary agreements they may have made. For instance, if a state is believed to have violated a compact of Union, the other states of that Union might declare their bonds of obligation to that state dissolved, and thus the offending state would be effectively expelled from their midst. This would not be a case of some states seceding from another, though, because the acting states would not be withdrawing from the Union. Instead, they would merely be declaring that a given state or states are no longer entitled to the benefits of the Union due to a violation of some type. The Union between compliant states could still remain intact through that process.

Also, if Lincoln felt that it was a travesty for several states to secede from one, as this would be akin to expelling that state from the Union, then we can furnish such a tragic example from "the seceders" of 1787. The nine states that first ratified the Constitution effectively broke up the American Union and, therefore, in the act of creating a new Union, seceded from the other four states. And finally, with the ratifications of Virginia, New York, and North Carolina, only Rhode Island was left alone. At this point, all of the ratifying states had effectively seceded from the one non-ratifying state. Thus the founders of the Republic are once again found to be at odds with the political ideology of Abraham Lincoln in that they had essentially "expelled" Rhode Island from the Union by 1790.

Position Four:

There is no such thing as 'State Sovereignty'

The following excerpts are from Lincoln's address to Congress on July 4, 1861:

> Having never been States, either in substance or name, outside of the Union, whence this magical omnipotence of "State rights," asserting a claim of power to lawfully destroy the Union itself? Much is said about the "sovereignty" of the States; but the word, even, is not in the national Constitution; nor, as is believed, in any of the State constitutions. What is "sovereignty," in the political sense of the term? Would it be far wrong to define it "a political community, without a superior?" Tested by this, no one of our States, except Texas, ever was a sovereignty. And even Texas gave up the character on coming into the Union...The States have their status in the Union, and they have no other legal status. If they break from this, they can only do so against law and by revolution.

We have already glimpsed the faults in Lincoln's argument that the Union is older than the states and is somehow perpetual; however, the specific issue of sovereignty – supremacy – remains, and was actually of far greater importance than slavery in starting the war between North and South (see Part Three, Position Three: Lincoln fought to end Slavery). Lincoln maintained that the Union extended sovereignty over the Southern states, while the Southern states maintained that they were sovereign and the Union was not. This issue is critical to our present discussion for that very reason, as it not only illuminates the type of government we live under today, but it was the direct cause of the War of Secession. Are the states sovereign, or is the Union sovereign?

We should start out by first defining the term *sovereignty*. Lincoln referred to a sovereign body as "a political community, without a superior," and this is quite a good definition reduced to the idea's simplest terms. Alexander Stephens, Vice-President of the Confederacy, agreed with the substance of Lincoln's definition when he defined sovereignty (or "paramount authority," as he sometimes called it) this way:

> That inherent, absolute power of self-determination, in every distinct political body, existing by virtue of its own social forces, which, in pursuit of the well-being of its own organism, within the limitations of natural justice, cannot be rightfully interfered with by any other similar body, without its own consent.[1]

Once again, the states perceived themselves to be sovereign bodies from the very beginning. Each state acted for itself, whether by virtue of its legislature or its people, in determining whether or not to sign the Declaration of Independence, ratify the Articles of Confederation, or ratify the Constitution. King George III acknowledged the American states as possessing sovereignty individually in the Treaty of Paris in 1783, and the states themselves pledged to protect their individual sovereignty in the Articles of Confederation. More to the point even, the nine states that seceded from the Articles to form a new Union under the Constitution implicitly recognized the sovereignty of the remaining four states by not attempting to force them into the new Union. Thus, despite Lincoln's denials, the states clearly were sovereign bodies at least up until their ratifications of the Constitution. They followed the stipulations described by both Lincoln and Stephens in acting of their own individual accord without acknowledging any superior entities. But what of the Union under the Constitution? Did the states finally surrender their sovereignty then?

At this point in our discussion, it should be noted that the states, in their act of ratifying the Constitution, must have either completely surrendered or completely retained their sovereignty. There can be no middle ground here. Sovereignty, as we have seen, is clearly defined as "absolute political authority". *Merriam-Webster* defines *absolute* as meaning: "Having no restriction, exception, or qualification; perfectly embodying the nature of a thing". The key concept to understand here is that there can be only one absolute kind of thing. You cannot have two things that are both absolute in the same manner, otherwise they condition (restrict) one another and neither is truly absolute. By token of this same principle, there can be only one absolute political authority in the American Union of States; either the Union is sovereign, or the states are sovereign. There are some who maintain that the Union and the states possess what they call "concurrent sovereignty," but this is, by definition, impossible. Sovereignty is an inherent, absolute condition, and thus, it is not divisible. It must exist in one entity alone.

However, even though the condition of sovereignty itself is indivisible, the powers that flow from it are another matter. Sovereign powers can be divided, shared, or delegated without compromising the original sovereignty of the one who is doing the dividing, sharing, or delegating. For example, a business owner can delegate power to an employee to act on his behalf or represent him in some capacity; and, in that way, the employee becomes a proxy of the employer, but he does not negate his employer's original, inherent authority. The employer can withdraw his grant of authority if he so chooses because he never surrendered it, he merely entrusted its exercise to another individual for a time. Alexander Stephens remarked on this subject as follows:

> Sovereign powers are divisible...Sovereignty itself, however, from which they all emanate, remains meanwhile the same unit...Nor is the delegation to another of the right to exercise a power of any kind, whether Sovereign or not, an alienation of it. The fact of its being delegated, shows that the source from which the delegation proceeds continues to exist.[2] [Emphasis in the original]

Under the Articles of Confederation, and later the Constitution, the states delegated some of their sovereign powers to the Union for it to manage on behalf of all the states via the federal government, while the states retained the full right to exercise all other powers. As a result of disputes that arose under the Articles, it was decided that, under the Constitution, the states should formally recognize that all powers delegated to the Union were to be exercised solely by the Union. Hence the origin of the Supremacy Clause and the requirement that public officials take an oath to support the Constitution. This was designed to correct faults that had arisen under the Articles, not to divest the states of the sovereignty that they clearly possessed as independent entities.

Consider the following comments from James Madison in Federalist 40. Speaking of arguments being offered against the Constitution, particularly that the Constitutional Convention overstepped its bounds of authority, Madison said:

> Will it be said that the *fundamental principles* of the Confederation were not within the purview of the convention, and ought not to have been varied? I ask, What are these principles? Do they require that the in the establishment of the Constitution the States should be regarded as distinct and independent sovereigns? They are so regarded by the Constitution proposed...

> Do these principles, in fine, require that the powers of the general government should be limited, and that, beyond this limit, the States should be left in possession of their sovereignty and independence? We have seen that in the new government, as in the old, the general powers are limited; and that the States, in all unenumerated cases, are left in the enjoyment of their sovereign and independent jurisdiction.

> The truth is that the great principles of the Constitution proposed by the convention may be considered less as absolutely new than the expansion of the principles which are found in the Articles of Confederation. The misfortune under the latter system has been that these principles are so feeble and confined as to justify all the charges of inefficiency which have been urged against it, and to require a degree of enlargement which gives to the new system the aspect of an entire transformation of the old. [Emphasis in the original]

In Federalist 40, Madison admitted that the states were to remain sovereign and independent in their own affairs under the Constitution, just as they had existed under the Articles of Confederation. The vital difference between the two systems would be that, under the Constitution, the Union would have greater powers than it had had before; but, as Madison said, the *fundamental principles* of the old Union were carried over intact to the new. The Constitution did not require the states to surrender their sovereignty, it merely required them to exercise fewer sovereign powers in favor of having those powers exercised by the Union. Consider the following two excerpts taken from the Constitution itself:

Article I. Section. I. All legislative Powers *herein granted* shall be vested in a Congress of the United States, which shall consist of a Senate and House of Representatives.

Amendment Ten: The powers not *delegated* to the United States by the Constitution, nor prohibited by it to the States, are reserved to the States respectively, or to the people.

If the states surrendered their sovereignty to the Union in the Constitution, we ought to find specific terminology to that effect somewhere in the document, but no such language exists in it. Instead we find words like *delegated* and *granted* where the powers of the Union are described, as in the above two examples; words that indicate, as Alexander Stephens argued, that the original source of the granting and delegating authority continues to exist intact. Therefore, the inescapable conclusion of the matter is that the states are sovereign bodies, even if they have pledged not to exercise all the powers of that sovereignty. It is also telling that the language of Amendment Ten describes powers not delegated to *the United States*, language that re-emphasizes the nature of the Union. This language speaks to the truth that the powers utilized by the federal government are not exercises of some inherent sovereignty of its own, but are rather a joint exercise of certain sovereign powers of all of the states. The federal government has no inherent power or standing of its own. It is merely the agent, trustee, or proxy of the states, and was created to manage the exercise of their joint powers.

Alexander Hamilton commented on this issue several times in his writings in the Federalist Papers. The following is an example taken from Federalist 32:

An entire consolidation of the States into one complete national sovereignty would imply an entire subordination of the parts; and whatever powers might remain in them would be altogether dependent on the general will. But as the plan of the convention aims only at a partial union or consolidation, the State governments would clearly retain all the rights of sovereignty which they before had, and which were not, by that act, *exclusively* delegated to the United States.

Beyond the general issue of sovereignty itself, however, nationalists often like to refer to the Constitution's "Supremacy Clause" in arguing that the states are impotent and have no choice but to bow in humble subservience to the greater authority of Washington D.C., no matter what the issue. But does the Constitution itself actually state this, or even imply it? Judge for yourself. The Supremacy Clause is found in Article Six of the Constitution, and it reads as follows: "This Constitution, and the Laws of the United States which shall be made in Pursuance thereof; and all Treaties made, under the Authority of the United States, shall be the supreme Law of the Land."

What nationalists fail to understand, in spite of the clear language we read above, is that it is the Constitution that is supreme, *not* the Union or the federal government that represents it, the officials of which are limited by the Constitution and sworn to uphold it. The founders were very clear on this point. Alexander Hamilton, for one, addressed this issue twice in the Federalist Papers, including in the following excerpt, which is found in Federalist 33:

> But it is said that the laws of the Union are to be the *supreme law* of the land. What inference can be drawn from this, or what would they amount to, if they were not to be supreme? It is evident they would amount to nothing. A LAW, by the very meaning of the term, includes supremacy. It is a rule which those to whom it is prescribed are bound to observe...

> But it will not follow from this doctrine that acts of the larger society which are *not pursuant* to its constitutional powers, but which are invasions of the residuary authorities of the smaller societies, will become the supreme law of the land. These will be merely acts of usurpation, and will deserve to be treated as such. Hence we perceive that the clause which declares the supremacy of the laws of the Union...only declares a truth which flows immediately and necessarily from the institution of a federal government. It will not, I presume, have escaped observation that it *expressly* confines this supremacy to laws made *pursuant to the Constitution;* which I mention merely as an instance of caution in the convention; since that limitation would have been understood, though it had not been expressed. [Emphasis in the original]

Thus, from Hamilton's remarks, as well as the others we have reviewed in previous sections, it becomes apparent that the Supremacy Clause of the Constitution does not mean that the federal government possesses unlimited authority to which the states must bow without question. On the contrary, as an agent of the states the federal government has very limited authority, beyond which the states are left with the full enjoyment of their sovereign powers. Considering this, it is easy to understand why men like Webster and Lincoln protested so vociferously that the states were not sovereign and that they did not create the Union. For if the states are sovereign, and they did create the Union, then they have every natural and legal right to withdraw their consent and dissolve what they have created, as they never surrendered the prerogative to withdraw their delegated powers.

Here are excerpts from the ratifications of three of the original thirteen states, New York, Rhode Island and Virginia. Note the language used, in light of our previous discussions:

New York: We, the delegates of *the people of the state of New York*, duly elected and met in Convention, having maturely considered the Constitution for the United States of America...Do declare and make known...That *all power is originally vested in, and consequently derived from, the people*, and that government is instituted by them for their common interest, protection, and security.

That *the powers of government may be reassumed by the people* whensoever it shall become necessary to their happiness; that every power, jurisdiction, and right, which is not by the said Constitution clearly delegated to the Congress of the United States, or the departments of the government thereof, remains to the people of the several states, or to their respective state governments, to whom they may have granted the same...

Rhode Island: We, the delegates of *the people of the state of Rhode Island and Providence Plantations*, duly elected and met in Convention, having maturely considered the Constitution for the United States of America...do declare and make known...That *all power is naturally vested in, and consequently derived from, the people*; that magistrates, therefore, are their trustees and agents, and at all times amenable to them. That *the powers of government may be reassumed by the people* whensoever it shall become necessary to their happiness...

Virginia: We, the delegates of the people of Virginia, duly elected in pursuance of a recommendation from the General Assembly...Do, in the name and in behalf of the people of Virginia, declare and make known, that the powers granted under the Constitution, being derived from the people of the United States, may be resumed by them, whensoever the same shall be perverted to their injury or oppression, and that every power not granted thereby remains with them, and at their will...

Daniel Webster attempted to use Virginia's ratification to bolster his claim that the Union was created by the people as a whole and could only be dissolved by the people as a whole; but we have seen abundant evidence that the understanding of the time was that the people had ratified the Constitution as "composing thirteen sovereignties," not as one aggregate mass. The people of the states delegated governmental powers individually and reserved their right to reclaim them individually. They could hardly have done otherwise. After all, how could the people of the individual states, who lacked any authority to delegate power for the people of any other state, reserve the right to reassume the powers that had been delegated by any other state, or by all of the individual states? Clearly, the people of each state gave only what was theirs to give, and reserved the right to reclaim only what was theirs to reclaim.

Virginia, North Carolina and Rhode Island were accepted into the Union via these ratifications. Would they have been, had the other states disagreed with their perspective concerning their status and powers under the Constitution?

Position Five:

Southerners were guilty of Rebellion and Treason

Abraham Lincoln claimed that the seceded Southern states were in rebellion against the government in 1861, and he called out troops against them accordingly. But, constitutionally speaking, is secession rebellion? Is it treason? Does the federal government have a legitimate right to act against secession on the basis that it is punishing acts of rebellion and treason?

The Constitution has the following to say in regard to treason and rebellion:

> Article I, Section 8. The Congress shall have Power...To provide for calling forth the militia to execute the Laws of the Union, suppress Insurrections and repel Invasions.

> Article I, Section 9. The Privilege of the Writ of Habeas Corpus shall not be suspended, unless in Cases of Rebellion or Invasion the public Safety may require it.

> Article III, Section 3. Treason against the United States, shall consist only in levying War against them, or in adhering to their Enemies, giving them Aid and Comfort. No Person shall be convicted of Treason unless on the Testimony of two Witnesses to the same overt Act, or on Confession in open Court. Congress shall have Power to declare the Punishment of Treason, but no Attainder of Treason shall work Corruption of Blood, or Forfeiture except during the Life of the Person attainted.

> Article IV, Section 2. A Person charged in any State with Treason, Felony, or other Crime, who shall flee from Justice, and be found

in another State, shall on Demand of the executive Authority of the State from which he fled, be delivered up, to be removed to the State having Jurisdiction of the Crime.

Merriam-Webster defines *rebellion* as: "opposition to one in authority or dominance," and "open, armed, and usually unsuccessful defiance of or resistance to an established government…an instance of such defiance or resistance." *Treason* is defined as: "the betrayal of a trust: TREACHERY," and "the offense of attempting by overt acts to overthrow the government of the state to which the offender owes allegiance or to kill or personally injure the sovereign or the sovereign's family."

Reduced to their simplest core elements, "rebellion" and "treason" have to do with resistance to, defiance of, or betrayal of an established authority or sovereignty to which one owes allegiance or obedience. Therefore, before seceded states can be accused of "rebellion" or "treason," we must first establish that they are subordinates to an established authority or sovereignty to which they owed allegiance and obedience.

We have already seen that the federal government has no sovereign authority over the states. It has only those powers that have been delegated to it by the states to exercise for the Union of all the states. The Constitution does not deny the right of secession to the states, nor does it empower the federal government to hold states in the Union by force. It requires no allegiance save the oath that elected officials take whereby they promise to uphold its provisions. Therefore, the seceded Southern states in 1861 could not have been guilty of either rebellion or treason against the Union. On what grounds could they be charged? What law did they violate? Where there is no authority, there can be no rebellion; where there is no allegiance, there can be no treason.

"But," say the nationalists, "the Constitution does say that treason against the United States 'shall consist only in levying war against them, or in adhering to their enemies, giving them aid and comfort.' It cannot be denied that the Southern states levied war against the United States, therefore, they were clearly guilty of treason." The reply to this objection depends upon which of the following two scenarios that you accept: 1) The Southern states were still members of the

Union during the war, or 2) The Southern states had, in fact, seceded and were no longer members of the Union during the war.

If you accept the first premise, then you agree with Abraham Lincoln, who, in his first inaugural address, claimed that the Union was unbroken (even though seven states had already seceded):

> I therefore consider that in view of the Constitution and the laws the Union is unbroken, and to the extent of my ability, I shall take care, as the Constitution itself expressly enjoins upon me, that the laws of the Union be faithfully executed in all the States.

This issue came back to haunt Lincoln many times during the course of the war. He was attempting to treat the Southern states as though they were still in the Union, yet he was also waging war against them and had to deal with the issue that they supposedly continued to have rights under the Constitution. If one holds the belief, as Lincoln did, that the Southern states were still in the Union during the war, then the situation becomes complicated indeed.

The founders understood that coercion is sometimes necessary to uphold the law; however, they viewed the idea of coercing a state of the Union as being contrary to the "spirit of Republicanism," and certain to lead to a calamity for liberty. In framing the Constitution, they sought to find a system that would allow the government to enforce its laws in the most benevolent ways possible. Consider the following excerpts demonstrating how the founders felt about the idea of federal coercion against a state or states, by which I mean states still in the Union and in violation of one or more constitutional provisions [Emphasis, where it appears, is mine]:

James Madison, from *Elliott's Debates*, May 31, 1787, during the Constitutional Convention:

> Mr. MADISON observed, that the more he reflected on the use of force, the more he doubted the practicability, the justice, and the efficacy of it, when applied to people collectively, and not individually. A union of the states containing such an ingredient seemed to provide for its own destruction. *The use of force against a state would look more like a declaration of war than an infliction of punishment,* and would probably be considered by the party attacked as a dissolution of all previous compacts by which it might be bound.[1]

Alexander Hamilton, from New York's ratification convention:

> Can any reasonable man be well disposed towards a government which makes war and carnage the only means of supporting itself – a government that can exist only by the sword? Every such war must involve the innocent with the guilty. This single consideration should be sufficient to dispose every peaceable citizen against such a government.[2]

Governor Edmund Randolph, from the Virginia ratifying convention:

> Have we lived to this, then, that, in order to suppress and exclude tyranny, it is necessary to render the most affectionate friends the most bitter enemies? – set the father against the son, and make the brother slay the brother? Is *this the happy expedient that is to preserve liberty? Will it not destroy it?*[3]

Oliver Ellsworth, from the Connecticut ratifying convention:

> I am for coercion by Law, that coercion which acts only upon delinquent individuals. *This constitution does not attempt to coerce sovereign bodies, States in their political capacity.* No coercion is applicable to such bodies, but that of an armed force. If we should attempt to execute the Laws of the Union by sending an armed force against a delinquent State, it would involve the good and bad, the innocent and guilty, in the same calamity.[4]

The above quotes make it quite clear that, even in a situation where a state or states were in violation of the Constitution, the founders perceived the idea of federal coercion against them as effectively inaugurating war and destroying liberty. And these emphatic words were spoken in regard to the federal government using coercion to force compliance with legitimate laws! Nevertheless, since Congress is granted the authority to make laws in pursuance of its delegated powers (taxation, etc), it naturally follows that force could legitimately be incorporated into those laws to ensure compliance; otherwise the act of passing a law would be reduced to a meaningless exercise. But this would apply only to those areas where the government was pursuing its legitimate, constitutional authority. And since it has no legitimate, constitutional authority where secession is concerned, it cannot justifiably employ coercion. Again, what law would it be enforcing?

If the President of the United States steps outside of his constitution-ally sanctioned powers, he is legally unempowered, and his actions amount to nothing more than usurpation. The founders certainly did not consider resistance to usurpation to be rebellion; and indeed, it makes no logical sense to do so. Rebellion is a resistance to rightful authority. Usurpation is acting outside of rightful authority. In forcing the Southern states back into the Union, Lincoln engaged in usurpa-tion; and, therefore, in resisting him even by force of war, the South-ern states could not have been guilty of rebellion.

This brings us to the second option: the idea that the Southern states were not in the Union during the war. This is a much more plausible line of reasoning, given that the Confederate States definitely func-tioned as an independent country with their own government and constitution for some four years. Also, secession was an event, not a process; the state ordinances of secession took effect immediately. The states proclaimed themselves out of the Union, effective immediately, and then proceeded to manage their affairs as independent entities from that point. Lincoln's assertion that the Southern states were still in the Union because they had no right to secede was rather like the following scenario: Person A draws a line on the ground and tells Person B that they have no right to cross the line. Person B crosses the line. Person A then states: "Because you have no right to cross the line, I declare that you have, in fact, not crossed it." This is hardly a pragmatic position.

Considering the Southern states to be out of the Union, a charge of rebellion or treason would be inadmissible once again due to the fact that acts of rebellion or treason, by definition, only find meaning with regard to the authority, sovereign, or government to which a person owes allegiance and obedience. If a Frenchman should commit an act of war against the United States, he can be tried for terrorism or an act of war; but since he is not a citizen of the United States, he cannot be tried for rebellion or treason, as he owes no allegiance or obedience to the United States. When the Southern states seceded and formed their own confederation, their people were no longer citizens of the United States, and thus could not be guilty of treason or rebellion against it.

Having reviewed these facts, it might well be asked here: "Well, if re-bellion or treason cannot be applied in the case of secession, when do they lawfully apply?" Consider the following three comments on the subject from Edmund Randolph, James Madison, and Alexander Hamilton:

Edmund Randolph, commenting on the fact that Congress could probably not act to rescue a state from internal rebellion under the Articles of Confederation:

> It would afford some consolation, if when rebellion shall threaten any state, an ultimate asylum could be found under the wing of Congress. But it as least equivocal, whether they can intrude forces into a state, rent asunder by civil discord, even with the purest solicitude for our federal welfare, and on the most urgent intreaties of the state itself.[5]

James Madison, from Federalist 43:

> Among the advantages of a confederate republic enumerated by Montesquieu, an important one is, "that should a popular insurrection happen in one of the states, the others are able to quell it. Should abuses creep into one part, they are reformed by those that remain sound."

Alexander Hamilton, from Federalist 29:

> In times of insurrection, or invasion, it would be natural and proper that the militia of a neighboring State should be marched into another, to resist a common enemy, or to guard the republic against the violence of faction or sedition. This was frequently the case in respect to the first object in the course of the late war; and this mutual succor is, indeed, a principal end of our political association.

Far from Lincoln's purpose, the founders perceived the power to put down insurrections and rebellions as being used with respect to individuals violating federal law or else threatening the states from within. This was not a power that was meant to be exercised against the states on the part of the federal government, but rather, *for* the states and the stability of the Union.

Position Six:

The Southern States might have formed non-Republican Governments

During his speech to Congress in special session on July 4, 1861, Lincoln said:

> The Constitution provides, and all the States have accepted the provision, that "the United States shall guaranty to every State in this Union a republican form of government." But if a state may lawfully go out of the Union, having done so, it may also discard the republican form of Government; so that to prevent its going out is an indispensable means to the end of maintaining the guarantee mentioned; and when an end is lawful and obligatory, the indispensable means to it are also lawful and obligatory.

The provision that Lincoln refers to is found in Article IV, Section IV of the Constitution, and must be read in its entirety to discern its full meaning and implications:

> The United States shall guarantee to every State in this Union a Republican form of Government, and shall protect each of them against Invasion; and on Application of the Legislature, or of the Executive (when the Legislature cannot be convened) against domestic Violence.

Here, as with every other provision of the Constitution, we must conclude that this provision can only apply to a state that is actually in the Union. The words "shall guarantee to every State *in this Union*," make that point rather self-evident, else why would it be worded that way?

Reading the full text of the provision, it becomes clear that it was meant to protect the states and the liberties of their people, not to hinder them. Consider the following two excerpts from Madison and Hamilton:

Alexander Hamilton, from Federalist 21:

> Without a guranty the assistance to be derived from the Union in repelling those domestic dangers which may sometimes threaten the existence of the State constitutions must be renounced. Usurpation may rear its crest in each State and trample upon the liberties of the people, while the national government could legally do nothing more than behold its encroachments with indignation and regret. A successful faction may erect a tyranny on the ruins of order and law, while no succor could constitutionally be afforded by the Union to the friends and supporters of the government. The tempestuous situation from which Massachusetts has scarcely emerged [Shay's Rebellion] evinces that dangers of this kind are not merely speculative.

James Madison, from Federalist 43:

> In a confederacy founded on republican principles, and composed of republican members, the superintending government ought clearly to possess authority to defend the system against aristocratic or monarchial innovations. The more intimate the nature of such a union may be, the greater interest have the members in the political institutions of each other; and the greater right to insist that the forms of government under which the compact was entered into should be *substantially* maintained...

> But the authority extends no further than to a *guaranty* of a republican form of government, which supposes a pre-existing government of the form which is to be guaranteed. As long, therefore, as the existing republican forms of government are continued by the States, they are guaranteed by the federal Constitution. Whenever the States may choose to substitute other republican forms, they have a right to do so and claim the federal guranty for the latter. The only restriction imposed upon them is that they shall not exchange republican for anti-republican Constitutions; a restriction which, it is presumed, will hardly be considered as a grievance. [Emphasis in the original]

Shay's Rebellion in Massachusetts is cited as an example of why this provision was incorporated into the Constitution, and these comments serve to further develop the truth that this provision was enacted as a means of protecting states from the overthrow of their governments by internal rebellions. It was never intended to restrain the states from acting in pursuit of their legitimate, reserved powers.

Also, note that Lincoln theorized that a state seceding from the Union, "*may* also discard the republican form of Government," and thus, the state could not be allowed to go. In other words, a state that left the Union *might* also adopt a non-republican form of government. Can we seriously be asked to believe that a war that cost the lives of more than half a million men and devastated the country was justifiably waged over something *that could have happened?* Extend this logic, if you will, to other areas of life in these United States. Would the federal government be justified in keeping standing armies in each of the states because it has a duty to guard each state against internal domestic violence, and who knows when that just might occur? Should people be forbidden to operate vehicles because they *might* exceed the speed limit or injure others? Can anyone envision a world in which we lived based on the assumption of what *might* happen to us or what we *might* do to others? It is safe to say that none of us would be allowed to walk the streets.

And let's review for a moment not what *might* have happened, but what actually *did* happen in 1861. Did the Southern states that seceded from the Union "discard the republican form" of government? Absolutely not. They maintained their own republican systems and then went so far as to replicate the U.S. Constitution's provision guaranteeing a republican form of government to each state in their own Confederate States Constitution. The provision appears in Article IV, Section IV of the Confederate Constitution and is nearly identical to its U.S. counterpart. It reads as follows:

> The Confederate States shall guarantee to every State that now is, or hereafter may become, a member of this Confederacy, a Republican form of Government; and shall protect each of them against invasion; and on application of the Legislature (or of the Executive, when the Legislature is not in session,) against domestic violence.

Far from discarding the provision to maintain republican governments in each state, the Confederate States actually protected this vision of the founders, and thereby demonstrated their steadfast loyalty to the ideal of republican government. Indeed, the secessions of the Southern states were an exercise in republican government. However, despite his claim to be fighting "a people's contest," and to be concerned with the preservation of "government of the people, by the people, for the people," Lincoln ignored the will of the people of the Southern states and compelled them to remain in the Union by military force. Lincoln's contradictory position is evident from his remarks concerning the State of Virginia in his July 4, 1861, speech to Congress:

> The people of Virginia have thus allowed this giant insurrection to make its nest within her borders; and this Government has no choice left but to deal with it where it finds it. And it has less regret, as the loyal citizens have in due form claimed its protection. Those loyal citizens this Government is bound to recognize and protect as being Virginia.[1]

Virginians had ratified their ordinance of secession by a vote of 132,201 to 37,451, and Lincoln, who had said that he who rejects the peaceful rule of the majority in a society "does of necessity fly to anarchy or to despotism," chose to support the minority of Virginians who voted against secession as somehow being "Virginia". Those who voted for secession were not even counted as being Virginians any longer. This is an incredible statement.

So much for being concerned with the possibility that the seceded states *might* subvert republican government, Lincoln actually did so. And he did so while invoking the name of republican government and the will of the people! This is an amazing hypocrisy. And what is still more amazing is that Lincoln, this man who supplanted a Union based on peaceful consent with a Union based on military force and coercion, continues to be venerated as the savior of "the Republic".

Position Seven:

The Southern States would have defaulted on the Debts and Obligations of the Union

The following is another excerpt from Lincoln's July 4, 1861, speech to Congress:

> The nation purchased with money the countries out of which several of these States were formed: is it just that they shall go off without leave and without refunding? The nation paid very large sums (in the aggregate, I believe, nearly a hundred millions) to relieve Florida of its aboriginal tribes: is it just that she shall now be off without consent, or without making any return?

Lincoln's indignation over the idea that the Southern states intended to secede without settling their debts to the Union or the Union's creditors is empty, and actually dishonest. In fact, the Southern states did attempt to settle such matters with the government of the United States, and sent commissioners to Washington bearing a letter from Jefferson Davis to President Lincoln that read:

> Sir: Being animated by an earnest desire to unite and bind together our respective countries by friendly ties, I have appointed Martin J. Crawford, one of our most esteemed and trustworthy citizens, as special Commissioner of the Confederate States to the Government of the United States; and I have now the honor to introduce him to you, and to ask for him a reception and treatment corresponding to his station, and to the purposes for which he is sent.[1]

The Confederate commissioners that arrived in Washington sent a letter of introduction to Secretary of State Seward that read, in part:

The undersigned are instructed to make to the Government of the United States overtures for the opening of negotiations, assuring the Government of the United States, that the President, Congress, and people of the Confederate States earnestly desire a peaceful solution of these great questions...[2]

Lincoln knew of the presence of these commissioners and their mission to settle all matters between the United States and the Confederate States, and he refused to have anything to do with them. Lincoln even referred to their attempts to negotiate with the United States in his second inaugural address:

While the inaugural address was being delivered from this place, devoted altogether to saving the Union without war, urgent agents were in the city seeking to destroy it without war; seeking to dissolve the Union and divide effects by negotiation.

So what we have here is Lincoln accusing the Southern states of attempting to leave the Union without paying their fair share of the debts, and then later priding himself before the country on having resisted their attempts to negotiate on those debts. Can anything be more disingenuous? The Confederate government did attempt to negotiate with Lincoln (see Position Nine: "The South Started It" for a detailed account), and even incorporated a clause in its provisional constitution underscoring its intentions to do so.

Article VI, Section II of the Provisional Confederate Constitution reads:

The Government hereby being instituted shall take immediate steps for the settlement of all matters between the States forming it, and their other late confederates of the United States, in relation to the public property and public debt at the time of their withdrawal from them; these States hereby declaring it to be their wish and earnest desire to adjust everything pertaining to the common property, common liability, and common obligations of that Union upon the principles of right, justice, equity, and good faith.

As you can see from these excerpts, the Confederate States did attempt to peacefully settle their debts to the Union, but these overtures were rejected. They continued these efforts until the war actually began and further attempts at negotiation became useless. Lincoln plainly lied to the country when he claimed that the South was not interested in making an equitable transition. He knew very well that Southern negotiators had been sent to Washington to do just that, and he knew that his administration had rejected their efforts.

Position Eight:

Secession is Anarchy

Speaking in his first inaugural address, Lincoln maintained that secession would lead to anarchy:

> If the minority will not acquiesce, the majority must, or the Government must cease. There is no other alternative, for continuing the Government is acquiescence on one side or the other...Plainly the central idea of secession is the essence of anarchy. A majority held in restraint by constitutional checks and limitations, and always changing easily with deliberate changes of popular opinions and sentiments, is the only true sovereign of a free people. Whoever rejects it does of necessity fly to anarchy or to despotism. Unanimity is impossible.

Unanimity is indeed impossible in any government, and Lincoln's statement regarding a minority acquiescing to a majority is true, as far as it goes. However, we must remember that the United States of America is a constitutional republic, and even the Supreme Law of the land itself may not change unless it is formally amended. This means that the majority cannot rule on all issues by a simple 51% margin of the vote, thereby requiring a minority to instantly surrender on any issue. The law is supreme in our American system, not the majority.

There are certain aspects of the law that are constitutionally given to Congress, and here a 51% vote of the majority is legal and proper. But should Congress step outside of its constitutional boundaries, its actions are illegal and void of authority. Therefore, it is possible for a majority to carry a vote on an issue and still have no legal authority for its actions. The Constitution was designed to protect the liberties of the people to the extent where it would take an overwhelming majority to amend the document and expand the powers of the central government. Lincoln himself identified with the truth of this when he said that the best government is that of a majority, "held in restraint by constitutional checks and limitations". Yes, but what of a government where the majority increasingly refuses to be "held in restraint by constitutional checks and limitations"? The Southern states believed that they were confronting such a government in 1861, and they acted upon that basis.

Some will answer here that Lincoln was referring to the Southern states rejecting him as President of the United States, that they overthrew the will of the majority by seceding after his election, but it is important to understand that secession and Lincoln's election are two entirely separate issues. The Southern states never denied that Lincoln won the election. They simply chose to separate from the United States of America, leaving Lincoln as President of that country, and to go their own way under political leadership of their own choosing. It was the Northern states that elected Lincoln to the presidency, and they got what they wanted. Southern secession did not interfere with that in any way. Nor could the Southern states be charged with thwarting the will of a majority of individual Americans, as it was the electoral vote that placed Lincoln in the White House in 1860, not the popular vote. In terms of the popular vote, Lincoln won more votes than any other candidate that year (coming in about half a million votes ahead of Stephen Douglas), but even so, he received only forty percent of the total vote. And as to secession itself, the United States never voted on that issue at all, so there is no way in which the Southern states could be legitimately charged with failing to 'acquiese to the will of the majority' where it is concerned.

Lincoln's claim that secession is the "essence of anarchy" is typical of nationalist politicians in general. He immediately seized upon the situation and took it to an unwarranted extreme in order to create fear and a justification for intervention. This is still a favorite tool of politicians today. It is not unusual for a politician whose favorite bill has just come under fire to predict all but the collapse of civilization itself if his legislation is defeated. We see examples of this every day in America, and Lincoln's argument was just as outlandish.

Merriam-Webster defines *anarchy* as an "absence of government…a state of lawlessness or political disorder due to the absence of governmental authority … DISORDER." What about secession makes it "the essence of anarchy," by this definition? Just because a state secedes from an established Union, does that necessarily mean that it cannot maintain or reorganize its own governmental structure? Must it automatically forsake government altogether and descend into lawlessness and bloody chaos? Is this what happened in the Southern states in 1860 and 1861?

Absolutely not. The Southern states seceded peacefully and maintained order within their borders. They met together in convention and created a confederated republic of their own, with a constitution very similar to the one they had just withdrawn from. They sent emissaries to Washington to amicably settle their outstanding affairs with the United States government, and emissaries abroad to develop relations with other nations. Plainly, order still prevailed in the South. The Confederacy was not in a state of anarchy, nor does the idea of secession itself equate to anarchy.

Position Nine:
The South started It

From Lincoln's address to Congress in special session, July 4, 1861:

> So viewing the issue, no choice was left but to call out the war power of the government, and so to resist force employed for its destruction by force for its preservation.

One of the most persistent myths surrounding the War of Secession is that the Confederacy started the war by committing a naked act of aggression of against the United States, namely by attacking Fort Sumter in Charleston, South Carolina. And while it is true that the Confederacy did attack Sumter, most Americans are unaware of the circumstances that led to the attack, including Lincoln's role in it. Thus, in evaluating this particular argument against the Southern states, I would like to provide some background information on the Sumter crisis and how the war came to be.

The Politics of Brinksmanship

Charleston on the Eve of War

In 1860, Charleston harbor was guarded by three key military installations: Fort Moultrie, Castle Pinckney, and Fort Sumter, the latter of which was located on an artificial island in the midst of the harbor and was unoccupied at that time. Major Robert Anderson, a Kentuckian, was in charge of the harbor's defenses, and both he and his garrison were stationed in Fort Moultrie. Anderson, whom Jefferson Davis later referred to as "a true soldier and a man of the finest sense of honor," was sympathetic to the Southern states but felt that his duty required him to act first and foremost as an officer in the United States military. For that reason, Anderson was troubled when it became apparent that South Carolina would likely secede in the wake of Abraham Lincoln's election to the presidency.

On November 28, 1860, Anderson wrote to his superiors in Washington and requested instructions. He was afraid that he and his garrison might come under attack if South Carolina seceded, and while he was "anxious...indeed, determined, so far as honor will permit-to avoid collision with the citizens of South Carolina," he had also determined that he would not surrender his garrison without a direct order from Washington.[1] Anderson also requested additional reinforcements and stated that he thought he could defend himself better if he were allowed to place troops in Fort Sumter.

On December 1, Adjutant-General Samuel Cooper responded to Anderson that he was, per the instructions of Secretary of War John B. Floyd, to defend himself if attacked, but otherwise to conduct himself in such a way "as to be free from the charge of initiating a collision".[2] These instructions were reiterated on December 11, when Anderson was visited by Don Carlos Buell, assistant to the Adjutant-General. Anderson's orders from Buell were as follows:

> You are carefully to avoid every act which would needlessly tend to provoke aggression; and for that reason you are not, without evident and imminent necessity, to take up any position which could be construed into the assumption of a hostile attitude. But you are to hold possession of the forts in this harbor, and if attacked you are to defend yourself to the last extremity. The smallness of your force will not permit you, perhaps, to occupy more than one of the three forts, but an attack on or attempt to take possession of any one of them will be regarded as an act of hostility, and you may then put your command into either of them which you may deem most proper to increase its power of resistance. You are also authorized to take similar steps whenever you have tangible evidence of a design to proceed to a hostile act.[3]

These orders were further reiterated in a personal letter from Secretary Floyd to Anderson on December 21, 1860, in which Anderson was ordered to "hold possession of the forts in the harbor of Charleston," and to defend himself if attacked but to "exercise a sound military discretion," and to do nothing provocative.[4]

South Carolina's state convention unanimously voted to secede from the Union on December 20, 1860, one day prior to the follow-up communication from Secretary Floyd to Anderson; and the state immediately dispatched commissioners to Washington to negotiate for the peaceful transference of Charleston's forts. At this time Anderson became especially vigilant regarding the attitude of South Carolinians toward his garrison, and grew more fearful of an impending attack with each passing day as the "Palmetto Republic" got underway. And while he was not certain what South Carolina's intentions toward him and his garrison might be in the long run, he definitely knew that the state wished no change in the "military situation" in the harbor, meaning that the state wanted Anderson and his men to stay where they were while negotiations were underway. This is evidenced for us by two particular incidents:

First, on the same day that South Carolina adopted her ordinance of secession, Captain John C. Foster of the Army Corps of Engineers, who was supervising local workmen at Fort Sumter, received a letter from Captain F. C. Humphreys, who was in charge of the United States Army ordnance stores in Charleston. Humphreys wrote to Foster on the basis of a concern expressed by Governor Pickens. Pickens had heard a rumor that troops had been transferred from Fort Moultrie to Fort Sumter, and he wanted to find out if there was any truth to the rumor. Humphreys requested that Foster respond to the governor on this matter, a request that Foster declined, stating that he felt he could not engage in official communications with the governor of a state that had just seceded from the Union. Nevertheless, Foster regretted the fact that such unfounded rumors had reached the governor's ear, and told Humphreys: "I, as the officer in charge of Fort Sumter, can assure you that no enlisted men have been transferred from Fort Moultrie to Fort Sumter."[5]

Second, Anderson himself wrote to Adjutant-General Cooper on December 22, indicating that it was his belief that South Carolina authorities were determined to keep him from occupying Fort Sumter:

> I have heard from several sources that last night and the night before a steamer was stationed between this island and Fort Sumter. That the authorities of South Carolina are determined to prevent, if possible, any troops from being placed in that fort, and that they will seize upon that most important work as soon as they think

there is reasonable ground for a doubt whether it will be turned over to the State...

No one call tell what will be done. They may defer action until their commissioners return from Washington; or if apprised by the nature of the debates in Congress that their demands will not probably be acceded to, they may act without waiting for them.[6]

These communications make it clear that Anderson understood South Carolina would look negatively upon any attempt to move his garrison. Yet he was also responsible for defending the forts in the harbor and for protecting his men, a responsibility that led him to believe that he might have to violate South Carolina's expectations, regardless of the political costs involved. Thus Anderson was caught in the unenviable position of having to exercise his discretion as to what constituted a threat against his command, and to act accordingly, while, at the same time, avoiding any actions that might be construed as provocative in the most highly charged political atmosphere in the history of the United States.

Four days following his letter to Adjutant-General Cooper, Anderson decided that he could wait no longer. He was convinced that he should abandon Fort Moultrie and place his garrison into Fort Sumter, where he thought South Carolina would "hardly be foolish enough to attack me" if negotiations did not go its way.[7] With this in mind, Anderson transferred his garrison from Moultrie to Sumter after sundown on December 26, deceiving most of his men as to their intended destination, lest any of them should be inclined to warn South Carolina authorities. He then wrote his superiors to notify of them of the move, stating that it was, in his opinion, "necessary to prevent the effusion of blood".[8]

On the morning of December 27, the city of Charleston awoke to find a United States flag waving over Fort Sumter and smoke emanating from Fort Moultrie, as Anderson had ordered his men to destroy gun carriages and whatever ammunition could not be transported to Sumter. South Carolina authorities reacted to Anderson's move by immediately taking possession of Castle Pinckney and Fort Moultrie and raising the Palmetto flag over those installations. Anderson's move created a flurry of activity. Newspapers, both North and South, accused the major of violating his orders and acting provocatively. South Carolina's commissioners expressed their outrage to President

James Buchanan, who advised that them that, while he understood that South Carolina believed Anderson had acted "not only without but against my orders," he would not command Anderson to give up Sumter now that the state had seized the harbor's remaining forts.[9] Secretary of War Floyd was indignant, as he believed that Anderson had acted provocatively; and, when it became clear that Buchanan would not order Anderson to return to Moultrie, Floyd resigned.

In the final analysis, due to the fact that Anderson's orders authorized him to hold the harbor, to occupy any fort necessary for accomplishing this directive, and to act based on his discretion in the matter, it must be said that he did not violate the "letter of the law" in moving to Fort Sumter. He did, however, violate the spirit of the law by knowingly taking action that would be viewed as provocative by the authorities at Charleston, and in the absence of any "evident and imminent necessity". It is true that Anderson feared South Carolina authorities might assail him at Fort Moultrie at any time, but he had been in fear of this since November, and South Carolina had taken no such action in all that time. Nor had it made any moves against either Pinckney or Sumter, which it might have done quite easily, seeing as neither installation was garrisoned.

Indeed, the fact that South Carolina authorities were so completely taken by surprise by Anderson's move, strongly indicates that they had no immediate intentions of assailing either Fort Sumter or Fort Moultrie. As it happened, it was not until after Anderson made his move that South Carolina made its move. Wondering whether the inhabitants of Charleston might not awake another morning to find a United States flotilla in the harbor, or some other such surprising state of affairs, state authorities seized control of the remaining forts and looked toward Washington with doubtful eyes. Ironically, Major Anderson had, by his actions in Charleston harbor, fostered a heightened attitude of suspicion and helped set the stage for the war that he himself wanted so very much to avoid.

The Star of the West

During the time when South Carolina's commissioners and President Buchanan were exchanging correspondence regarding the situation in Charleston harbor, Winfield Scott, hero of the Mexican War and General-In-Chief of the United States Army, was working behind the

scenes, urging Buchanan to authorize a secret shipment of reinforcements, arms, and supplies to Fort Sumter. Buchanan, who found himself the subject of stinging accusations of spinelessness and disloyalty
for failing take a hard line on South Carolina's secession, already
looked favorably upon the idea, and had spent time discussing the
matter with his cabinet. Buchanan suggested using the *USS Brooklyn*
for the mission, but General Scott felt that the presence of a warship
would be too provocative under the circumstances. Instead, he rec-
ommended using a merchant ship for the effort. Buchanan approved
this plan and General Scott secured the services of *The Star of the West*,
a merchant ship with a regular coastal run, to carry out the re-supply
operation.

This sort of reinforcement and re-supply mission was exactly what
South Carolina authorities were determined to prevent, thus great
pains were taken to keep the *Star's* mission a secret, as is evident in
orders issued to Lieutenant Charles R. Woods – U.S. Ninth Infantry –
by Assistant Adjutant-General Lorenzo Thomas on January 5, 1861.
Woods was the officer placed in command of the reinforcements destined to arrive at Fort Sumter via the *Star*. "The duty upon which you
are now placed by direction of the General-in-Chief," wrote Thomas,
"will require great care and energy on your part to execute it successfully":

> For it is important that all your movements be kept as secret as
> possible. Accordingly on approaching the Charleston bar, you will
> place below decks your entire force, in order that only the ordi-
> nary crew may be seen by persons from the shore or on boarding
> the vessel. Every precaution must be resorted to prevent being
> fired upon by batteries erected on either Sullivan's or James Is-
> land.[10]

In spite of efforts to keep the mission a secret, however, details of the
Star of the West expedition soon leaked to the newspapers, and readers
in Charleston had an account of the operation a full day before the
Star was scheduled to arrive.[11] With South Carolina authorities thus
alerted to the details of the *Star's* mission, any hopes for its success
were effectively dashed. When she appeared in Charleston harbor
early on the morning of January 9, with her contingent of reinforcements concealed below decks, South Carolina batteries promptly
opened fire and forced the *Star* to retreat.

Major Anderson, who had seen a newspaper account of the *Star* expedition, but had not received any official notice from Washington, refused to fire on the South Carolina batteries that morning for fear of inadvertently starting a war. He regretted that decision once he discovered that the *Star* had indeed been sent by the United States government to aid him, and immediately wrote to Governor Pickens, demanding an explanation:

> Two of your batteries fired this morning upon an unarmed vessel bearing the flag of my Government. As I have not been notified that war has been declared by South Carolina against the Government of the United States, I cannot but think that this hostile act was committed without your sanction or authority. Under that hope, and that alone, did I refrain from opening fire upon your batteries. I have the honor, therefore, respectfully to ask whether the above mentioned act...was committed in obedience to your instructions, and to notify you, if it be not disclaimed, that I must regard it as an act of war, and that I shall not, after a reasonable time for the return of my messenger, permit any vessels to pass within range of the guns of my fort.[12]

Pickens responded to Anderson by reiterating the fact of South Carolina's secession, by stating that President Buchanan had been warned that any attempt to send troops into Charleston harbor would be regarded as "an act of hostility," and by explaining that the Star had been fired upon only after disregarding warnings not to enter the harbor. [13]

Anderson communicated his exchange with Governor Pickens to the newly installed Secretary of War, Joseph Holt, who expressed regret that Anderson had not been informed of the *Star's* mission and labeled South Carolina's actions "an act of war".[14]

But while Secretary Holt accused South Carolina of committing an act of war, there was to be no war at this time. For the moment, Anderson remained at Fort Sumter with his small garrison, South Carolinians constructed various artillery batteries around the harbor perimeter, General Winfield Scott changed his mind about the wisdom of resupplying U.S. forts in Southern territory, and more states left the Union.

The Changing of the Guard

Beginning with Mississippi, five additional Southern states seceded during the month of January 1861. At the request of South Carolina, the seceded states met together in Montgomery, Alabama, on February 4 and set about forming a provisional, confederated government to unite their interests. At the top of the new Confederate government's list of priorities was the issue of peacefully settling all outstanding matters with the United States. To the furtherance of that end, Southern leaders commissioned three men: A.B. Roman, Martin J. Crawford, and John Forsyth, to travel to Washington and open negotiations with the United States government. These men had been prominent members of the three parties running in opposition to the Republican Party in the election of 1860, and they were chosen in the hope that their previous political affiliations would give them a broad appeal to the non-Republican members of the federal government, since Republicans had shown no interest in negotiations thus far.

At the same time as the Confederacy was organizing down South, the United States were preparing to inaugurate a new president; and millions of eyes, both Northern and Southern, turned to President-elect Lincoln to see what stance he would take on secession. Lincoln had been outspoken during his campaign, flatly denying any possibility of secession and intimating that he might deal with potential secessionists "as old John Brown has been dealt with". Yet, during the months between his election and inauguration, Lincoln was mysteriously silent on the issue, a fact which was, by itself, a source of unease on both sides of the Mason-Dixon line in those uncertain days.

When the time for answers finally came on March 4, 1861, inauguration day, Lincoln unveiled a policy that was very simple and very hard-line in its implications. He considered secession impossible. The Union, he said, was "unbroken," thus nothing in the relationship between the Southern states and the federal government had changed; and while he would not invade the seceded states, he promised to "hold, occupy, and possess the property and places belonging to the Government and to collect the duties and imposts," as if secession had never taken place. If war came, Lincoln said, it would come only as a result of the seceded states preventing him from peacefully fulfilling his constitutional responsibilities:

In doing this there needs to be no bloodshed or violence, and there shall be none unless it be forced upon the national authority... beyond what may be necessary for these objects, there will be no invasion, no using of force against or among the people anywhere...

In your hands, my dissatisfied fellow-countrymen, and not in mine, is the momentous issue of civil war. The Government will not assail you. You can have no conflict without being yourselves the aggressors. You have no oath registered in heaven to destroy the Government, while I shall have the most solemn one to 'preserve, protect, and defend it'.

Lincoln's inaugural address stirred mixed reactions throughout the country. Republicans and Unionists in the North were emboldened by Lincoln's words, as they felt this was their assurance that the President intended to stand firm against the South. Southern secessionists were enraged by Lincoln's comments, as they felt he was ignoring their peace overtures. They had no intention of surrendering any of the former federal properties they now held in their possession, nor were they going to pay duties and imposts to Washington, a city they now considered as housing a foreign government. Under these conditions, if both sides held firm, war was inevitable, and secessionists viewed Lincoln's statements as a de facto declaration of war against them. At Fort Sumter, Captain John Foster took note of how Lincoln's speech was received in Charleston and wrote to the U.S. Army Engineer's office on March 6 concerning it: "We have not yet received the inaugural address of President Lincoln," Foster commented, "although it is reported from town that it is coercive in its character, and that much excitement prevails."[15]

Unionists in the South and border states were also somewhat dismayed by Lincoln's address, as they readily recognized the threat of coercion that it contained. Such threats, they understood, reduced chances for peacefully restoring the seceded states to the Union, and also held tremendous potential for swaying more states, particularly Virginia, into the Confederacy.

Days of Development and Decision

In the days following his inauguration, Lincoln took in the situation in Charleston harbor with great interest, examining Major Anderson's dispatches and inquiring of his staff for opinions as to how the matter should be handled. From his dispatches, it appeared that Anderson would be out of supplies within a few weeks. Lincoln realized that if Anderson ran out of supplies he would be forced to surrender his garrison, and the new President was determined to hold the fort at all costs, as he believed that abandoning Sumter would be a vindication of secession.

With this conviction in mind, Lincoln determined to find some way in which to re-supply Sumter, and the first person he turned to on the matter was General Winfield Scott. On March 15, Lincoln wrote to Scott concerning a re-supply plan proposed by one Gustavus Fox – a former navy officer whom Lincoln would eventually make Assistant Secretary of the Navy – and asked: "Assuming it to be possible to now provision Fort Sumter, under all the circumstances is it wise to attempt it? Please give me your opinion in writing on this question."[16] Scott reviewed the President's question and reluctantly concluded that, "it would be unwise now to make such an attempt":

> The proposition presented by Mr. Fox, so sincerely entertained and ably advocated, would be entitled to my favorable consideration if, with all the light before me and in the face of so many distinguished military authorities on the other side, I did not believe that the attempt to carry it into effect would initiate a bloody and protracted conflict...[17]

Scott went on to quote a letter from Major Anderson in which Anderson stated that it would take a force of no less than 20,000 "good and well-disciplined men" to seize control of Charleston harbor and effectively re-supply Fort Sumter. Scott also made it clear that the majority of his advisors concurred with Anderson's opinion and advised against attempting such a mission. He then concluded his response to Lincoln with the following notation:

> No practical benefit will result to the country or the Government by accepting the proposal alluded to, and I am therefore of opinion that the cause of humanity and the highest obligation to the public interest would be best promoted by adopting the counsels of those brave and experienced men whose suggestions I have laid before you.[18]

Another military advisor, Brigadier General Joseph G. Totten, Chief of

Army Engineers, expressed agreement with Scott, informing Lincoln that, "This attempt like any other, will inevitably involve a collision."[19]

Lincoln was disappointed with the military appraisal of his plans and turned to his cabinet, only to be disappointed again when he found the majority were in agreement with General Scott. Secretary of State William H. Seward was of the firm belief that any attempt to re-supply Sumter would "provoke combat, and probably initiate a civil war".[20] Attorney General Bates, while he believed that South Carolina had already "struck the first blow" was, nevertheless, reluctant to do anything "which may have the semblance...of beginning a civil war, the terrible consequences of which would, I think, find no parallel in modern times".[21] Only Postmaster Montgomery Blair felt differently, arguing that a re-supply effort would "vindicate the hardy courage of the North" and reaffirm the authority of the Union.

The presence of such strong opposition in the cabinet and the military forced Lincoln to hesitate and re-evaluate his options somewhat, and he decided to gather more information before making a final decision on the future of Sumter. As part of that process, Lincoln sent Gustavus Fox to visit Sumter and decide for himself whether his re-supply plan was actually feasible. Fox left Washington on March 19, visited Fort Sumter and conferred with Major Anderson, although he did not inform Anderson of his plans. Fox then reported back to Lincoln on March 25, that, after having viewed the situation in Charleston harbor first-hand, his re-supply plan seemed "very feasible".

In addition to Fox, Lincoln also sent two other scouts to South Carolina. One of these was his Charleston-born friend, Stephen A. Hurlbut, whose mission was to confer with friends and acquaintances and report back on the strength of Union sentiment in South Carolina, particularly in the city of Charleston. Arriving back in Washington two days after Fox, Hurlbut reported to the President that, "separate Nationality" was "a fixed fact" in the South.[22] The seven seceded states were "irrevocably gone," he said, and, further, it was his opinion that any attempt to "fulfill the duties of the Executive Office in enforcing the laws and authority of the U.S. within their limits will be War".[23]

The second of Lincoln's two scouts was also another personal friend, Ward Hill Lamon. Lamon took a different tack than Hurlbut, not only visiting Fort Sumter, but also speaking with South Carolina Governor Francis Pickens. Although he was very devoted to Lincoln – and would eventually serve as his bodyguard – Lamon favored the peace policies of Secretary of State Seward in the Sumter affair, and actually went so far as to inform Major Anderson and Governor Pickens that no relief expedition would be attempted for Sumter. When Lincoln heard of Lamon's promises to Anderson and Pickens, he was outraged and declared that Lamon had never been given authority to make any such statements.[24] Still, due to his stubborn refusal to communicate with representatives from the seceded states (who, as he knew, were in Washington seeking an audience with him even then), Lincoln made no attempt to correct Lamon's misinformation. Governor Pickens, Major Anderson, and the Confederate States government proceeded under the assumption that Sumter would be given up, believing that they had the authority of a presidential representative to that effect. They also had other assurances to this effect, which we will see shortly.

Following the reports of his scouts, Lincoln hesitated yet again. He actually give some thought to abandoning Sumter, and seemed willing to do so if he were promised that Virginia would remain in the Union, as he felt that exchanging a state for a fort was "no bad business". But Virginia's adherence to the Union was fragile, and pressure was mounting on Lincoln to move forward with strong measures. Ardent Unionists were concerned that the United States government not appear weak and indecisive. Additionally, there were concerns about a growing peace movement in the North, as it was garnering some prominent support.

Chief Justice Roger Taney was known to be opposed to the use of force against the South. Former Constitutional Union Party Vice Presidential candidate, Edward Everett, declared that "to hold States in the Union by force is preposterous."[25] James S. Thayer, a New York Democrat, stated that the peaceful separation of North and South, though "painful and humiliating," should be pursued "so that we may yet be left in a comparatively prosperous condition, in friendly relations with another Confederacy."[26] Fiery abolitionist William Lloyd Garrison had called for a convention of the free states to "organize an independent government upon free and just principles," and hoped they would "say to the slave states – 'Though you are without excuse for your treasonable conduct, depart in peace! '"[27] *New York Tribune* editor Horace Greeley stated, "We hope never to live in a republic whereof one section is pinned to the residue by bayonets."[28] Additionally, talk of secession was cropping up in such places as New Jersey and California, and there was even some suggestion of turning New York City into a "free city".[29] Perhaps most alarming of all for Lincoln and his cabinet, however, was the revelation that General Winfield Scott was in favor of abandoning Fort Sumter *and* Fort Pickens, in order to stave off the threat of war.

By the end of March 1861, Lincoln's cabinet reversed its position and sided with the proposed re-supply mission for Sumter. Most still believed that such a mission was likely to result in war, but they now expressed opinions that the risk of war would be worthwhile, and if there was to be war, that it might as well start on their terms. Secretary Chase reflected this opinion when he remarked that, if war was to come:

> I perceive no reason why it may not be best begun in consequence of military resistance to the efforts of the administration to sustain troops of the Union stationed, under authority of the Government, in a Fort of the Union, in the ordinary course of service.[30]

Lincoln openly acknowledged the inevitability of conflict where his plan was concerned but, with his cabinet behind him, was determined to press forward with it in spite of the consequences. As Allan Nevins observes in his *War for the Union*: "To a friend he remarked that he was 'in the dumps' – for he knew that he must try to relieve Sumter, and relief meant war."[31] When Major Anderson heard that a re-supply fleet was on the way, he, too, knew what the end result must be, and wrote the following to his superiors:

> I had the honor to receive by yesterday's mail the letter of the honorable Secretary of War, dated April 4, and confess that what he there states surprises me very greatly...I trust that this matter will be at once put in a correct light, as a movement made now, when the South has been erroneously informed that none such will be attempted, would produce most disastrous results throughout our country.
>
> It is, of course, now too late for me to give any advice in reference

to the proposed scheme of Captain Fox. I fear that its result cannot fail to be disastrous to all concerned...

I ought to have been informed that this expedition was to come. Colonel Lamon's remark convinced me that the idea, merely hinted at to me by Captain Fox, would not be carried out. We shall strive to do our duty, though I frankly say that my heart is not in the war which I see is to be thus commenced. That God will still avert it, and cause us to resort to pacific measures to maintain our rights, is my ardent prayer.[32]

Failed Negotiations

As mentioned previously, Confederate peace emissaries were sent to Washington in the hope of beginning negotiations between the United States and Confederate States governments, and bearing an introductory letter from Confederate President Jefferson Davis to that effect. Martin J. Crawford, the first of three Confederate commissioners, arrived in Washington D.C. three days prior to the inauguration of Abraham Lincoln. Out-going U.S. President James Buchanan had evidently agreed to receive Crawford, or to at least refer him to the United States Congress; however, given the increasing stridence of Northern opinion against Buchanan's administration, the President had come to fear for his own personal safety, as well as the safety of his home. Consequently, he refused to either see Crawford or refer him to the Senate.[33]

Thus unable to meet with President Buchanan, and cognizant of the pressures under which the new administration would be assuming office, Crawford waited until the arrival of the second Confederate commissioner, John Forsyth, before attempting formal contact with the Lincoln administration. Of course, the Confederate commissioners knew of Lincoln's position on secession through his inaugural address, and were aware that Lincoln might refuse to negotiate directly with them. However, they entertained hopes that the President might be willing to confer with them through the auspices of Secretary of State Seward, who was known to be the Lincoln administration's foremost advocate of a peaceful resolution to the secession crisis.

With this hope, the Confederate commissioners attempted to contact Seward through the services of a series of intermediaries, starting with New York lobbyist Sam Ward, and Senators Gwin of California and Hunter of Virginia. Through these men, Seward requested a delay of twenty days in negotiations, a request the Confederate commissioners assented to on the condition that there be no change with regard to the existing military situation at Forts Sumter and Pickens. Although he had no authority to make such a promise, Seward nonetheless agreed to the terms. The Confederate commissioners then reported back to the Confederate capital on March 9, indicating that the Lincoln administration appeared to be readying itself to evacuate Fort Sumter, a view commonly held by those close to the administration at the time.

On March 12, the Confederate commissioners sent a formal introduction of themselves and their purpose to Secretary Seward through an intermediary, advising that "the President, Congress, and people of the Confederate States earnestly desire a peaceful solution...of all questions growing out of this political separation, upon such terms of amity and good-will as the respective interests, geographical contiguity, and future welfare of the two nations may render necessary".[34] Seward drafted a response to the Confederate commissioners upon receiving their letter, but delayed sending it to them until April 8, as the commissioners had agreed to allow him twenty days to make his official response. In the meantime, and after supposedly consulting with Lincoln, Seward advised the commissioners that he could not communicate directly with them. For that reason, all future communications between Seward and the Confederate commissioners were conducted through the auspices of two members of the United States Supreme Court: Justice Campbell of Alabama, and Justice Nelson of New York. Campbell and Nelson met with Seward on several occasions throughout the Sumter crisis, and it was through their services that Seward communicated the information that gave the Confederacy false hopes regarding Sumter.

The first example of such an assurance from Seward came on March 15, 1861, the same day that Lincoln polled General Scott and his cabinet about Sumter. Seward told Judge Campbell that Jefferson Davis would find out "by telegram" – likely sometime within three days – that the order to abandon Sumter had been given.[35] No doubt Seward thought Lincoln would cave under pressure from his cabinet and the military and quickly give the order for Sumter to be evacuated.

On March 20, five days following Seward's assurance to Campbell, the Confederate commissioners learned that, not only had Fort Sumter not been evacuated, but Major Anderson was still actively working on its defenses. Justices Campbell and Nelson again approached Secretary Seward, and conducted two interviews with him on this new development. Seward assured them that the delay was "accidental," that the evacuation would still take place, and that they would know as soon as any changes were made in the status of either Fort Sumter or Fort Pickens.[36] This is interesting when you consider that, just one day prior to Seward's renewed assurances, Gustavus Fox had left to survey the situation in Charleston harbor. Fox had left on his mission with the knowledge of General Winfield Scott, Secretary of War Cameron, and Postmaster Blair in addition to President Lincoln. Given the extent of his involvement in the administration, it is extremely implausible to believe that Seward was not aware of Fox's mission. Yet, in spite of the fact that Lincoln had sent a scout to evaluate a re-supply effort, Seward continued to promise that the fort would be evacuated, even doing so in a "buoyant and sanguine" manner, as recounted by Campbell, and claiming that the delay was "accidental".

Still, given Seward's mistaken assessment of his place in the administration, and his underestimation of Lincoln's determination, it is likely that he thought he would ultimately have his way. This explanation might serve to excuse Seward from charges of duplicity in his dealings with the Confederate emissaries; however, it was not long before Seward knew of Lincoln's intentions, leaving him without excuse for his continued assurances.

For its part, the Confederacy continued to wait based upon Seward's word, as indicated by a letter sent from the three commissioners to Confederate Secretary of State, Robert Toombs, on March 20, 1861:

> You have not heard from us because there is no change. If there is faith in man we may rely on the assurances we have as to the status. Time is essential to a peaceful issue of this mission. In the present posture of affairs precipitation is war. We are all agreed.[37]

Not having heard anything from Ward Hill Lamon since his departure from South Carolina, Governor Pickens telegraphed the Confederate commissioners on March 30 (one day following Lincoln's final cabinet meeting before approving the Fox mission), and requested to know why Fort Sumter had not yet been evacuated as promised. The commissioners turned this telegraph over to Justice Campbell, who met with Secretary Seward on April 1, 1861. Seward informed Campbell that Lamon had acted without authority in promising that Fort Sumter would be evacuated. This was the first time the Confederates were informed that Lamon's assurances were worthless. Seward then advised Campbell that, "the Government will not undertake to supply Fort Sumter without giving notice to Governor Pickens," an announcement that took Campbell by surprise given Seward's previous assurances that the fort would, in fact, be evacuated. But when Campbell asked the secretary if there had been "a change in his former communications," Seward's reply was "None."

At this point, the commissioners were nearly out of patience, and rumors concerning an expeditionary force planned for Charleston harbor (size and intent unknown) had already leaked to the public. Judge Campbell wrote to Secretary Seward again concerning the subject and, once again, received assurances that all was well. "Faith as to Sumter fully kept," Seward famously replied. "Wait and see."[38]

This last communication between Campbell and Seward took place on April 7. By this time, Seward undoubtedly knew that Lincoln had approved the Fox expedition (this had been done on March 30), and that the expedition was to set sail at any time. In fact, just the day before, April 6, Lincoln had dispatched Robert S. Chew, an employee of Seward's State Department, to South Carolina with a message to Governor Pickens:

> I am directed by the President of the United States to notify [you] to expect an attempt will be made to supply Fort Sumter with provisions only, and that if such attempt be not resisted, no effort to throw in provisions, arms, or ammunition will be made without further notice or in case of an attack upon the fort.

Seward could not have been unaware of this, and it is rather telling that he changed his tune somewhat in communicating with Campbell, as he remarked that no attempt would be made to re-supply Fort Sumter, "without giving notice to Governor Pickens". Obviously, Seward knew that the relief expedition was already in progress, and yet, he continued to provide assurances to the apparent contrary with, as historian Shelby Foote says, "the straight-faced solemnity of a man delivering an April fool pronouncement".[39]

By now Seward was in over his head. He had been passing false assurances along to the Confederate commissioners based on inaccurate assumptions of his own power in the Lincoln administration. Now that the cabinet had shifted in its viewpoint, events had moved beyond his control. This, combined with the fact that Seward had come under unwanted scrutiny for his peace policies (it was suspected that he was influencing General Scott to give up the forts), made the situation such that there was little he could do except attempt to cover his tracks and parse his statements so that he could not be accused of having outright lied to the commissioners. Still, no matter the situation, from his words it is quite evident that Seward intended the commissioners to believe that Sumter would be evacuated in accordance with his previous statements.

The Confederate commissioners were not entirely drawn in by Seward's reassurances, however. News of the Fox expedition in the media, delays in Seward's promised evacuation of Sumter, and particularly the sudden denial of Lamon's assurances to Governor Pickens, had served to make them more than a little suspicious of the administration. Details concerning the makeup of the Fox expedition, including troop strength, were soon available to the public, to the dismay of the Lincoln administration and the consternation of Confederate authorities. Governor Pickens was not even permitted to reply to the message delivered by Chew stating that Sumter would be resupplied. When he asked to do so, Chew told Pickens that he was "not authorized to receive any communications from him in reply".[40]

Then, on April 8, the commissioners finally received Seward's response to their introductory letter of March 12. In his letter, Seward informed the commissioners that he could not recognize the "so-called Confederate States" as an entity with which "diplomatic relations ought to be established," and, as a result, could not "recognize them as diplomatic agents, or hold correspondence or other communication with them." Seward advised the commissioners that he had submitted his written reply to President Lincoln, who "sanctions the Secretary's decision declining official intercourse" with the commissioners.[41]

Having received Seward's formal response to their letter, the Confederate commissioners sent a telegram to General P.G.T. Beauregard, who had assumed command of the Confederate forces in Charleston, to the effect that:

> Accounts are uncertain, because of the constant vacillation of this Government. We were reassured yesterday that the status of Sumter would not be changed without previous notice to Governor Pickens, but we have no faith in them. The war policy prevails in the Cabinet at this hour.[42]

The commissioners then sent a written response to Seward's letter through Justice Campbell on April 9, 1861. In it, they argued that they did not ask the United States government to recognize Confederate independence, but "only asked audience to adjust, in a spirit of amity and peace, the new relations springing from a manifest and accomplished revolution in the Government of the late Federal Union". The administration's refusal to treat with the commissioners, while, at the same time, preparing "active naval and military" operations to forcefully re-supply Fort Sumter could, as the commissioners put it, only be treated as "a declaration of war against the Confederate States," due to the fact that Lincoln understood that Sumter could not be re-supplied without conflict.[43]

Seward replied to this last communication on April 10, but only to the extent of referring to his former letter indicating that he could not hold official negotiations with the commissioners, and acknowledging receipt of their reply to that letter. Their efforts to obtain an audience with the administration to the end of peaceful negotiations thus frustrated, the commissioners left Washington on April 11, 1861, and reported back to the Confederate government at Montgomery, Alabama. "We never had a chance to make Lincoln an offer of any kind," John Forsyth informed Jefferson Davis. "You can't negotiate with a man who says you don't exist."[44]

On April 12, with the Fox expedition known to be underway, with the expedition's intent uncertain, and with negotiations having failed, Confederate batteries opened fire on Fort Sumter. On April 13, a frustrated Judge Campbell wrote to Secretary Seward to ask for an explanation as to why Seward had continued to assert that Sumter would be evacuated when he knew that a re-supply operation was already in the works. Campbell informed Seward that the Confederate commissioners, as well as their government, felt that they had been "abused" by Seward's continued reassurances, and that the "proximate cause" of the outbreak of violence at Fort Sumter was due to "the equivocating conduct of the Administration."[45] Seward did not reply.

Much debate has taken place over the years as to exactly how much Abraham Lincoln knew about Secretary Seward's informal negotiations with the Confederate commissioners, and what he might have approved. In his *Rise and Fall of the Confederate Government*, Jefferson Davis argues that Lincoln must have known about Seward's dealings with the Confederate commissioners, dealings which took place over nearly a month's time and were conducted through sitting justices of the Supreme Court. Indeed, Davis mentions one particular occasion where Judge Campbell reported that Seward excused himself in order to confer with Lincoln, and then returned with what he said was the President's official word.[46]

Further, Davis argues that Lincoln must have known and approved of Seward's actions, if for no other reason, because he took no punitive steps against Seward once the background of the Sumter affair became public knowledge.

> Yet the Secretary of State was not impeached and brought to trial for the grave offense of undertaking to conduct the most momentous and vital transactions that had been or could be brought before the government of the United States, without the knowledge and in opposition to the will of the President, and for having involved the government in dishonor, if not disaster.[47]

"Stand and Deliver"

While growing up, I was taught the story of Fort Sumter and how America's bloodiest conflict was initiated by Southern guns in a contest for possession of that tiny island fortress; however, I never knew anything of the negotiation and manipulation that took place behind the scenes until I unearthed the information for myself. Up until that time, I had thought that, no matter whether the Southern states had the right to secede, the attack on Fort Sumter was a naked act of aggression. Given the information we have just reviewed, I have come to think differently on the matter.

The attack on Fort Sumter was certainly ill advised and unnecessary, and it played into Lincoln's purpose. As we have seen, Lincoln, his military advisors and his cabinet, all knew very well that any effort to relieve Sumter would result in war. They had the precedent set by the *Star of the West* incident, which told them that the Confederates would open fire on any force that entered the harbor without permission; and, further, this time they knew that Major Anderson would return fire. With war made inevitable by his head-in-the-sand approach to secession, and by his refusal to negotiate with the Confederate commissioners, Lincoln's challenge was to find a way in which to provoke Southerners into firing that first, fatal shot. Only then could he unite the reluctant factions of the Northern states on the basis of repelling Southern aggression.

Lincoln had laid the groundwork for this policy in his first inaugural address, in which he had indirectly threatened the Confederate states with his talk of "you can have no conflict without yourselves being the aggressors". This is interesting when you consider that, during his presidential campaign, he had chided the South for using a very similar type of indirect threat. Speaking in reference to Southern threats to secede should he be elected President, Lincoln had said: "A highwayman holds a pistol to my head and mutters through his teeth, 'Stand and deliver, or I shall kill you and then you will be a murderer.'"[48] Then, having won the election, Lincoln informed Southerners that they would give him what he wanted or there would be war and it would be their fault: "In your hands, my dissatisfied fellow-countrymen, and not in mine, is the momentous issue of civil war. The Government will not assail you. You can have no conflict without being yourselves the aggressors." Translation: "Stand and deliver".

Lincoln was advised to employ this tactic by his friend Senator Orville Browning of Illinois, among others, and for the very purpose of attempting to place the Southern states in the wrong, as illustrated by the following excerpt from one of Browning's letters to Lincoln:

> In any conflict...between the government and the seceding States, it is very important that the traitors shall be the aggressors, and that they be kept constantly and palpably in the wrong. The first attempt...to furnish supplies or reinforcements to [Fort] Sumter will induce aggression by South Carolina, and then the government will stand justified, before the entire country, in repelling

that aggression, and retaking the forts. [49]

Writing to Orville Browning after the Confederacy attacked Fort Sumter, Lincoln stated: "The plan succeeded…They attacked Sumter – it fell, and thus, did more service than it otherwise could."[50] To Gustavus Fox, the architect of his re-supply plan, Lincoln wrote:

> You and I both anticipated that the cause of the country would be advanced by making the attempt to provision Fort Sumpter, even if it should fail; and it is no small consolation now to feel that our anticipation is justified by the result.[51]

The question to ask here is how could Lincoln claim to be "justified" by the result of his plan when the result was war? Unless, of course, that *was* the plan. True to Browning's advice, Lincoln had placed the Confederacy on the horns of a most unpleasant dilemma. If the Confederates allowed Fort Sumter to remain in Union hands, they would have essentially surrendered their claims to independence. They would also have been allowing a foreign government to retain control of a key defensive position in the midst of one of their few good ports. On the other hand, if they did strike out at the fort, they risked being labeled as aggressors, and, in the words of Browning, the United States government would "stand justified…in repelling that aggression, and retaking the forts". Either way, Lincoln won and he knew it. In the words of Shelby Foote, Lincoln's plan was to "await an act of aggression by the South, exerting in the interim just enough pressure to provoke such an act, without exerting enough to justify it".[52] Historian James McPherson has referred to Lincoln's strategy as "a stroke of genius," remarking that, "in effect, he was telling Jefferson Davis, 'heads I win, tails you lose'".[53]

Some in the South saw the inevitable consequences of an attack on the fort and counseled against it. Confederate Vice President Alexander Stephens – who had argued against secession in his home state of Georgia – favored delaying action on Sumter, as did Secretary of State Robert Toombs, who objected to the use of force in terms that proved to be famously prophetic:

> The firing on that fort will inaugurate a civil war greater than any the world has ever seen. Mr. President, at this time it is suicide, murder, and will lose us every friend at the North. You will wantonly strike a hornet's nest which extends from mountains to

ocean, and legions now quiet will swarm out and sting us to death. It is unnecessary; it puts us in the wrong; it is fatal.[54]

Yet there were others who felt that striking a blow at Sumter would ensure Confederate unity and probably bring indecisive border states into the fold, if they saw that the infant Southern republic was capable of sustaining itself. There were also defensive considerations. The port of Charleston was one of the South's few good ports. If Major Anderson should decide to do so, he could effectively close the port by firing on any ship within range of his guns, as he had threatened to do after the *Star of the West* incident. There was also the fact that the true mission of the relief expedition was unknown. The Confederates suspected that Lincoln might be intending to retake all of the forts in Charleston harbor, or even to invade the city itself. For that reason, they decided to take control of Sumter before the fleet could arrive, lest they find themselves confronting the guns of a naval flotilla in combination those of Anderson. "A deadly weapon has been aimed at our heart," Jefferson Davis said in summary of the Confederate position, "only a fool would wait until the shot has been fired."[55]

Still, despite all of this, it seems that Lincoln did at least make a good-faith effort to reveal his intentions by sending that eleventh hour note to Governor Pickens, advising that he was going to send supplies to Sumter – and only supplies. Why then was this assurance not sufficient to prevent the Confederate attack? Jefferson Davis, writing in his *Rise and Fall of the Confederate Government*, explains that the Southern government was not impressed with Lincoln's assurances for a number of reasons.

First of all, Davis argues that there was no reason to believe Lincoln's Assurances, given the *Star of the West* incident and the "deceptions practiced upon the Confederate commissioners in Washington". Although Lincoln stated that the Confederates had been "expressly notified" that he intended to place only provisions in Sumter at that time, Davis points out that the Confederates had been "just as expressly notified"(by Lamon and Seward) that Sumter would be evacuated, and that "it would be as easy to violate the one pledge as it had been to break the other". Secondly, Davis stated that the note to Governor Pickens was "a mere memorandum, without date, signature, or authentication of any kind". In Davis' opinion, the note seemed to be "carefully and purposely divested of every attribute that could make it binding and valid," in case Lincoln decided to deny that he had ever sent it.

"Cryptic Utterances"

Robert Toombs was correct when he argued that the attack on Sumter put the South in the wrong and would lose it friends in the North. In retrospect, the South should either have allowed the fort to be re-supplied (since it was already in Union hands, it would not have been a loss to them), or it should have officially denied the re-supply fleet entrance to Charleston Harbor, thus putting the issue of force back into the Union's corner. But the Confederates were angry, fearful, and out of patience. They had been ignored by Lincoln, led astray by Seward, misinformed by Lamon, and alarmed by news of an approaching fleet. Still fresh in their memory was Anderson's surprise move to Sumter from Moultrie and Buchanan's attempt to secretly land troops on Sumter. Again, the Confederates did not wish to confront the guns of a hostile fleet combined with those of Anderson, and there was no way for them to know what the fleet's objective truly was at that time. The only assurances they had came from a government they by then – and not without good reason – believed to be dishonest and manipulative. They lashed out at Sumter, partially in anger, partially in panic, partially hoping that the border states would see their resolve and join them.

In fact, based on the evidence we have seen and how it points to Lincoln's attempts to provoke the South into firing that first shot, it is not altogether unreasonable to wonder if Lincoln allowed Seward to provide the South with his false assurances that Sumter would be evacuated. As Jefferson Davis argued, Lincoln must have known what Seward was up to, and he must have realized that the Confederates would be confused and angry when it was revealed that Seward had misled them. Adopting such a tactic certainly increased the chance that the South would act preemptively, which is apparently what he wanted.

Still, Lincoln's defenders have argued that he really never intended to provoke the South into starting a war at all, and it is fitting that we should examine that perspective before concluding our discussion on this topic.

One of Lincoln's defenders where this subject is concerned is his noted biographer David Donald. In his book *Lincoln*, Donald states that the "cryptic utterances" Lincoln made to Browning and Fox about the firing on Fort Sumter did not actually mean that his purpose was to provoke war with the Confederacy. Lincoln was in a "contradictory position," Donald says, because he had vowed "not to be the first to shed fraternal blood. But he had also vowed not to surrender the forts":

> The only resolution of these contradictory positions was for the Confederates to fire the first shot. The attempt to relieve Fort Sumter provoked them to do just that.[56]

Donald starts out by essentially saying that Lincoln did not really mean what he said, and then goes on to prove that Lincoln meant just what he said after all. Donald states that Lincoln was in a contradictory position, and this much is certainly true. Lincoln could not peacefully hold the forts and collect the revenues from a group of people who felt that he had no authority over them. Ultimately, Lincoln would have been compelled to use force.

Donald is also correct in stating that Lincoln attempted to resolve "these contradictory positions" by provoking the Confederates to shoot first, which is astounding when you consider that he is saying this in an effort to argue that Lincoln did not want to provoke war. Donald completely contradicts himself here, arguing that Lincoln did not want to provoke war, and then immediately demonstrating why he did just that, and why he had every reason to do it. Despite his best effort to demonstrate otherwise, Donald merely reaffirms the fact that Lincoln actively sought to provoke the South into firing that first shot, setting him at liberty to dub Southerners "aggressors" and to "call out the war power of the government" against them. There is simply no way around the matter. In the above excerpt, Donald is forced to acknowledge the very thing he is attempting to disprove.

Beyond this point, however, Donald also claims that Lincoln made "repeated efforts to avoid collision in the months between his inauguration and the firing on Fort Sumter," and I have to ask: what precisely did Lincoln do? In *all* of my considerable research into this subject, I have yet to find a single example of any act on Lincoln's part that was genuinely designed to avoid conflict. How could he have worked for peace when he would not treat with the representatives of other side, not necessarily to the point of recognizing their political independence, but simply to the point of avoiding hostilities? As John Forsyth put it, Lincoln acted as if the Confederate commissioners did not even exist. Also, Lincoln made no secret of the fact that his proclamation of rebellion was based on George Washington's proclamation from the 1794 Whiskey Rebellion. But it was a well-known fact even in Lincoln's day that, prior to issuing his proclamation calling forth the militia in that situation, President Washington sent emissaries to the insurrectionists to try and negotiate a peaceful end to the crisis. Why did Lincoln follow Washington's overall pattern and yet omit this all-important step? Even his letter to Governor Pickens was a half-hearted, eleventh-hour effort at best, and was issued after he had already set his plans in motion, plans that he knew were certain to lead to war.

Lincoln did have opportunities to reach a peaceful resolution to the secession crisis, even apart from dealing with the Confederate commissioners, but he chose not to avail himself of them. Robert Johannsen, author of *Stephen Douglas*, illustrates one such instance for us in describing Lincoln's refusal to help Douglas, his old political foe from Illinois and supporter during the war, to salvage the Virginia Peace Conference in February, 1861. "The task of the Peace Conference was not only formidable," says Johannsen, "it was hopeless":

> The selection of delegates in some northern states was so manipulated by Republican governors and legislatures as to prevent an adjustment, and some delegates were instructed to resist compromise...Douglas appealed to Lincoln to intervene with the Republicans in order to save the conference, but his gesture was not successful.[57]

Oddly enough, David Donald agrees with Johannsen's assessment of the potential for peace in 1861. He states that Lincoln might have intervened in negotiations and brought about some type of reconciliation were it not for the fact that Lincoln "considered these compromise schemes bribes to the secessionists".[58] The Louisville *Journal* condemned Republican leaders for what it called their "unconciliatory and defiant course," and claimed that it was, "beyond dispute the principle cause of the fearful distrust of the North which now possesses and inflames the Southern breast."[59] Noah Brooks, a reporter and personal friend of Lincoln's, wrote that Lincoln would not negotiate with the Confederates because he would not "permit himself to be seduced into recognizing any persons as ambassadors or emissaries sent from the so-called President Davis," as Lincoln denied the legitimacy of the Confederate government. Beyond this point, however, Brooks went on to say that there was no reason for Lincoln to negotiate anyway because, "Negotiation implies that the rebellion was not without cause and that the Government stands ready to make just concessions; it argues governmental inability to conquer a peace".[60]

Lincoln defenders have also cast doubt upon the sincerity of the South's attempts at negotiation, as Allan Nevins demonstrates for us here in this excerpt from his *War for the Union*:

> But that the [Confederate] commissioners themselves attempted to delude and deceive Seward by tacitly encouraging his belief in eventual Southern return there is no doubt! [Martin] Crawford admitted as much when early in March he notified Toombs that he had acquiesced in Seward's plea for delay, on condition that the existing status be rigidly preserved. "His reasons, and my own, it is proper to say, are as wide apart as the poles; he is fully persuaded that peace will bring about a reconstruction of the Union, whilst I feel confident it will build up and cement our Confederacy, and put us beyond the reach of either his arms or his diplomacy." He did not tell Seward that![61]

In answer to Nevins, first I would have to point out that Crawford was unable to tell Seward much at all because Seward would not speak with him! Clear communications between the two men were rendered virtually impossible by the Lincoln administration's stubborn insistence on remaining deaf and dumb toward the South.

Second, the Confederate commissioners were sent to Washington for the very purpose of facilitating peaceful separation, not for reunification. Seward was certainly not blind to that fact, nor was he blind to the fact that the Confederacy would continue to establish itself during the time he had requested for a delay. He could not have reasonably expected the Confederates to simply sit back and hold their breath for a month. The fact that Seward wanted peace in order to reconstruct the Union was well known to the commissioners; and the fact that the commissioners wanted peace in order to further construct the Confederacy and solidify their independence was not lost on Seward, as his ultimate response to them indicates. In granting his request for a delay, the commissioners did not entertain any false hopes that Seward might have had. Their purpose for being in Washington never changed, nor did they ever say that it had. The man Nevins calls "the wily Seward" certainly knew why they were there; his own correspondence with the commissioners proves that beyond question.

Lincoln's Final Case for War

In the following excerpts from his message to Congress in special session, July 4, 1861, Lincoln fabricated a case for war against the South based on the incident at Fort Sumter. I would like to examine these last few of his remarks on the subject before we move on:

> It is thus seen that the assault upon and reduction of Fort Sumter was in no sense a matter of self defense on the part of the assailants. They well knew that the garrison in the fort could by no possibility commit aggression upon them.

As we have seen, all that Southerners knew for certain at the time was that a secret military expedition had been assembled and was being sent in their direction. Due to the vacillation and stubborn tactics of the administration in Washington, they could not be certain what mission the fleet was sent to accomplish. Also, as indicated earlier, Sumter was not defenseless. In his letter to Governor Pickens following the *Star of the West* incident, Major Anderson had clearly threatened to close Charleston harbor, as virtually any vessel entering the harbor would "pass within range of the guns of my fort". Sumter's location in the harbor had been chosen for precisely this purpose, so that it might deny entrance to enemy vessels attempting to attack Charleston. Anderson's threat clearly demonstrated that Fort Sumter was, in fact, capable of "committing aggression" if its commander so ordered. And it must also be remembered that the Confederacy was dealing with the possible threat of having to contend with the guns of Fort Sumter in concert with a federal flotilla, if it turned out that Lincoln had decided to land troops in Charleston.

Lincoln continues:

> They knew – they had been expressly notified – that the giving of bread to the few brave and hungry men of the garrison was all which would on that occasion be attempted, unless themselves, by

resisting so much, should provoke more.

The Confederates believed they had been expressly notified of a number of things on a number of occasions; and, as Jefferson Davis asked, how could they be any more certain that the Lincoln government was sincere this time around? As to the matter of food, Anderson had no intention of starving his command to death in an effort to hold the fort.

On the afternoon of March 11, 1861, two of General Beauregard's aids were dispatched to Anderson with a letter advising him that Beauregard had been ordered to take possession of Sumter. Anderson declined to surrender the garrison, but stated to Beauregard's aids that if the Confederates did not "batter us to pieces" the garrison would be starved out in a few days anyway.[62] Beauregard included this information along with Anderson's written response in a transmission to the Confederate government, and received the following reply from Secretary of War Walker:

> We do not desire needlessly to bombard Fort Sumter. If Major Anderson will state the time at which, as indicated by him, he will evacuate, and agree that in the mean time he will not use his guns against us, unless our should be employed against Fort Sumter, you are authorized thus to avoid the effusion of blood. If this or its equivalent be refused, reduce the fort as your judgment decides to be most practicable.[63]

Beauregard informed Anderson of Secretary Walker's reply, and early on the morning of April 12, 1861, Anderson responded as follows:

> GENERAL: I have the honor to acknowledge the receipt of your second communication...and to state, in reply, that, cordially uniting with you in the desire to avoid the useless effusion of blood, I will, if provided with the proper and necessary means of transportation, evacuate Fort Sumter by noon on the 15th instant, should I not receive, prior to that time, controlling instructions from my Government, or additional supplies; and that I will not in the mean time, open my fire upon your forces unless compelled to do so by some hostile act against this fort, or the flag of my Government, by the forces under your command, or by some portion of them, or by the perpetration of some act showing a hostile intention on your part against this fort or the flag it bears.[64]

Jefferson Davis later stated that Beauregard could not accept Anderson's terms due to the fact that the re-supply mission would arrive well before noon on April 15, as well as the fact that any confrontation with those ships entering the harbor would release Major Anderson from his agreement not to fire on the Confederates. For these reasons, Beauregard determined that he had no other choice but to open fire and "reduce" Fort Sumter before the re-supply fleet could arrive. The fleet did, in fact, arrive at Charleston harbor on the morning of April 12, but was unable to enter due unfavorable weather conditions.

Clearly, Anderson was not intent upon starving his garrison in order to hold Sumter. On the contrary, he intended to evacuate the fort when his supplies ran out. Lincoln knew of the critical supply shortage, hence his urgent desire to re-supply the garrison; however, there was a more fundamental cause underlying his concern than that of "the giving of bread to the few brave and hungry men of the garrison," as he stated in the following:

> They knew that this Government desired to keep the garrison in the fort, not to assail them, but merely to maintain visible possession, and thus to preserve the Union from actual and immediate dissolution – trusting, as hereinbefore stated, to time, discussion, and the ballot-box, for final adjustment; and they assailed and reduced the fort for precisely the reverse object – to drive out the visible authority of the Federal Union, and then force it to immediate dissolution.

Thus Lincoln once again confirms the political reasons behind Fox's relief mission to Sumter: to hold the fort for the Union. Interestingly, Lincoln states that this was in order "to preserve the Union from actual and immediate dissolution". Once again, I would point out that the entire Union was not facing dissolution simply because the Southern states were departing. The Northern states were still united under the Constitution. And surely the loss of one more fort could not have been as catastrophic to Washington as the loss of seven entire states! Nor was Sumter worth the inevitable loss of the border states or the loss of the hundreds of thousands who would die in the war.

Also, Lincoln's comments about trusting "to time, discussion, and the ballot-box" are almost humorous here. Lincoln was the one rushing pell-mell toward war; and *who*, precisely, was it that he intended should discuss the situation, since his administration would not confer with Southern representatives? A vote? He never once called for a vote, or a convention of the states, or any action by Congress. In his inaugural, he suggested that the American people could do what they wished with the Union, but he certainly never tried to present the issue to them for a decision. He acted on his own.

And, lastly, we see Lincoln refer back to the trap he had set for the Confederacy:

> And having said to them in the inaugural address, "You can have no conflict without being yourselves the aggressors," he took pains not only to keep this declaration good but also to keep the case so free from the power of ingenious sophistry that the world should not be able to misunderstand it. By the affair at Fort Sumter, with its surrounding circumstances, that point was reached. Then and thereby the assailants of the Government began the conflict of arms, without a gun in sight or in expectancy to return their fire, save only the few in the fort, sent to that harbor years before for their own protection, and still ready to give that protection in whatever was lawful. In this act, discarding all else, they have forced upon the country the distinct issue, "immediate dissolution or blood."

The Simple Matter of a Choice

If Lincoln had no other choice but war in meeting the issue of secession, it was he who put himself in that position. There were other alternatives available, including negotiation. The South was certainly willing to negotiate. It actively tried to negotiate. It had nothing to lose, and everything to gain, from negotiation. Nor would holding negotiations with the Confederates have been equivalent to recognizing their independence or granting them some sort of legitimacy. Again, President Washington attempted negotiation with the Whiskey Rebellion insurgents in 1795 but, in doing so, he certainly did not recognize their movement as legitimate, nor did anyone believe that he had. Lincoln appealed to other precedents set by Washington at that time – why not this one as well?

In the final analysis, Lincoln made a very simple, informed choice concerning the matter of secession. He *did* have options other than war. He could have referred the matter to Congress, called for a constitutional conference, or suggested a special election to ascertain the will of the American people. He did none of these things. Instead, he determined that he would adopt one course and pursue it inflexibly. The facts of the situation and the opinions of his friends and advisors were before him; he understood the implications. He went forward, knowing what the result would be, and trying to color the circumstances so they would be as favorable to his cause as possible.

But this was Lincoln's way. It was an established part of his personality. He subscribed to fatalistic notions regarding his own behavior, commenting almost as though he had no will of his own but could only act in an automatic, pre-programmed and unchangeable fashion. And lest the reader find this notion far-fetched or unfair, consider the following quote from Lincoln: "I claim not to have controlled events, but confess plainly that events have controlled me." Another example of Lincoln's fatalism comes from his second inaugural address: "Both parties deprecated war, but one of them would make war rather than let the nation survive, and the other would accept war rather than let it perish, and the war came." Here Lincoln states that "one of them" (the South) "would *make* war," and "the other" (Lincoln and the North) "would *accept* war..." In other words, the North had nothing to do with starting or conducting the war, it just participated out of necessity after the South made war against it. This despite the fact that almost any historian, regardless of ideological stripe, would be forced to admit that the Southern states fought on the defensive, and for the purpose of securing independence from the North, not conquering it. Yet, Lincoln spoke as though he had no hand in the matter, as if the war was an approaching thunderstorm that he could do nothing about except to watch and weather. The facts differ with that assessment.

Admittedly, the South should not have attacked Sumter. It should have waited, thus effectively calling Lincoln's bluff, confirming its peaceful intentions, and handing the issue of force back to Lincoln while the peace movement continued to grow in the North. So, yes, the Confederates certainly share part of the blame here. They allowed themselves to be manipulated to their own detriment. But I hope this discussion has demonstrated that Lincoln *did* seek to anger them, *did* attempt to manipulate and provoke them, and *does* bear the primary blame for pursuing a course that he knew would lead to war when his opponent was sincerely trying to offer him other options. At the very least, I hope we have demonstrated that Lincoln was not an innocent, aggrieved party in the Sumter affair.

In concluding my analysis, I quote from Alexander Stephens. Stephens readily admitted that the fact that the Confederacy fired the first shot was, "a great truth that will live forever". However:

> You must allow me to say that in personal or national conflicts, it is not he who strikes the first blow, or fires the first gun that inaugurates or begins the conflict. Hallam has well said that "the aggressor in a war (that is, he who begins it,) is not the first who uses force, but the first who renders force necessary".

> Which side, according to that high authority…was the aggressor in this instance? Which side was it that provoked and rendered the first blow necessary? The true answer to that question will settle the fact as to which side began the war.[65]

Part Three:

The Modern Case against Secession

"We still read today of how [Confederate Colonel John Singleton] Mosby had the gall to operate 'in the shadow of the dome.' Perhaps it is necessary to point out that such a shadow was cast on the sovereign state of Virginia, the home of Washington, Jefferson, Madison, Monroe, Henry and Randolph. The gall was on the other side, and it still is."

– Fitzhugh Lee, *General Lee*

"Don't the winners of wars have the right to sanitize their conduct as well as possess the spoils of war? With time, history's final verdict will be rendered, and the sanitation brigade will have to face up to its falsehoods and errors, however laudable its motivations of patriotism may have been."

– Charles Adams, *When in the course of Human Events*

Having examined the Webster-Lincoln case against the Compact Theory of the Union, and Lincoln's case against the secession of the Southern states, let's turn to the more modern arguments that have been advanced against secession (both secession in general and southern secession in 1860-1861). Most of those who advance these arguments also support the old viewpoints favored by Lincoln and Webster; however, they generally go one or two steps further while building on that same unstable foundation.

Position One:

Secession is un-American

Secession is un-American. Anyone who advocates the idea that states can or should withdraw from the Union is not a patriot and not a true American. American patriotism is inseparable from American unity.

This is an argument generally advanced by those who love their country very much but hold to mistaken ideas about how it came into being and what is necessary for its survival. For many the United States of America is a great geographical expanse stretching from "sea to shining sea". For many it is a flag with fifty stars embedded in a field of blue and flanked by thirteen red and white stripes. For many it is the Fourth of July, Veterans Day parades, impressive marble monuments, patriotic songs, field trips to battlefields, the great interstate highway system, the world's most powerful military force, the world's highest standard of living, and the general "can-do" feeling of being an American.

There is nothing wrong with any of this, but it must be realized that everything we have come to know and love as the United States of America today is based upon the ideals of a group of patriots who once put their lives, fortunes, and sacred honor on the line to obtain the greatest prize of all: liberty.

America is Different for a Reason

Other nations have their own colorful flags, patriotic holidays and songs, larger-than-life heroes, expansive dominions, tremendous military machines, and what-have-you, but none have America's history of devotion to liberty. In this aspect, she stands virtually alone. The world has both admired and envied her, and more than a few have come to these shores seeking the promise of liberty. The great ideal that made this possible was the concept that government is a creature of the people, not vice versa. Take away the aspects of liberty and equality before the law, and America is reduced to just another powerful, industrial country seeking to hold itself together for its own sake, and at times with brute force.

The history of much of the rest of the world has been that of kings and tyrants who have used their peoples to further their own notions of greatness, regardless of the cost. In ancient Egypt and Rome, the pharaohs and emperors often oppressively taxed their populations in order to build lush palaces and monuments while their people lived in squalor. This pattern was repeated throughout the Middle Ages by kings and popes who cared only for themselves and greedily took whatever they wanted from the people to finance endless wars and other self-serving schemes. Unfortunately, the history of political systems has been one long parade of varying degrees of the oppression of the people at large for the advancement of a select few. Not so with America.

She was the result of nearly a thousand years of bloody struggle on the part of the English-speaking peoples to bring the king under the law and make him equal to the people. In America, government was not to be supreme; the law was to be supreme. As we have seen, it was, and to this day is still required that all government officials, federal and state, take an oath to defend and uphold the Constitution. The founders of this country understood that for a tyrant to arise, he must first rise above all others, and in order for one man to rise above another, he must first subvert the law that makes all men equal. It was to this end that the Union was established, to guard the liberties of the people and to keep them at peace amongst themselves and with all of mankind. Speaking in Federalist 14, James Madison said:

> We have seen the necessity of the union as our bulwark against foreign danger, as the conservator of peace among ourselves, as the guardian of our commerce and other common interests, as the only substitute for those military establishments which have subverted the liberties of the old world, and as the proper antidote for the diseases of faction, which have proved fatal to other popular governments...

Speaking to the American people in his Farewell Address on September 17, 1796, George Washington stated:

I shall carry it with me to my grave as a strong incitement to unceasing vows that Heaven may continue to you the choicest tokens of its beneficence; that your union and brotherly affection may be perpetual; that the free Constitution, which is the work of your hands may be sacredly maintained...

The founders believed that the Union ought to endure for as long as possible, lest the states separate from one another and fall into endless wars like the European nations. Nevertheless, as we have already seen reflected in the mind of Benjamin Franklin, the founders understood that the Constitution could not last forever. And as we have seen reflected in the mind of Thomas Jefferson, the earth is for the living; each generation has the right to fashion its institutions as it pleases without regard to the wishes of men who are long dead and gone. There is no magic in the word "Union" that empowers it to the defense of liberty or our natural affection, thus union should not be a goal in and of itself where free people are concerned. Consider the Axis Powers in World War II, or the former Soviet Union. Both were unions of a type, but neither was anything we would care to emulate.

American patriotism is much more than pledging allegiance to a flag, and certainly more than dedicating ourselves to the preservation of the Union for its own sake. It is an unswerving loyalty to the fundamental doctrine that the United States of America was formed to protect: the idea that all human beings have an inherent right to life, liberty, and the pursuit of happiness. This is the core set of ideas that compelled the founders to declare independence from Great Britain, to form the Articles of Confederation, and later, to form the Constitution. To say that secession is "un-American" or "unpatriotic," is to deny the very means by which this country came into existence. What is secession except for a political separation of one party or parties from another? Is this not what the founders did? Can the act that enabled the creation of the United States of America itself be labeled "un-American"? Can the men that we call the first American Patriots have become what they were by means of a belief that we would now call "unpatriotic"? If so, then all of our foundational ideals and documents are monuments to political heresy.

Can we afford to be a country at war with – or in denial of – its own core ideology?

As we have seen, Abraham Lincoln once said that the idea that no man was good enough to rule another without that other's consent was "the leading principle – the sheet anchor of American republicanism." Yet, having said this, Lincoln then set about to establish the rule of his government over not just one person, but many millions of persons who no longer consented to it. It was he who betrayed "the leading principle" of American republicanism in 1861, not those who seceded to form their own government. The Southern states were of the opinion that their liberties and safety were no longer protected by the Union. Since the Union was created to guarantee those liberties, it had effectively lost the justification for its own existence in their eyes; therefore, they elected to discard it as their forefathers had done with their own connection to Great Britain and their first Union under the Articles of Confederation.

But the Lincoln-era generation in the Northern states had forgotten their patriotic birthright as well as their own ancestors' promises to secede, if necessary, to defend their rights. Those who dared espouse the doctrines of Washington, Jefferson, Madison, Franklin and other founders in 1861 were labeled "rebels" and "traitors" to be suppressed and shamed at any cost. Consider an example:

Mary Custis Lee, better known as Mrs. Robert E. Lee, was Martha Washington's great-granddaughter. As part of her inheritance from her father, Mrs. Lee had received various items that originally belonged to George and Martha Washington, including furniture, items used during the Revolutionary War, and even a set of china presented to Mrs. Washington by the Marquis de Lafayette. These items had been kept in the Lee home at Arlington, Virginia, which later became Arlington National Cemetery.

Lee's home was captured by Union soldiers during the early days of the war, and all of these family heirlooms were confiscated by the government. After the war, Mrs. Lee wrote to President Andrew Johnson in an attempt to have these items returned to her family. Johnson agreed, and made arrangements through the Secretary of the Interior to have this done; however, radical Republicans in Congress learned of the matter and acted to prevent Johnson from returning Mary Lee's belongings. The following excerpt, from Charles Bracelen Flood's *Lee: the Last Years*, explains what actions the radicals took, and their justification for them:

The Radicals leapt on this...A resolution was quickly introduced on the floor of the House, asking "by what right the Secretary of the Interior surrenders these objects so cherished as once the property of the Father of his Country to the rebel general-in-chief."[1]

How strange and unfortunate it was that, by 1868 when this event occurred, Congress had forgotten that, in his day, George Washington was the "rebel general-in-chief". Oddly enough, it was Richard Henry Lee, the father of Robert E. Lee, who memorialized Washington as "first in war, first in peace, and first in the hearts of his countrymen". Given Robert E. Lee's popularity in the South, a popularity which remains solid to this day, we can only imagine that, had the South succeeded in securing her independence, Lee might very well have become "the Father of his Country" to the new Southern nation.

History is replete with such ironies. Had the British won their war against the American colonies, it's likely that Washington would have continued to be remembered as the "rebel general-in-chief," and the colonial patriots of the day would have been vilified as "traitors" just as Confederates were following the War of Secession. Had the South won the War of Secession though, the Confederate leaders of the day would have become her founding patriots, and would have been remembered, by Southerners, as fondly as the Founding Fathers of the United States are remembered by Americans today.

The Conduct and Philosophy of Lincoln's War

Those who view Abraham Lincoln and his allies as true American patriots in the fight against secession should take care to consider the spirit and manner in which the war was waged. For as much as Lincoln and company are praised on the basis that they fought for the flag, very little is said concerning the decidedly un-American extremes they went to in order to achieve their goal of "preserving the Union". Many are quick to recite Lincoln's kind letter to Mrs. Bixby or his plea that government of, by, and for the people should not perish from the earth (hypocritical as that statement was in its context); but far fewer are willing to quote Republican Congressman Thaddeus Stevens, who declared that if the entire South had to be "laid waste and made a desert, in order to save this Union from destruction, so be it". "Abolition – Yes!" Stevens declared:

Abolish everything on the face of the earth but this Union; free every slave – slay every traitor – burn every rebel mansion, if these things be necessary to preserve this temple of freedom to the world and to our posterity.[2]

In the beginning, when it was commonly believed that the war could not last more than a year or so – if that long – Lincoln and his commanders more or less followed what General George McCellen termed a "constitutional and conservative policy" in prosecuting the war. An active effort was made to confine hostilities to the competing armies and to avoid harming civilians and civilian infrastructure when possible. However, as the war continued and casualties mounted, that restrained ideal gave way to cruel expediency, and some of the darkest chapters in American history were written.

"We are not only fighting hostile armies, but a hostile people," General William Tecumseh Sherman declared in 1864, "and must make old and young, rich and poor, feel the hard hand of war, as well as their organized armies."[3] This is precisely what Sherman, Grant and other Union leaders did in those latter years of the war. With the knowledge and approval of both Lincoln and the Congress, they spread misery and destruction among the Southern people in order to, as Sherman put it, make Southerners so "sick and tired" of war that they would eagerly "come to the emblem of our nation, and sue for peace". "I would not coax them, or even meet them halfway," Sherman declared in a letter to General Henry Halleck, the U.S. Army Chief of Staff. Instead, he preferred to make them "so sick of war that generations would pass away before they would again appeal to it".[4]

Sherman is certainly the most famous, or infamous, of Lincoln's "total warriors". To this day, his campaigns in Georgia and South Carolina rank among the most ruthless and brutal in the history of the American military. Sherman set out to "make Georgia howl," as he famously wrote to General Ulysses S. Grant in 1864, and it cannot be disputed that he succeeded in that goal. During his Georgia campaign, Sherman ordered his men to destroy infrastructure, to burn crops and kill what livestock could not be used for the army's purposes, and to seize foodstuffs. "If the people raise a howl against my barbarity and cruelty, I will answer that war is war, and not popularity-seeking," Sherman wrote to Halleck. "If they want peace they and their relatives must stop the war." Sherman later remarked that he knew the people of the South would derive two conclusions from this policy: "One, that we were in earnest; and the other, if they were sincere in their common and popular clamor 'to die in the last ditch,' that the opportunity would soon come".[5]

The destruction and grief wrought by Sherman's forces in Georgia and South Carolina would seem unimaginable to modern Americans. Indeed, even those among Sherman's own host were stricken by what they saw in those days. "It was a very pitiable sight to behold little children almost naked and many women barefooted," recalled "Cy" Titus, 19th Regiment Michigan Volunteers, while in Atlanta. "I could not help but feel sorry from the very bottom of my heart to see what destitution this cruel war has brought upon these people."[6] Charles Brown, 21st Michigan, wrote of Sherman's passage through South Carolina and said that if any army had done the same in his home state as what he had seen in the South, "I would never live as long as one of the invading army did. I do not blame the South and shall not if they do go to guerrilla warfare".[7]

Sherman himself plainly saw the result of his own ideology in practice and resolved to, as he said, "harden my heart to these things". Sherman made this remark to Major Henry Hitchcock concerning a Georgia woman who appealed to him to prevent the theft of her livestock. "That poor woman today," Sherman lamented, "how could I help her? There's no help for it. The soldiers will take all she has...Jeff Davis is responsible for all this."[8] On another occasion, Sherman wrote to his wife that he doubted whether the "deep and bitter enmity of the women of the South" had any parallel in history.

> No one who sees them and hears them but must feel the intensity of their hate. Not a man is seen; nothing but women with houses plundered...desolation sown broadcast, servants all gone and women and children bred in luxury, beautiful and accomplished, begging with one breath for the soldiers' rations and in another praying that the Almighty or Joe Johnston will come and kill us, the despoilers of their homes and all that is sacred.[9]

Still, despite such attacks of conscience, Sherman deliberately and fixedly pursued his course. "My aim then was, to whip the rebels," he wrote in later years. "To humble their pride, to follow them to their inmost recesses, and make them fear and dread us. Fear of the Lord is the beginning of wisdom".[10] Others, such as Henry Hitchcock, agreed that Sherman was doing the right thing, despite the consequences, as it was felt that such actions would hasten the war's end. "It is a terrible thing to consume and destroy the sustenance of thousands of people," Hitchcock wrote, "and most sad and distressing to see and hear the terror and grief and want of these women and children...But if that terror and grief and want shall help to paralyze their husbands and fathers who are fighting us...it is mercy in the end".[11]

Mercy for who, Mr. Hitchcock? Certainly not for the Georgia mother who pleaded with a group of Sherman's soldiers to leave her the last few chickens left by other foraging parties, as they were all that stood between her children and starvation. Her pleas earned her a smile from one soldier who famously replied, "Madam, we're going to suppress this rebellion if it takes every last chicken in the Confederacy."[12]

On December 18, 1864, General Halleck wrote to Sherman, who was about to start his campaign through South Carolina at that time, and made a coy suggestion regarding Charleston. "I hope that by *some accident* the place may be destroyed," Halleck wrote [Italics in the original]. "And, if a little salt should be sown upon its site, it may prevent the growth of future crops of nullification and secession".[13] Sherman replied that he would keep Halleck's suggestion in mind, but did not think salt would be necessary to effectively destroy Charleston under the circumstances. "The whole army is burning with an insatiable desire to wreak vengeance upon South Carolina," Sherman wrote. "I almost tremble at her fate, but feel that she deserves all that seems in store for her.[14]

As for Sherman, while his deeds earned him timeless hatred in the South, they brought him acclaim in the North, as evidenced by this joint resolution of Congress, dated January 14, 1865, congratulating Sherman on his "march to the sea":

> *Be it resolved by the Senate and House of Representatives of the United States of America in Congress assembled,* That the thanks of the people and of the Congress of the United States are due and are hereby tendered to Major-General William T. Sherman, and through him to the officers and men under his command, for their gallantry and good conduct in their late campaign from Chattanooga to Atlanta, and the triumphal march thence through Georgia to Savannah, terminating in the capture and occupation of that

city; and that the President cause a copy of this joint resolution to be engrossed and forwarded to Major-General Sherman.[15]

Similar acclaim awaited Generals Grant and Sheridan, who were unleashing scorched earth warfare in parts of Virginia while Sherman was rampaging farther south. Of particular interest in Virginia was the Shenandoah Valley. On August 28, 1864, General Grant wrote to General Sheridan and ordered him to turn the valley into "a barren waste" by destroying railroads and crops and carrying off "stock of all descriptions, and negroes, so as to prevent further planting".[16] Writing to General Halleck, Grant stated that Confederate forces should be pursued through Virginia by men who would "eat out Virginia clear and clean as far as they go, so that crows flying over it for the balance of the season will have to carry their provender with them".[17] One federal soldier who was tracking down Confederate guerrillas in Virginia suggested that the best means for dealing with "these citizen soldiers" was the scorched-earth warfare of "Attila, King of the Huns".[18]

Virginia, which had already suffered greatly from four years of near constant fighting on its soil, was further devastated by the total-war policies of such men as Grant and Sheridan. In some instances, entire families were forced to leave the state or face starvation in the war's aftermath. One such family was the Pattons, who accepted the generous assistance of a relative and moved to California, where George S. Patton, hero of World War II, was later born. Others were not fortunate enough to escape the calamity, a grim fact that some apparently found humorous, as recounted in this story from Admiral Raphael Semmes, CSA, commander of the famed Confederate warship *Alabama*. In this excerpt, Semmes quotes from Joseph Wright, former governor of Indiana, and then comments on the quotation:

> Wright – 'Leave Virginia alone, that can't sprout a black-eyed pea. Scripture teaches us that no people can live long where there is no grass. The question then is only, whether they can live thirty or sixty days'.
>
> Semmes – "Thus, amid the laughter and jeers of an unwashed rabble, did an ex-Governor, and an ex-U.S. Minister, gloat over the prospect of starving an entire people, women and children included. Did we need other incitement on board the Alabama, to apply a well-lighted torch to the enemy's ships?"[19]

What motivated men like Sherman, Grant and Sheridan to resort to such tactics? The following excerpts from a letter from General Sherman to General Halleck, dated September 17, 1863, may shed some light on the philosophy behind the evolution of the Union's scorched earth warfare policy:[20]

> Can we whip the South? If we can, our numerical majority has both the natural and constitutional right to govern them. If we cannot whip them, they contend for the natural right to select their own government, and they have the argument...

> I would banish all minor questions, assert the broad doctrine that as a nation the United States has the right, and also the physical power, to penetrate to every part of our national domain, and that we will do it...that we will remove and destroy every obstacle, if need be, take every life, every acre of land, every particle of property, every thing that to us seems proper; that we will not cease till the end is attained; that all who do not aid us are our enemies, and that we will not account to them for our acts...

> The issues are made, and all discussion is out of place and ridiculous. The section of thirty-pounder Parrott rifles now drilling before my tent is a more convincing argument than the largest Democratic meeting the State of New York can possibly assemble at Albany...

> We must succeed – no other choice is left us except degradation. The South must be ruled by us, or she will rule us. We must conquer them, or ourselves be conquered. There is no middle course. They ask, and will have, nothing else, and talk of compromise is bosh; for we know they would even scorn the offer.

In his *Memoirs*, General Sherman referred to the above quoted letter to General Halleck, with its genocidal ideology and absurd claims, and made it clear that Abraham Lincoln approved of it entirely:

> General Halleck, on receipt of this letter, telegraphed me that Mr. Lincoln had read it carefully, and had instructed him to obtain my consent to have it published. At the time, I preferred not to be drawn into any newspaper controversy, and so wrote to General Halleck; and the above letter has never been, to my knowledge, published; though Mr. Lincoln more than once referred to it with marks of approval.[21]

As much as this letter says of Sherman, Lincoln's approval of its contents, to the point where he wanted to have it published for public consumption, says much of Lincoln as well. Government of the people and the laws indeed! Lincoln-admirer Stephen Oats comments that Lincoln completely approved of Sherman's total war policy and deliberately brutalized the Southern states into submission because that was "the surest way he knew to shorten the conflict, end the killing, and salvage his American dream."[22] But can a "dream" salvaged at such a price be anything but a nightmare? Can we really be led to believe that the men who crafted the Constitution to "secure the blessings of liberty to ourselves and to our posterity," and who opposed the idea of government sustaining itself by sword, would have sanctioned the "terror, grief and want" of women and children to keep the United States flag flying over the Southern states? Would Madison have sanctioned the actions and ideology of Sherman and Lincoln? Would Jefferson, Washington, Franklin, or even Hamilton have concurred with it? Was this their notion of patriotism? Was this their idea of America?

Writing in the *Boston Herald* on April 19, 1999, columnist Don Feder compared Yugoslav President Slobodan Milosevic's brutal tactics to those of Abraham Lincoln. Commenting frankly on the carnage and human suffering that accompanied Northern armies into the Southern states, Feder made it clear that Lincoln's tactics were indeed cruel; however, he then virtually brushed them aside with a statement that it all turned out for the best in the end. "Lincoln did what was necessary to preserve the Union," Feder commented. "America, the greatest force for good in this century, would have been reduced to a basket case if the rebellion had succeeded."[23]

It is incredible enough that Lincoln and his generals who committed these atrocities have been essentially deified in American history, but it is even more incredible that modern authors and historians are so readily prepared to excuse Lincoln's actions in the name of patriotism and spreading the light of freedom. The reason for this is very likely the same reason for which so many Northerners came to venerate Lincoln following his assassination. It was not that the Northern people had no idea what was going on in the South – their soldiers were writing home about it and their politicians were extolling it – it was the very fact that it was all happening down South and *not* in the

North.

Most Northerners never saw the devastation and suffering their boys in blue visited on the Southern people. There were no twenty-four hour cable stations to broadcast the images of burned homes and blasted fields, or to conduct interviews with survivors and refugees in that day. All that Northerners really knew was that the rebels had been taught a lesson, the flag had been avenged, and the great American empire had been held together. To be sure, they could not escape the fact that over 300,000 of their fathers, sons, and brothers had died in the war; but in time, this was reconciled as a great sacrifice for the American dream. Had the same devastation been visited upon the North as took place in the South, however, the Northern masses might not have forgiven Lincoln so easily.

This is also quite likely why men like Don Feder and Stephen Oats – the latter of whom comments that Lincoln "turned the war into the very thing he cautioned against: a remorseless revolutionary struggle whose concussions are still being felt"[24] – are so readily prepared to overlook the atrocities of which Lincoln and his forces were guilty. As I understand their way of thinking, Lincoln's end goal was so supremely important that no sacrifice was too great to achieve it. But then what are the sufferings of people long gone to men like Feder and Oats? They didn't live during that time. It was not they or their family members, friends, or neighbors who endured Sherman's wrath in Georgia and South Carolina, or starved in Virginia during the winter of 1865; they were not prosecuted by military courts for the use of "disloyal" language; it was not they who were thrown in prison for printing 'seditious' opinions in the newspapers. Perhaps they and others like them would be willing to undergo such trials, however, if they could only be assured that academics and politicians one hundred and forty years from now will dismiss their sufferings as the price tag for national advancement, and money well spent at that.

I, for one, won't be placing any bets on that assumption. My guess is that they would be every bit as outraged by such treatment as Southerners were in their day; but with the war and its casualties now safely in the distant past, they can go on praising Lincoln, who in the words of Oats, "still ranks as the best President Americans have had".[25]

There is truly no comparison here when it comes to the question of which side of the North/South conflict most approximated America's foundational ideals. Southerners who engaged in secession, whether one agrees with their reasons or not, were exercising the sacred right of self-government upon which the founders had conceived and built the country. Lincoln and his followers, on the other hand, violated every sacred American creed in levying a war of terror against a people who no longer consented to be governed by them, all the while maintaining that they fought for freedom and government of, by, and for the people.

Lastly, by way of contrast, consider General Robert E. Lee's General Order No. 73, which was issued to the Army of Northern Virginia during the Gettysburg Campaign:

> It must be remembered that we make war only on armed men, and that we cannot take vengeance for the wrongs our people have suffered without lowering ourselves in the eyes of all whose abhorrence has been excited by the atrocities of the enemy, and offending against Him to whom vengeance belongeth, without whose favor and support our efforts must all prove in vain.
>
> The Commanding General therefore earnestly exhorts the troops to abstain, with the most scrupulous care, from unnecessary or wanton injury to private property, and he enjoins upon all officers to arrest and bring to summary punishment all who shall in any way offend against the orders on this subject.[26]

To be fair, similar orders were issued by Union generals. Even Sherman himself ordered that civilians in Georgia be left with "a reasonable portion" of supplies "for their maintenance". However, as we can tell to some degree from the examples that we have seen, such orders were obviously not worth a great deal in practice. When confronted with the reality of what his soldiers were doing to civilians, Sherman simply said that he could do nothing about it and would have to harden his heart toward it. Lee's army, on the other hand, largely lived up to its general's directive to make war only on soldiers. Students of the war can well reflect here that the Army of Northern Virginia did not lay waste to Maryland and Pennsylvania during its two invasion attempts in 1862 and 1863. Chambersburg, Pennsylvania was partially burned by some of Lee's men during the

Gettysburg campaign, but even this destructive act was done in direct retaliation to Sherman's wanton annihilation of Meridian, Mississippi.

Now some may choose to quibble with my selection of various quotations from General Sherman, as the man does have a rather unsavory reputation, even among Lincoln loyalists. They might argue that including his viewpoints on the war really cannot accurately reflect upon the kindly Mr. Lincoln or the Northern cause in general. However, I remind the reader that Sherman was the leader of a major Union army engaged in a major overland campaign. Congress honored him for the "gallantry and good conduct" of that campaign, and Abraham Lincoln himself approved of Sherman's actions and the ideology behind them. Sherman made no effort to conceal the havoc his men wrecked in Georgia and South Carolina. On the contrary, he was proud of it. We have seen his words on the subject, and his view of how a strong majority may bludgeon a minority with impunity. Atrocities have occurred in virtually every war ever fought, but in 'modern' times such things are generally a deviation from established policy. With men like Sherman, atrocity *was* the established policy, and Lincoln and his Republican colleagues applauded it.

These examples are but a token sampling of the many that are available to demonstrate that Lincoln, his generals, and the radicals in Congress were prepared to win their war by any means possible, no matter what the human cost. Unsettling though the question may be, what does the fact that Congress and the President honored such brutality and the ideology behind it tell you about the Congress and the President of the time? And, in an even more general sense, are the quotations that we have just reviewed from Northern leaders and soldiers during the war consistent with your impressions of what constitutes American patriotism, or fighting an honorable war to preserve a free country? Is this a legacy worth celebrating?

Position Two:

The Constitution and the Laws
were suspended under Lincoln

Since secession is not addressed by the Constitution, it is reasonable to say that the Constitution had effectively been suspended at the time of the war, and thus, whatever steps Lincoln took cannot be regarded as unconstitutional or illegal. Secession was an unprecedented situation and the Constitution did not provide any guidelines for handling it.

The "Political Religion of the Nation"

In his early days, Abraham Lincoln expressed what appeared to be an unswerving devotion to the principles and maintenance of the law, as the following quote illustrates:

Let every American, every lover of liberty, every well wisher to his posterity, swear by the blood of the Revolution, never to violate in the least particular, the laws of the country; and never to tolerate their violation by others. As the patriots of seventy-six did to the support of the Declaration of Independence, so to the support of the Constitution and Laws, let every American pledge his life, his property, and his sacred honor; – let every man remember that to violate the law, is to trample on the blood of his father, and to tear the character of his own, and his children's liberty...in short, let it become the political religion of the nation.[1]

Lincoln's self-professed love of the law was put to the ultimate test during the War of Secession, and even his most devoted admirers have been forced to admit that his constitutional legacy is doubtful at best. But before we examine the question of whether or not the Constitution could be considered "suspended" during the war, and whether this exonerates Lincoln's questionable actions, we should first review exactly what constitutional violations allegedly occurred under Lincoln. The first action we will examine is Lincoln's proclamation of rebellion and his decision to call for 75,000 troops to be used against the seceded states.

Lincoln and Presidential War Powers

The Constitution says the following in reference to the military powers of the President:

> Article II, Section II, Clause I: The President shall be Commander in Chief of the Army and Navy of the United States, and of the Militia of the several States, when called into the actual Service of the United States...

This is the Constitution's sole provision with respect to the military powers of the President. The President has power to serve as "Commander in Chief" of the armed forces, and militia as well when they are called "into the actual service of the United States"; but does this mean that the President may actually make use of the military or call out the militia whenever he wishes? The Constitution itself answers this question in Article I, Section VIII, where it lists the following as ranking among the powers of Congress:

> Clause 11: To declare War, grant Letters of Marque and Reprisal, and make Rules concerning Captures on Land and Water;

> Clause 12: To raise and support Armies, but no Appropriation of Money to that Use shall be for a longer Term than two Years;

> Clause 13: To provide and maintain a Navy;

> Clause 14: To make Rules for the Government and Regulation of the land and naval Forces;

> Clause 15: To provide for calling forth the Militia to execute the Laws of the Union, suppress Insurrections and repel Invasions;

> Clause 16: To provide for organizing, arming, and disciplining, the Militia, and for governing such Part of them as may be employed in the Service of the United States, reserving to the States respectively, the Appointment of the Officers, and the Authority

of training the Militia according to the discipline prescribed by Congress…

Thus we see that, according to the express language of the Constitution, Congress, not the President, has power to raise armies and call for the militia to resist invasion, execute the laws of the Union, and suppress insurrections. However, it became obvious early on in our history that a crisis might threaten the country at a time when Congress was not in session. Due to the slow rate of travel and communication in the early days, it was possible that an invading enemy might get the better of American forces – or an insurrectionary force might get the better of a state government – before Congress could be convened to raise an army and respond to the threat.

These considerations moved Congress to pass the Militia Act of 1792, in which it delegated some of its constitutional authority over the military and the militia to the President. Under this act, the President had authority to call out the militia under certain restrictions:[2]

- To defend the United States against a foreign invader or an Indian attack.

- To suppress an insurrection against a state government, but only upon request of that state's legislature (or the governor, if the legislature could not convene).

- To enforce the laws of the Union should they be "opposed or the execution thereof obstructed, in any state, by combinations too powerful to be suppressed by the ordinary course of judicial proceedings, or by the powers vested in the marshals by this act, the same being notified to the President of the United States, by an associate justice or the district judge." This could only be done when Congress was not in session.

Congress also required that, prior to actually calling out the militia to suppress an insurgency or rebellion, the President was to issue a proclamation to "command such insurgents to disperse, and retire peaceably to their respective abodes, within a limited time."

In 1794, George Washington became the first President to call out the militia to suppress an insurrection. This was on the occasion of what became known as the Whiskey Rebellion, an eruption of violence in western Pennsylvania in which several hundred insurgents forcefully opposed a federal excise tax on liquor. Washington conferred with his cabinet and presented information on the situation in Pennsylvania to Supreme Court associate justice James Wilson, who agreed that "the ordinary course of judicial proceedings" and "the powers vested in the marshal" were insufficient to quell the growing insurrection. Washington then issued a proclamation on August 7, 1794, referring to his authority under the Militia Act of 1792, and commanding the insurgents to disperse.

The President then went one step further to avoid violence: he dispatched commissioners to meet with the insurgents in the hope of reaching a peaceful solution to the crisis. When this final effort proved fruitless, and the requirements of the law had been met, Washington called out militia units from Pennsylvania, New Jersey, Maryland and Virginia to suppress the insurrection, and Washington himself marched with the troops for part of the way in his role of Commander in Chief. In the end, the insurrection was put down by these units, and two of the insurgents who were convicted of treason were later pardoned by Washington. Congress, seeing that the President should be able to respond even more even rapidly to a crisis, then enacted the Militia Act of 1795, which removed the requirement that the President had to wait for official sanction from a judge before he could act against an insurrection.

Another significant change in the law came on March 3, 1807, when Congress passed an act allowing the President to use the regular United States army and navy to assist in the suppression of insurrections should the President deem it necessary to do so, and as long as he first "observed all the pre-requisites of the law in that respect," meaning the conditions set by the acts of 1792 and 95.

Although these various acts of Congress gave the President great freedom with regard to using the militia and the regular military, he was still restrained by the letter of the law. This issue came to light in 1833 when Andrew Jackson was threatening military force against South Carolina during the nullification crisis. Despite his ardent opposition to nullification in principle, Daniel Webster sharply criticized any attempt at coercive action on the part of Jackson's administration. Webster commented as follows:

For one, Sir, I raise my voice beforehand against the unauthorized employment of military power, and against superseding the authority of the laws, by an armed force, under pretence of putting down Nullification. The President has no authority to blockade Charleston; the President has no authority to employ military force, till he shall have been duly required so to do by the law, and by the civil authorities. His duty is to cause the laws to be executed. His duty is to support the civil authority. His duty is, if the laws be resisted, to employ the military force of the country, if necessary, for their support and execution; but to do all this in compliance only with law, and with decisions of the tribunals.[3]

Webster's protest was mainly aimed at the idea that the President seemed to have no intention of peacefully resolving the nullification crisis, that he could not act until he was notified that the laws could not be enforced in South Carolina by the courts or the marshals, and until he had first ordered the insurgents to disperse. At the time, it appeared that Jackson might act without satisfying these prerequisites.

Now, having reviewed the provisions of the Constitution and the laws with regard to the military powers of the President and his authority to quell insurrections, let's compare our findings against the situation in 1861:

Lincoln, quoting the Militia Acts of 1792 and 1795, as well as Washington's proclamations, issued his own proclamation of rebellion against the seceded states "in virtue of the power in me vested by the Constitution and the laws". But were Lincoln's actions truly in keeping with the Constitution and the laws? Let's examine the requirements that had to be met at that time before the President could act to suppress an insurrection in any of the states:

1. The laws of the United States must either be opposed or their execution obstructed:

What laws were opposed or obstructed in the seceded states? Nationalists argue: "The Constitution itself was opposed and obstructed! The seceded states no longer acknowledged the authority of the Supreme Law of the land". But does the Constitution, in its role as the Supreme Law of the land, say that no state can secede from the Union? Does it give the federal government the right to hold states in the Union? Absolutely not. Secession is not covered in the Constitution; and, as we have seen, any power not addressed in the Constitution must lie with the states or with the people of the states.

Nationalists also argue: "But the Southern states were not paying taxes or adhering to other requirements under Federal law." True, but then a seceded state is not in the Union and is not subject to the laws of the Union. Clearly, the Southern states had not violated the Constitution or any laws of the United States by seceding from the Union, thus they were not in a state of insurrection.

2. The laws must either be opposed or their execution obstructed by "combinations too powerful to be suppressed by the ordinary course of judicial proceedings, or by the powers vested in the marshals".

In 1794, neither the courts in Pennsylvania nor the federal marshal were able to execute the laws, as the Pennsylvania insurgents proved too powerful to suppress by these ordinary means. For this reason, Washington was able to step into the situation with the full authority of the law. But where was this in 1861? No courts had attempted to suppress secession; no federal marshal had been appointed to stop it. Consequently, neither the courts nor the marshals had reported an inability to enforce the laws against the seceded states.

Stephen Douglas, Lincoln's old debate opponent, spoke to these facts before the United States Senate on March 15, 1861, while refuting charges that he thought, at the time, were outrageous claims being made concerning how Lincoln intended to handle the secession crisis. Little could Douglas have known that the outrageous and illegal behavior he condemned as unthinkable in his speech would soon become public policy. Speaking of situations in which the President had legal authority to use the military against an insurrection, Douglas said the following:

> Where is your Judge in the Seceded States? Where is your Marshal? You have no civil authorities there, and the President, in his inaugural, tells you he does not intend to appoint any. He said he intended to use the power confided to him, to hold, occupy, and possess the Forts, and collect the revenue; but beyond this he did not intend to go. You are told, therefore, in the inaugural, that he is going to appoint no Judges, no Marshals, no civil officers, in the

Seceded States, that can execute the law; and hence, we are told that he does not intend to use the Army, the Navy, or the Militia, for any such purpose. Then, Sir, what cause is there for apprehension, that the President of the United States is going to pursue a war policy, unless he shall call Congress for the purpose of conferring the means? I presume no Senator will pretend that he has any authority, under the existing law, to do anything in the premises except what I have stated, and in the manner I have stated.[4]

Unfortunately, Douglas was wrong. He did not then understand that Lincoln intended to act without having met this prerequisite concerning the courts and the marshals.

3. The President must "command the insurgents to disperse, and retire peaceably to their respective abodes within a limited time".

In his proclamation, Lincoln did "command the persons composing the combinations aforesaid to disperse and retire peaceably to their respective abodes within twenty days from this date". In doing so, Lincoln basically copied Washington's proclamation from 1794, which read:

> Therefore, and in pursuance of the proviso above recited, I. George Washington, President of the United States, do hereby command all persons, being insurgents, as aforesaid, and all others whom it may concern, on or before the 1st day of September next to disperse and retire peaceably to their respective abodes.

In 1794, Washington was dealing with a few hundred insurgents at most. In 1861, if Lincoln's accusation of rebellion is taken seriously, the President was dealing, at first, with seven states and millions of insurgents, and later, with eleven states and millions more insurgents. But how is it possible to order entire states and millions of persons to "disperse and retire to their respective abodes"?

Clearly, the laws of 1795 and 1807 were never designed to treat a secession movement as a common rebellion or insurgency. No legal foundation for suppressing a secession movement had ever been adopted by Congress because the Constitution did not authorize Congress to make war upon seceding states. Lincoln's attempt to use the Militia Act of 1795 to suit his purpose in 1861 was not in keeping with the Constitution or the laws of the United States at all, but was an unlawful usurpation of power and a perversion of the law. This third provision of the Militia Act cannot even be applied to the situation in 1861, and thus could not be met as a prerequisite for calling out the militia and the military to suppress a secession movement.

Some will argue that Lincoln had to act quickly because he was dealing with an emergency situation, but it should be pointed out that the secession crisis did not materialize over night. It had been well underway even before Lincoln entered office. Yet, at no time did he approach Congress with any of his plans or request any type of assistance with preparations to meet the situation. The House of Representatives adjourned shortly after Lincoln's inauguration, but the Senate remained in session until March 28, 1861, only two days before Lincoln ordered a re-supply mission to proceed to Fort Sumter, setting in motion the chain of events that would lead to war (refer to Part Two, Position Nine: "The South Started It" for details).

In fact, on March 25, 1861, the Senate passed a resolution requesting that the President provide copies of Major Robert Anderson's communications from Fort Sumter so that they could examine them and assess the situation before adjourning. Lincoln replied:

> I have received a copy of a resolution of the Senate, passed on the 25th instant, requesting me, if, in my opinion, not incompatible with the public interest, to communicate to the Senate the dispatches of Major Robert Anderson to the War Department during the time he has been in command of Fort Sumter.

> On examining the correspondence thus called for, I have, with the highest respect for the Senate, come to the conclusion that, at the present moment, the publication of it would be inexpedient.[5]

Had Lincoln provided Anderson's dispatches, the Senate would have seen that the situation in Charleston was approaching a crisis point sooner than originally anticipated; and senators might have extended their session and taken some sort of action. But it is well known that Lincoln saw traitors hiding in every closet in Washington at this time and was trying to proceed as secretly as possible. Conferring with Congress would not only have exposed his plans, it would have invited congressional interference.

If the President had been truly concerned about fulfilling his duty to ensure that the laws were faithfully executed, why did he act so flippantly with regard to his own actions in light of those laws, particularly in an unprecedented and clearly volatile situation? This was typical of Lincoln, however. He tended to act by himself and upon his own justifications. Once he had taken certain actions, he would claim that it was too late to undo them because they were already in motion, as we will see in the upcoming section: *A Blockade of Southern Ports*. And politicians today, fancying themselves to be made in Lincoln's image, consistently do the same. Usurpation is now held up as "leadership" and "vision".

Speaking of Lincoln in his address to the Senate on March 15, 1861, Stephen Douglas addressed this very matter:

> But it may be said that the President of the United States ought to have the power to collect the revenue on ship-board, to blockade the ports, to use the military to enforce the law. I say, it may be said he ought to have that power. Be that as it may, the President of the United States has not asked for that power. He knew that he did not possess it under the existing laws – for we are bound to presume that he is familiar with the laws which he took an oath to execute…We are bound to presume that, when he said he would use the power confided to him to hold, occupy, and possess the Forts and other property of the United States, he knew he could not call out the militia for any such purpose, under the existing law. We are bound to presume that he knew of this total absence of power on all these questions.[6]

So we see that, although Lincoln expected violence to break out during this unprecedented period in American history, at no time did he seek any type of legitimate, extended authority for dealing with it. Lincoln allowed Congress to adjourn, and even though he did call them into session following the bombardment of Fort Sumter, he called them to report to Washington on July 4, 1861. The date of Lincoln's proclamation was April 15! This meant that Congress would not report to Washington for three months; and in the meantime, Lincoln would essentially be accountable to no one but himself. Lincoln then not only did call the military into service, he actually expanded it on his own authority, in spite of the fact that, per Article II, Section VIII of the Constitution, only Congress can raise armies and provide for the Navy.

A Blockade of Southern Ports

Shortly after his initial proclamation of rebellion and call for troops, Lincoln issued a proclamation announcing a blockade of Southern ports. This proclamation, which Lincoln claimed was issued "in pursuance of the laws of the United States and the laws of nations," astounded even some of those who supported Lincoln's war effort, and members of his own administration as well as congressional Republicans protested the measure, as there were serious legal problems with it. Lincoln, however, was unperturbed by these cautions. When Republican Congressman Thaddeus Stevens confronted Lincoln over the matter, Lincoln replied he did not know anything about the law of nations but thought that his proclamation was "all right":

> I'm a good enough lawyer in a Western law court, I suppose, but we don't practice the law of nations up there, and I supposed Seward knew all about it, and I left it to him. But it's done now and can't be helped, so we must get along as well as we can.[7]

The problem that Stevens and others pointed out to Lincoln was that the law of nations recognized blockades as existing only between belligerent powers, meaning that, in order to legally employ a blockade against the seceded states, Lincoln would have to recognized the Confederacy as a "belligerent," a hostile power. This would have essentially meant recognizing the independence of the Confederacy and its status as a separate country. There was no other way the Confederacy could be a "belligerent" power, no other way in which the blockade could be legal. Yet, Lincoln maintained that the seceded states were still in the Union and that the Confederates were "rebels". This meant that, as Thaddeus Stevens protested, the United States of America was essentially blocking itself.

Despite his claims to the contrary in his proclamation, Lincoln must have understood that his actions were not "in pursuance of the laws of the United States and the laws of nations," certainly after his own colleagues confronted him about the matter. There was no legal basis for his actions whatsoever; and despite the fact that Lincoln knew this, we see that he did it, nonetheless. We also see that he publicly attempted to justify his actions on a legal basis while privately joking that he really did not care that he had no legal basis for it.

Lincoln continued this two-facedness in his address to Congress on

July 4, 1861, given three months after his proclamation of a blockade:

> Recurring to the action of the Government, it may be stated that at first a call was made for seventy-five thousand militia; and rapidly following this a proclamation was issued for closing ports of the insurrectionary districts by proceedings in the nature of a blockade. *So far all was believed to be strictly legal.*[8] [Emphasis mine]

Lincoln had a habit of doing whatever suited him, regardless of whether it was legal, and this fact stands in stark contrast to the picture that Lincoln-apologists have painted of the sixteenth President over the years: that portrait of a virtuous man who always did what was right and good. Noah Brooks, Lincoln's journalist friend who was quoted earlier, once described Lincoln's character in that same storybook fashion: "With him the question was not, 'Is it convenient? Is it expedient?' but, 'Is it right?'"[9] Mr. Brooks aside though, we have clearly seen examples of Lincoln choosing what was convenient and expedient over what was right. We shall soon see more evidence of it.

Before moving on, let's see one more comment from Stephen Douglas' speech of March 15, 1861:

> But we are told that the country is to be precipitated into war by blockading all the Southern ports; blockading ports within the United States; blocking our own ports with our own Army and Navy! Where is the authority for that? What law authorizes the President of the United States to blockade Federal ports at discretion? He has no more authority to blockade New Orleans or Charleston than he has to blockade New York or Boston... The intimation that he is to do this, implies a want of respect for the integrity of the President, or an ignorance of the laws of the land on the part of those who are disturbing the harmony and quiet of the country by threats of illegal violence.[10]

Keep in mind here that Douglas made his comments prior to the outbreak of war and any of these actions on the part of Lincoln. At the time, Douglas was attempting to persuade doubters that the President would not do any of these things because, legally, he could not do them. He was arguing that senators should have more respect for the President than to assume that he would do such outrageous things.

A Downward Spiral

Lincoln's proclamations calling for 75,000 militiamen and imposing a blockade were certainly startling; however, they were by no means the only unconstitutional acts of this President. Having set out on the path of usurpation, Lincoln continued the downward spiral of the laws in other areas as well. On April 27, 1861, Lincoln quietly authorized the commanding general of the United States Army to suspend the right to a writ of habeas corpus in the greater Washington area, and, in that single order, one of our Constitution's most important provisions was overthrown.

Habeas Corpus is a Latin phrase meaning "bring out the body," or "present the body". First introduced by the Magna Carta, the writ of habeas corpus allows a judge to order that a prisoner be brought before a court in order to determine whether that person has been lawfully arrested. In other words, it is a protection that prevents governments from holding political prisoners. Once it was introduced, the writ quickly became one of the most sacred aspects of English law because it prevented rulers from forcefully silencing or otherwise taking vengeance against their political opponents. Consider the following quote from Alexander Hamilton, as found in Federalist 84, concerning the importance of the writ:

> The observations of the judicious Blackstone...are well worthy of recital: "To bereave a man of life [says he] or by violence to confiscate his estate, without accusation or trial, would be so gross and notorious an act of despotism as must at once convey the alarm of tyranny throughout the whole nation; but confinement of the person, by secretly hurrying him to jail, where his sufferings are unknown or forgotten, is a less public, a less striking, and therefore a *more dangerous engine* of arbitrary government." And as a remedy for this fatal evil he is everywhere peculiarly emphatical in his encomiums [words of praise] on the habeas corpus act, which in one place he calls "the BULWARK of the British Constitution." [Capitalization in the original]

Lincoln's first actual *public* proclamation authorizing a suspension of the right to a writ habeas corpus came on May 10, 1861, when he authorized military officials in Florida to suspend the writ and to "actually remove," from the vicinity of the United States fortresses all dangerous or suspected persons". Lincoln did this on the basis that: "An insurrection exists in the State of Florida, by which the lives, liberty, and property of loyal citizens of the United States are endangered". He justified his actions to Congress on July 4, 1861, as follows:

> It was not believed that any law was violated. The provision of the Constitution that "the privilege of the writ of habeas corpus shall not be suspended unless when, in cases of rebellion or invasion, the public safety may require it," is equivalent to a provision – is a provision – that such privilege may be suspended when, in case of rebellion or invasion, the public safety does require it... Now, it is insisted that Congress, and not the Executive, is vested with this power. But the Constitution itself is silent as to which or who is to exercise the power; and as the provision was plainly made for a dangerous emergency, it cannot be believed the framers of the instrument intended that in every case the danger should run its course until Congress could be called together; the very assembling of which might be prevented, as was intended in this case, by the rebellion.[11]

It is also unbelievable that the framers, having drafted a protection for times of a "dangerous emergency," should have been so careless as to not stipulate who was to exercise that important power. The provision concerning suspension of the writ of habeas corpus is part of Section Nine under Article I of the Constitution, which is headed: "All legislative powers herein granted shall be vested in a Congress of the United States..." Thus, since it is found in Article I (and the powers of the President are separately catalogued under Article II) the power to suspend the right to a writ of habeas corpus is clearly a power of Congress alone. Lincoln quoted Article I, Section Nine during his address to Congress, and thus he obviously knew that it was listed among those powers specifically delegated to Congress. Abraham Lincoln was many things, but he was not a fool.

The most celebrated controversy regarding habeas corpus to arise under Lincoln is undoubtedly the case of John Merryman, a Maryland man who was arrested on suspicion of being involved in armed resistance against the Union war effort. At two o'clock on the morning of May 25, 1861, an armed party entered Merryman's home, took him from his bed, and carried him off to Fort McHenry in Annapolis.[12] Merryman's arrest was an entirely arbitrary affair; no court had issued a warrant for him, nor were any formal charges filed in court against him. The military simply seized him.

Word of this situation reached United States Chief Justice Roger Taney, who granted a writ of habeas corpus to Merryman, obligating General George Cadwalader, the commander at Fort McHenry, to bring Merryman before the court. Cadwalader refused the writ, citing Lincoln's orders to suspend the writ of habeas corpus as he (Cadwalader) saw fit "for the public safety". Taney was left with no option that could free the prisoner without violence, and was forced to confine his actions to issuing an opinion in which he condemned the Lincoln administration for what amounted to an act of despotism.

Concerning Lincoln's proclamation, Taney remarked, "I certainly listened to it with some surprise, for I had supposed it to be one of those points of constitutional law upon which there was no difference of opinion, and that it was admitted on all hands, that the privilege of the writ could not be suspended, except by act of congress."[13] In his opinion, Taney cited the case of Aaron Burr's conspiracy and stated that even then, when Thomas Jefferson considered a suspension of the writ necessary, he did not take the matter upon himself but referred it to Congress. Taney also cited the opinions of Supreme Court justices Joseph Story and John Marshall, opinions in which they affirmed that the right to suspend the writ rested with Congress alone.

Taney also accosted Lincoln for violating the Constitution's guarantees concerning due process of law and, in so doing, for usurping the role of the judicial branch.[14] He pointed out that one of the causes that compelled the founders to declare independence from England was King George III's attempt to "render the military independent of, and superior to, the civil power," and warned of dire consequences should such usurpations continue:

> These great and fundamental laws [the due process provisions of the Bill of Rights], which congress itself could not suspend, have been disregarded and suspended, like the writ of habeas corpus, by a military order, supported by force of arms. Such is the case now before me, and I can only say that if the authority which the constitution has confided to the judiciary department and judicial officers, may thus, upon any pretext or under any circumstances, be usurped by the military power, at its discretion, the people of

the United States are no longer living under a government of laws, but every citizen holds life, liberty and property at the will and pleasure of the army officer in whose military district he may happen to be found.[15]

A copy of Taney's decision was provided to Lincoln, who, according to his friend Ward Hill Lamon, responded by issuing a warrant to arrest the Chief Justice![16] The federal marshal to whom the arrest warrant was given wisely chose not to execute it; nevertheless, this is a remarkable event in American history, and it has received precious little attention.

As is often the case, the collapse of one liberty soon led to the fall of others. By 1863, Lincoln, with a complicit Congress in his corner, had extended his suspension of the writ of habeas corpus to cover the entire country, effectively instituting martial law. Northerners who openly expressed sympathy for Southerners or the Confederate cause were subject to accusations of "disloyalty," and many thousands of citizens were charged and convicted of treason and imprisoned by military fiat. Just how many citizens were imprisoned for political reasons during the war may never be known, as even the federal government itself was never able to establish an approximate number.

Crusading Union officials closed an estimated three hundred anti-Lincoln newspapers in the Northern states during the war, an action which was perhaps a bridge too far, as it generated protest among even "loyal" citizens. For that reason the administration eventually started throwing troublesome newspaper editors into prison instead of closing their papers entirely, a tactic which allowed the Union government the luxury of silencing its media critics without generating so much negative publicity.[17] The situation in the supposedly free American media eventually deteriorated to the point that, by 1864, the Cincinnati *Enquirer* was able to remark that the press was muzzled by a "censorship as rigid as that of Austria or France."[18]

Lincoln's militarism quickly plunged the country into the founders' worst nightmare: fratricidal war and despotism. Constitutional government existed only in the form thereof, but lacked any sort of real power whatsoever. The country was firmly under the control of the Lincoln administration and completely subject to its whims. Secretary of State William H. Seward once boasted to Britain's Lord Lyons that:

"My lord, I can touch a bell on my right hand and order the arrest of a citizen of Ohio. I can touch the bell again and order the arrest of a citizen of New York. And no power on earth except that of the president can release them. Can Queen Victoria do as much?"[19] Even the supposedly sacred electoral process was subject to interference at this time in our history. Voters were sometimes required to identify themselves by party affiliation or swear loyalty oaths to the Union, and Democrats often failed to reach the ballot boxes. Union generals also had a tight grip on the electoral process in their respective areas of occupation in the Southern and border states, and did all they could to keep "disloyal" persons from casting votes.

In particular, the border states of Maryland, Kentucky and Missouri felt the grip of Lincoln's "people's contest" early on, and played host to some of the more memorable assaults on freedom and the Constitution. Maryland was of special interest to federal authorities early in the war due to the fact that it surrounded most of Washington DC. Since Washington was already bordered by Confederate Virginia on the south, if Maryland seceded the Union capital would have found itself isolated deep within enemy territory. Maryland was considered a Southern state at that time; however, although there were pro-Confederates in its legislature, and although much of the state's population was sympathetic to the seceded Southern states, Maryland itself took no steps to secede. Indeed, it attempted to remain neutral, officially declining to aid either North or South. In spite of this neutral stance though, Maryland became the first state to taste the new war upon its soil. A group of Union volunteers passing through Baltimore on their way to Washington on April 19, 1861, clashed with Southern sympathizers in an encounter that left twenty-six people dead and many more injured. This impromptu skirmish occurred, oddly enough, on the anniversary of the Battle of Lexington during the Revolutionary War.

Although Maryland never took any official strides toward secession, Washington eventually acted to preempt the possibility. On September 11, 1861 – with a meeting of the Maryland legislature scheduled to take place within six days – Lincoln's Secretary of War, Simon Cameron, ordered Union General Banks to prevent Maryland's secession by arresting "all or part" of the legislature's members, if necessary. "Exercise your own judgment as to the time and manner," Cameron wrote, "but do the work effectually."[20] Arrests began on September 17, eventually resulting in the imprisonment of thirty-one members of the legislature and the mayor of Baltimore. At election time in November, federal marshals policed the polls to keep Southern sympathizers from voting, and Maryland soldiers serving in the Union army were granted leave to go home and vote. Thus Union leaders ensured that Maryland's new legislature, and therefore the state itself, would remain staunchly loyal to the Union cause from that point forward.[21]

Kentucky, Lincoln's home state, was of desperate importance to the President, who felt that losing that state to the Confederacy would essentially be the loss of the war. As a result, federal authorities in Kentucky clamped down on "disloyal" sentiment wherever and however they could, to the point of censoring sermon content and sheet music.[22] As the war progressed, Kentucky found itself in the rather strange position of having two governments, one loyal to the South and one loyal to the North. Kentucky's Southern sympathizing government managed to convene a convention and pass an ordinance of secession, but superior Union forces held the state in the Union for the duration of the war.

Meanwhile, the state of Missouri found itself in the midst of a true civil war that would leave it, "seething with hatreds, divided county by county, even farm by farm, and racked with internecine war".[23] Missouri saw entire populations displaced by Union efforts to counter guerrilla warfare, and even faced an incident similar to the one that claimed more than twenty lives in Baltimore. On May 10, 1861, fanatical Unionist Nathaniel Lyon surrounded a militia encampment with artillery and, claiming them to be a budding secessionist force, compelled them to surrender. Lyons then marched his captives through the city of St. Louis where a riot ensued and Lyons' men began firing into the crowd as Union volunteers had done in Baltimore. Sadly, this clash produced nearly the same number of fatalities as the Baltimore riot.

The Man without a Country

Clement Vallandingham, a United States Congressman from Ohio, was severely critical of the Lincoln administration's war policies, a stance that ultimately earned him a visit from federal troops, who entered his home in the dead of night and brought him before a military court. Vallandingham was convicted of the "crime" of having spoken against the war, and was imprisoned. Eventually, public indignation forced Lincoln to release Vallandingham, whom he then exiled to the Confederacy; an act where Lincoln effectively sent a man to a place that he maintained did not exist. Vallandingham later returned to the United States, and this fact was shared with the President in 1864. Lincoln found it difficult to believe that Vallandingham had returned but thought he could be ignored as long as he kept a low profile. "So long as he behaves himself decently," Lincoln said, "he is as effectually in disguise as a slovenly man who went to a masquerade party with a clean face."[24]

The Vallandingham affair eventually became the basis for *The Man Without a Country*: a popular story about a man who has spoken out hatefully against his country and is forced to spend his days in exile, where no one is permitted to give him any news of his homeland. At the end of the story, the man repents of his errors and desires that someone should at last tell him something of his country's recent history before he dies. I saw this story performed as a play while in junior high school, and it was explained to us at the time that we should all be good patriots who love our country unconditionally and are willing to do anything for it. Looking back on that time, I can only wonder if those who presented the play and its lessons knew that it was based upon the story of a man who did nothing more than exercise his constitutional right of free speech in protest against the illegal actions of Lincoln's regime. I can only wonder if they ever considered that, if Lincoln was right in what his government did to Clement Vallandingham, then the Patriots of the American Revolution who denounced the British government and separated from it were nothing more than disloyal agitators who deserved the same treatment as *The Man Without a Country*.

Lincoln's Legacy of Executive Usurpation

Writing in *Lincoln: The Man Behind the Myths*, Stephen Oates comments that Lincoln was "no dictator". Indeed, Oates claims that the idea of dictatorship "appalled him, for it violated everything he held sacred in government."[25] According to Oats and other Lincoln admirers, the fact that Lincoln placed himself above the law and assumed virtually all of the powers of a dictator did not actually make him a dictator. But if the very idea of being a dictator appalled Lincoln, it did not appall him enough; for, he was ever ready to assume that role in pursuit of his goals, a pursuit that held nothing sacred in government except for government itself.

This affinity for Lincoln and the Lincoln legacy, particularly on the part of advocates of limited, constitutional government, is truly an American enigma. American politicians often roundly criticize foreign governments for employing Lincolnesque tactics; and yet, these same politicians who criticize such measures as being destructive of liberty often have no shortage of words in praise of Lincoln. President George W. Bush has even been compared with Abraham Lincoln on many occasions since the terrorist attacks of September 11, 2001. On April 12, 2002, during an evening's entertainment at Ford's Theater in Washington, Bush was honored by one speaker on the basis that he had defended America against enemies of freedom just as Abraham Lincoln had once done when confronted with "rebel flags" just across the Potomac. I was watching from home at the time and noted that this speaker, in the act of transforming Lincoln into a defender of American liberty, had just performed a greater magic trick than David Copperfield, who had performed for the same audience only moments before. For his part, Bush just gravely nodded his head and accepted the honor of being compared to Lincoln as a nun might beam at being compared with Mother Theresa.

Congress eventually met and took action to approve many of Lincoln's actions, but the President certainly did not trouble himself to wait for this approval. On his own authority, he deliberately took steps that propelled the country into the most violent conflict it had ever seen. This war was waged in the name of the Constitution, the laws, and government of the people; but when victory came it was not a victory for the Constitution, the laws, and government of the people. It was a victory for authoritarianism brought about by brute force. Jeffrey Hummel, author of *Emancipating Slaves, Enslaving Free Men*, comments:

> The Civil War represents the simultaneous culmination and repudiation of the American Revolution…In the years ahead, coercive authority would wax and wane with year-to-year circumstances, but the long-term trend would be unmistakable. Henceforth there would be no more major victories of Liberty over Power.[26]

"Law is organized justice," wrote Frederic Bastiat in his classic 1850 work, *The Law*. Commenting on the true nature of the law and its applications for society in general, Bastiat declared that law is force and can only be legitimately used in regard to the defense of individual rights. "For truly," asked Bastiat, "how can we imagine force being used against the liberty of citizens without it also being used against justice, and thus acting against its proper purpose?"[27]

Lincoln's use of the law as force against freedoms that the law was created to protect was a travesty of justice, and we embrace his ideals today only at our own continued peril. For if we embrace Lincoln's ideology, then government, and not the law, is absolute; and there is no appeal that a citizen might make to the law for protection that might not then be answered with the ancient maxim: *"Necessitas non habet legem,"* or "Necessity has (or knows) no law." And what will our future leaders feel is "necessary"? What actions will they attempt to justify with appeals to the example of Lincoln and other usurpers?

Former United States Supreme Court Chief Justice William Rehnquist has already illustrated this idea for us somewhat in recent comments he made concerning civil liberties during times of crisis. He has essentially stated that there are no restraints the government must acknowledge, the Constitution not withstanding, in attempting to meet such a situation. After commenting on violations of civil liberties employed during both the War of Secession and World War II, Rehnquist hailed Lincoln as "the greatest of American Presidents," and Franklin Roosevelt as ranking "high among the runners up" because they were willing to violate the Constitution in order to do what they thought was necessary at the time. Says Rehnquist:

> The courts, for their part, have largely reserved the decisions favoring civil liberties in wartime to be handed down after the war was over. Again, we see the truth in the maxim <u>Inter Arma Silent Leges</u> – in time of war the laws are silent.
>
> To lawyers and judges, this may seem a thoroughly undesirable state of affairs, but in the greater scheme of things it may be best for all concerned. The fact that judges are loath to strike down wartime measures while the war is going on is demonstrated both by our experience in the Civil War and in World War II. This fact represents something more than some sort of patriotic hysteria

that holds the judiciary in its grip; it has been felt and even embraced by members of the Supreme Court who have championed civil liberty in peacetime... While we would not want to subscribe to the full sweep of the Latin maxim – <u>Inter Arma Silent Leges</u> – in time of war the laws are silent, perhaps we can accept the proposition that though the laws are not silent in wartime, they speak with a muted voice.[28]

In so saying, Rehnquist has presented us with the possibility of future Clement Vallandingham's being forcefully silenced for the "public good," and other actions being taken by the government to overthrow what our founders considered "unalienable rights". In his speech, Rehnquist does try to reassure us that civil liberties are usually reinstated and unconstitutional privations overturned after the conflict is over; however, while the crisis is underway, it would appear that we are at the mercy of lawless dictators engaging in whatever they feel is "necessary". And what is to stop usurpers made in Lincoln's image from putting our country into perpetual states of emergency in order to facilitate their bids for greater power? If you find that statement outlandish, consider that government officials have openly told us that the War on Terror is a conflict with no apparent end in sight. Meanwhile, they continue to appropriate more and more power, all supposedly in our best interest; and, if you question them, they question your patriotism and tell you to get in line.

Most recently (as of 2006), President George W. Bush was able to build on Lincoln's foundation of executive usurpation in order to invade a sovereign country – Iraq – overthrow its government, set up a new government, and then entirely rebuild the country. His actions have had worldwide repercussions, and have resulted in the loss, to date, of over two thousand American lives, tens of thousands of Iraqi lives, and the spending of multiplied billions of dollars (the latest estimates indicate the total price tag of the war may exceed $1 trillion); and he was able to do all of this without either an act of hostility on the part of Iraq or a declaration of war by Congress. In addition, President Bush has declared, via various "signing statements" that he has the right to ignore laws of Congress in regard to such issues as torturing prisoners of war and upholding civil privacy rights, if he decides that "national security" mandates such. This in spite of the fact that the Constitution requires the President to "take care that the laws be faithfully executed". These developments would have astonished our country's founders. Indeed, the military powers that presidents exercise today would have seemed kingly to them. They specifically limited the powers of American presidents in the Constitution because they had learned the hard lessons taught by centuries of bloodletting courtesy of the crowned heads of Europe. Under the American system, presidents were to be limited chief executives, not absolute monarchs.

Today, however, if you argue that the President does not have authority to involve this country in undeclared wars, or toss the Constitution and the laws out like yesterday's newspaper, the powers-that-be look upon you as little better than the enemy itself. Former Attorney General John Ashcroft spelled this out for us in no uncertain terms on December 7, 2001, when he stated that those who question the President's actions in the War on Terror are effectively aiding America's enemies:

> To those who scare peace-loving people with phantoms of lost liberty, my message is this: Your tactics only aid terrorists for they erode our national unity and diminish our resolve. They give ammunition to America's enemies and pause to America's friends.[29]

Consider also the words of a 1939 memo written by Frank Murphy – US Attorney General, and later Supreme Court Justice, under Franklin Roosevelt – words approvingly quoted by former Attorney General Ashcroft. Concerning the wartime powers of the President, Murphy wrote that these powers "have never been specifically defined and, in fact, cannot be – since their extent and limitations are largely dependent on conditions and circumstances."[30]

With all due respect to Murphy, Ashcroft, and stolid defenders of Presidents Lincoln, Wilson, Franklin Roosevelt and George W. Bush, the powers of the President of the United States – wartime or not – are specifically and totally defined by Article II of the Constitution. I have quoted the relevant clause already. The President is Commander in Chief of the armed forces of the United States and the militias of the states when they are called into the service of the United States. This gives the President supreme authority as a sort of commanding general of all U.S. armed forces in their constitutional role of providing for the common defense. It makes him Commander in Chief of the United States military, but *not of the United States themselves*. This is a crucial distinction. Being Commander in Chief of the armed forces makes the President a unifying military leader; being Commander in Chief of the United States would make him a dictator.

The founders clearly intended the former, not the latter. They intended that the President should be able to direct our country's defenses so that our armed forces might operate as a unified front against an aggressor; but they never intended that a President should overthrow the Constitution he was sworn to uphold or ascend to the headship of all civilian government. The idea is simply preposterous, for several compelling reasons:

1. If the founders meant for the President to have unquestioned authority to suspend the Constitution, institute martial law and assume the leadership of civil government, I would think that it would have been important enough a point for them to have clearly mentioned it somewhere in the Constitution. They did not. They made the President "Commander in Chief," not Dictator in Chief. In fact, Article IV, Section IV of the Constitution precludes martial law when it declares that, "The United States shall guarantee to every State in this Union a Republican Form of Government". Republican government is civil, representative government; martial law is military rule. The two are incompatible, and the Constitution specifically protects the former, thereby precluding the latter.

2. The Constitution, as we have seen, is the Supreme Law of the land, and it stipulates that the President must swear to uphold its provisions. But how can he both suspend it and uphold it? The answer is that he cannot; he is obligated to uphold the integrity of the Constitution or else he violates his oath of office and is impeachable.

3. While the Constitution gave the President power to be Commander in Chief of the military, it actually gave the war power of the country, and that of raising armies, to Congress. So it would then seem logical to ask, if the Commander in Chief role was meant to be all encompassing where the "national security" is concerned, why were war powers denied to the President?

Clearly, he was not meant to have absolute control over the country's military machine; and if he does not even have total control over military affairs as the stipulated Commander in Chief, how can he possibly be said to have authority superior to civil government, which is nowhere mentioned in the "Commander in Chief" clause?

4. The idea of presidential supremacy totally overthrows the Constitution's most fundamental and distinguishing characteristics: the rule of law, the separation of powers, and the clear fact that the federal government's powers were delegated by the states and their people, to whom all other powers are summarily reserved. If the President holds supreme power, what reserved powers could the states and the people possibly have? Supreme power is total power; it leaves nothing in reserve.

Presidents may claim that they act by virtue of "necessity," but the great difficulty here is that, while "necessity" (which is a very subjective term) may not depend upon the law, freedom does. The founders understood this. Governments have economies and great engines of war at their disposal, but the common man has only the law to protect him. Once the law is breached, no matter what the pretext, the common people no longer have rights, and the ambitious no longer have limitations. A President who places himself above the law, for whatever reason, has become a law unto himself. Government is then transformed from an agent designed to protect the rights of the people into the actual originator of those rights. Beginning with Lincoln, our Republic has been altered on this basis to the point where government has taken on a life and purpose of its own that the people are expected to serve, its direction guided not by the boundaries of the law but by whatever political agenda happens to control Washington DC at any given time.

It is true that the world has changed since the Constitution was written, and there are now dangers that we must face that the founders could not have envisioned. However, it is also true that the founders understood they could not account for everything that might come down the pike, and that the people might desire to change the Constitution. This is why they provided an amendment process, to allow the laws to be changed to account for new situations and new desires on the part of the country. If there is a need for the President or the Congress to do more, then the Constitution should be amended. If the need is that vital and pressing, surely the states and the American people will approve such measures. We as a country have made mistakes and are sometimes frustratingly apathetic, but we are not exactly a suicidal people.

All of this is said to illustrate a particularly disturbing and far-reaching aspect of the Lincoln legacy. Through his extra-constitutional actions, Lincoln set the precedents by which American presidents are operating today. And if we as a country travel the same road as our ancestors did under Lincoln, we should not be surprised if we find ourselves at the same place and in the same predicament. Phrases like "necessity knows no law" and "in time of war the laws are silent," are not the fundamental doctrines of free peoples. They are the anthem of empires, the banner of dictators, the crowner of kings.

Was the Constitution Suspended?

Having examined Lincoln's unconstitutional actions, let's try to answer the question that began the discussion: was the Constitution suspended at the time of the war; and, if so, does this excuse Lincoln's behavior?

If the Constitution was suspended at the time of the war, then we must necessarily ask how it came to be suspended. It could only have been suspended in one of two ways: either as a direct action of some type on the part of Lincoln or the government; or as a direct result of the circumstances of the time (i.e.: the entire secession situation was not covered by the Constitution and thus America effectively stepped outside of the Constitution from 1861-1865, or until 1877 if Reconstruction is considered).

In addressing these two potential grounds for suspension, first it should be noted that presidents have no authority to suspend the Constitution. For that matter, neither does Congress or the Supreme Court. Congress can propose amendments and a convention can be called by the states, but there is no mention of any means of suspending the document. The reason is obvious: the Constitution represents the Supreme Law of the land, the only means by which the federal government derives its powers, and the sole basis of the Union itself. Thus, if you suspend the Constitution, you literally suspend the United States of America. You effectively dissolve the Union because you render its only unifying agent inert, depriving the government of its authority to peacefully enforce the laws and removing any obligation on the states and people to obey those laws. Remember the quotes we saw from the founders where they stated that the only legitimate powers of the federal government flow from the Constitution.

The founders did not see any reason that would have justified a provision for suspending the Constitution. If a new situation arose, or if the people desired a change, the Constitution could be amended. If the people desired to radically alter or abolish the document, a convention could be called. Either of these two constitutional provisions is capable of handling the continued administration or abolition of the Constitution.

Furthermore, it should be noted that neither Lincoln nor the Congress took any official action actually designed to suspend the Constitution. Lincoln was not shy about doing what he pleased for whatever reasons he pleased. If he had desired to suspend the Constitution, it is safe to say that he would have. As it happened, Lincoln actually claimed that he was defending the Constitution and the laws, and his proclamations appealed to the Constitution and the laws (albeit in vain) for authority to prosecute the war. Had Lincoln considered the Constitution suspended, it would not have made any sense to continuously appeal to it for his authority in office.

No, it must be concluded that Lincoln did not suspend the Constitution. Not only did he not ever issue any kind of edict to that effect, but he clearly stated that he considered the Union "unbroken" and the laws still applicable to the Southern states. If the laws are not in effect, then there can be no insurrection against the laws, and Lincoln's justification of going to war against the South was on the basis that it was in a state of insurrection.

That said, however, Lincoln did maintain that he could legitimately exercise powers not granted to him by the Constitution because "measures, otherwise unconstitutional, might become lawful, by becoming indispensable to the preservation of the constitution through the preservation of the nation".[31] By this logic, even Lincoln's illegal actions were technically legal because they were necessary to uphold the Constitution. His July 4, 1861, address to Congress underscores this idea:

> He [Lincoln referring to himself] desires to preserve the Government, that it may be administered for all, as it was administered by the men who made it. Loyal citizens everywhere have the right to claim of this Government, and the Government has no right to withhold or neglect it. It is not perceived that, in giving it, there is any coercion, any conquest, or any subjugation, in any just sense of those terms.
>
> The Constitution provides, and all the States have accepted the provision, that "the United States shall guaranty to every State in this Union a republican form of Government." But if a State may lawfully go out of the Union, having done so, it may also discard the republican form of Government; so that to prevent is going out is an indispensable means to the end of maintaining the guarantee mentioned; and when an end is lawful and obligatory, the indispensable means to it are also lawful and obligatory.[32]

"Are all the laws but one to go unexecuted," Lincoln asked Congress during the same address, "and the Government itself to go pieces, lest that one be violated?" Lincoln's argument is an example of a logical fallacy known as 'false dilemma'. The situation he presented as justification for his actions simply did not exist. Secession violated no laws and the government was not going to pieces. The end he sought, forcing the Southern states to remain in the Union, was not lawful itself, and thus could not be lawfully pursued. Nevertheless, Lincoln's persistence in all of these examples demonstrates his view of the Constitution and the laws as remaining in effect during the war.

We then arrive at our second potential scenario. If Lincoln and Congress did not suspend the Constitution, then did the very nature of the unprecedented circumstances in which the country found itself serve to effectively suspend the document?

The answer to this question is found in another, which reduces the matter to its simplest elements: does secession interfere with the functioning of the Constitution? After all, what is a suspension of the Constitution but an interference with its operation? But secession, as a reserved right of the states, is constitutionally consistent, and thus cannot interfere with the Constitution's operation. Considering the situation in 1861, did the fact that eleven states departed the Union prevent the other twenty-two from assembling together in Congress, supporting the President, convening the Supreme Court, or exercising foreign and domestic policies? Not at all. Congress continued to meet. The President held his office and legitimate powers. The Supreme Court continued to meet and rule on the questions presented to it. New states were added to the Union. Commerce continued. The government of the United States continued to exist and to function without hindrance.

In conclusion, the Constitution does not authorize its own suspension, nor did Southern secession in 1860 and 1861 interfere with the Constitution's functionality or validity; thus, the Constitution could not have been legitimately suspended at the time of the war. The truth of the matter is that Lincoln violated it, repeatedly, deliberately, and callously.

"Nearly all men can stand adversity, but if you want to test a man's character give him power."

– Abraham Lincoln

Position Three:

Lincoln fought to end Slavery

Lincoln was right in waging war against the Southern states because he was trying to end slavery, and ending slavery was more important than any right the South might have had to secede from the Union.

Ask any school child today what caused the war between North and South and you will almost certainly hear, "Slavery," in reply. For most, this answer seems a given, as obvious a fact as one's own name; however, like so much else associated with Lincoln, it simply is not true. That statement will undoubtedly seem absurd to some who read this because it diminishes Lincoln's standing in what is generally considered an unimpeachable part of his legacy; however, as always, I ask that you consider the facts and judge for yourself.

Contrary to popular belief, the causes of Southern secession and the causes of the war were interrelated but not interdependent. Slavery played a part in secession, to some degree, but not in starting the war itself. To illustrate that point, I offer a discussion concerning the history of slavery in the sectional debate, followed by a discussion of what North and South thought they were fighting for during the War of Secession. The history of slavery and sectionalism in the United States is a complex issue that has inspired entire volumes. I cannot hope to do justice to every nuance of those issues in the space available here, but I will endeavor to cover the pertinent highlights.

A Brief Overview of Slavery & the Sectional Controversy

Early Developments

Slaves were first brought to America in the early 1600s, and were present in every colony by 1776 – with a greater concentration in the South due to issues related to climate and geography. These factors made slavery more profitable in the South than in the North. As a result, anti-slavery feeling was stronger in the North than in the South, but this is not to suggest that the North played no part in establishing the institution on these shores. For an example of this, consider the fact that certain delegates at the Independence Congress in 1776 refused to support Thomas Jefferson's initial draft of a declaration of independence due, partly, to the fact that it attacked King George III where slavery was concerned. Jefferson explains the reasons for that refusal as follows:

> The clause, too, reprobating the enslaving of the inhabitants of Africa [which Jefferson blamed on George III] was struck out, in compliance to South Carolina and Georgia, who had never attempted to restrain the importation of slaves, and who, on the contrary, still wished to continue it. Our northern brethren, also, I believe, felt a little tender under those censures; for, though their people have very few slaves themselves, yet they had been pretty considerable carriers of them to others.[1]

Indeed, Northern shipping had prospered from the slave trade, and Northern industry would continue to prosper from slave labor well into the 19th Century, but the institution itself was on its way out in the North at the time of the Revolution. In 1777, Vermont, although it was not yet a state, was first to abolish slavery. By 1804, Massachusetts, New Hampshire, Rhode Island, Connecticut, Pennsylvania, New York and New Jersey had either outlawed slavery or enacted gradual emancipation laws.

In 1790, various anti-slavery allies – including, indirectly, Benjamin Franklin[2] – attempted to persuade Congress to abolish slavery throughout the entire country. A heated debate immediately ensued. The Constitution gave the federal government no power to interfere with slavery beyond a provision allowing Congress to outlaw the slave trade after 1808. Indeed, the Constitution itself would likely never have come into being, or have been ratified by all of the states, had it not been for various compromises favorable to slavery. Not unexpectedly, rumblings of secession were heard in the South during this debate, and it is likely that the Union would have sundered had the effort to outlaw slavery succeeded. Ultimately, of course, the effort was unsuccessful, but Congress did outlaw the international slave trade once it was constitutionally free to do so.

Slavery as an institution was certainly an issue in early America, as the previous example indicates; however, it was primarily the aspect of slavery in the territories that really set North and South on a collision course. Why? Because the territories were the regions from which new states would be formed and added to the Union. In the beginning, North and South were almost perfectly balanced in their representation in the federal government. As the years progressed, however, the Northern states grew in population much more quickly than the Southern states, giving them potential to control the population-based U.S. House of Representatives. Only by balancing the number of Northern and Southern states in the U.S. Senate, could the South keep the federal government from falling entirely into Northern hands. Thus, as Americans migrated westward, it was important to the South that Southerners be allowed to take their slaves with them into the territories. If they were unable to do so, it would ultimately mean that no new slave-holding states would be added to the Union. Eventually the number of free-labor states would exceed the slave-holding states and the South would lose its influence in the federal government.

Thus the battle for the territories was key to the overall sectional debate, and it began relatively early in American history.

Spain and the Mississippi River Controversy

In 1786, when the United States were still under the Articles of Confederation, a treaty was proposed that would have guaranteed certain trade benefits to the United States in exchange for surrendering exclusive control of the Mississippi River to Spain for twenty years or more. This situation created something of a scandal. The seven Northern states of the confederation appeared ready to ratify the treaty while the six Southern states were decidedly opposed to the idea. James Madison wrote to Thomas Jefferson on August 12, 1786, asking him to consider what effect a treaty restricting access to the Mississippi would have on Virginia, which Madison described as "already jealous of northern policy". Indeed, Madison believed that Spain was trying to capitalize on that budding sectional animosity in order to, as he put it, "work a total separation of interest and affection between the western and eastern settlements and to foment the jealousy between the eastern and southern States."[3] Controversy over the matter was such that James Monroe wrote privately to Patrick Henry, warning of a possible secession of the states "east of the Hudson...and the erection of them into a separate government".[4]

The Louisiana Purchase

The next major clash over sectional issues came in the year 1803, during the administration of Thomas Jefferson. It was in that year that French emperor Napoleon Bonaparte made the United States an offer it seemingly could not refuse: the acquisition of that vast area of land that would ultimately be called the Louisiana Purchase, an opportunity to more than double the territory of the United States. Once again, the balance of power between the Southern and Northern states became the subject of heated debate, and once again, rumblings of secession were heard. George Cabot, then senator from Massachusetts and a leading Federalist, identified the sectional interests behind his state's objection to the acquisition of Louisiana when he stated that "the influence of our part of the Union must be diminished by the acquisition of more weight at the other extremity".[5] Other Federalists in the North at that time were involved in a plot to elect Aaron Burr as governor of New York in order that the state might secede and take New England with it.

In 1811, when the question of admitting a small section of the Louisiana Territory, the present State of Louisiana, into the Union arose, Massachusetts Representative Josiah Quincy, who would later support Abraham Lincoln and the Northern cause during the War of Secession, declared that the bill's passage would result in a virtual dissolution of the Union. "It will free the States from their moral obligation," Quincy declared, "and, as it will be the right of all, so it will be duty of some, definitely to prepare for a separation, amicably if they can, violently if they must. "[6]

The Hartford Convention

A more significant consideration of secession from the Union was later entertained, again by Northern states, in the famous Hartford Convention of December 5, 1814 – January 5, 1815, in which George Cabot presided (and which subsequently ruined his political career and that of the Federalists in general). As always, the differing interests of the manufacturing and agricultural states readily fanned the flames of sectional tension, but this time the primary catalyst was foreign rather than domestic: the War of 1812. Prior to the war, the Northern states enjoyed a thriving trade with Great Britain, but the war disrupted this comfortable state of affairs and led to the call for a convention to enunciate the grievances of the Northern states.

The restoration of friendly relations with England arrived with the United States Senate's approval of a treaty to end the war in February of 1815, effectively reducing the Hartford Convention to an exercise. Overall though, the greatest significance of the convention was that the delegates had actively considered secession. And even though the option of secession was voted down in the end, the Hartford Convention did serve to identify causes for which secession would be justified and stated them as follows:

> Events may prove that the causes of our calamities are deep and permanent. They may be found to proceed, not merely from the blindness of the prejudice, pride of opinion, violence of party spirit, or the confusion of the times; but they may be traced to implacable combinations of individuals or of States to monopolize power and office, and to trample without remorse upon the rights and interests of commercial sections of the Union. Whenever it shall appear that the causes are radical and permanent, a separation by equitable arrangement will be preferable to an alliance by constraint among nominal friends, but real enemies.[7]

The Missouri Question – A "Firebell in the Night"

In 1818, when Missouri applied for admission to the Union, the issue of slavery factored more directly into the territorial dispute, setting off a debate in Congress that lasted for two years. The central point of contention lay with an amendment introduced by James Tallmadge of New York. This amendment required that no more slaves could be introduced into Missouri upon its admission to the Union, and that all children born to slaves in Missouri after its admission would be declared free upon reaching their twenty-fifth birthday.

Writing to James Monroe on February 10, 1820, James Madison spoke for many in the South when he maintained that Congress had no authority to regulate slavery as Tallmadge's amendment sought to do in

Missouri. Stating that he had been, "truly astonished at some of the doctrines and deliberations to which the Missouri question has led," Madison remarked that the Constitution's clause concerning congressional authority to regulate the migration and importation of slaves could not be applied to Missouri.

> I should deem it impossible that the memory of any one who was a member of the General Convention [the Constitutional convention of 1787], could favor an opinion that the terms did not exclusively refer to Migration and importation into the U.S. Had they been understood in that Body in the sense now put on them, it is easy to conceive the alienation they would have there created in certain States; And no one can decide better than yourself the effect they would have had in the State Conventions, if such a meaning had been avowed by the Advocates of the Constitution.[8]

Nevertheless, debate over the Missouri question raged on until a final compromise was reached. Under the terms of the Missouri Compromise, the brainchild of Kentuckian Henry Clay, Congress agreed to admit Missouri as a "slave state," prohibited slavery elsewhere north of the 36-30 latitude in the territory of the Louisiana Purchase, and admitted Maine to the Union as a "free state".

While open sectional hostility cooled after the adoption of the compromise, the entire issue had set the stage for renewing the battle again and again as the United States expanded to the Pacific Ocean. John Quincy Adams of New England recognized the political quagmire to come for what it was and prophesied that the worst had yet to be seen. "The discussion of the Missouri question," Adams maintained, "disclosed a secret; it revealed the basis for a new organization of parties. Here was a new party ready-formed – terrible to the whole Union, but portentously terrible to the South."[9] Adams' "ready-formed" new party would be the Republican Party of 1854, which ran the first sectional ticket in American history in the apocalyptic, four-way election of 1860. Both the Republican President and Vice Presidential candidates hailed from the North: Lincoln from Illinois, and Hannibal Hamlin from Maine. In the past, one candidate had always been from the North and one from the South.

In the aforementioned letter to James Monroe, James Madison remarked that the act of admitting Missouri by coupling it with Maine was, "to say the very least, a doubtful policy," and then went on to agree with Monroe that political power was the true object of the Missouri struggle, not concern over the status of slavery:

> I find the idea is fast spreading that the zeal with which the extension, so called, of slavery is opposed, has, with the coalesced leaders, an object very different from the welfare of the slaves, or the check to their increase; and that their real object is, as you intimate, to form a new state of parties founded on local instead of political distinctions; thereby dividing the Republicans of the North from those of the South, and making the former instrumental in giving to the opponents of both an ascendancy over the whole.[10]

Thomas Jefferson was also alarmed by the Missouri debate and stated that its implications, "like a fire bell in the night, awakened and filled me with terror. I considered it at once as the knell of the Union."[11] Writing to William Short on April 22, 1820, Jefferson predicted that the compromise would never last and that each new quarrel would only further deepen the sectional rift. "This is a reprieve only," Jefferson argued, "not a final sentence. A geographical line, coinciding with a marked principle, moral and political, once conceived and held up to the angry passions of men, will never be obliterated; and every new irritation will mark it deeper and deeper."[12] And later, writing to Albert Gallatin on December 26, 1820, Jefferson echoed the thoughts of Madison and John Quincy Adams on the nature of the Missouri debate. In Jefferson's view, the Federalists, after losing the election of 1800, did away with the old political divisions "of whig and tory" and "devised a new one of slave-holding and non-slave-holding states". This, Jefferson thought, was calculated to separate the Northern states from the Southern, and to gain the Federalists new allies by forcing those who might disagree with them otherwise to join them through mutual opposition to slavery.

> It served to throw dust into the eyes of the people and to fanaticise them, while to the knowing ones it gave a geographical and preponderant line of the Potomac and Ohio, throwing twelve States to the North and East, and ten to the South and West. With these therefore it is merely a question of power: but with this geographical minority it is a question of existence.[13]

The predictions made by these men during the Missouri Compromise era were soon proven true. The compromise itself was only a reprieve in the sectional cold war. Each time a new state was formed the same debate sprang up; and each time the debate resurfaced, it grew more hostile. As Jefferson pointed out, the Federalists, those who favored a strong national system, had gone down to defeat with his election to the presidency and had since been in search of a new political home. Northern manufacturing interests made those states natural allies with a more energetic form of government; and, as a result, the heirs of the old Federalist ideology were able to make inroads there. And slavery, since it had become a geographically defined institution in the United States, helped to separate North and South even further. Political party lines still overlapped the two sections, but once anti-slavery was wedded to manufacturing interests, the overlap began to shrink. Whether the Federalists actively worked toward that end, as Jefferson and Madison believed, is debatable; however, ultimately, circumstances did seem to work to their advantage.

In the end, these events conspired to make the North more of an advocate of political activism and consolidation, while the South became the advocate of limited government and states' rights, particularly as its influence in the federal government shrank. The stage was thus set for a complicated and bitter power struggle, one that left the Northern majority, in Jefferson's words, with a "question of power," while the Southern minority would be faced with "a question of existence".

South Carolina and the "Tariff of Abominations"

In 1828, a new crisis developed. The main players in this drama were President Andrew Jackson and the State of South Carolina, the latter represented mostly in the person of then Vice President John C. Calhoun. The issue in question was the Tariff of 1828, which was what is known as a "protective tariff," one designed to increase the price of foreign goods so as to provide domestic manufacturers with a competitive edge in the market place.

The Northern states favored protective tariffs due to their manufacturing interests, but matters were quite different in the agrarian South. The Southern states depended heavily upon the exportation of their agricultural goods, and thus the reception those goods received in foreign markets was of paramount interest to them. If the United

States enacted a high protective tariff, other countries might retaliate with protective tariffs of their own, potentially leading to trade wars that could harm the Southern economy. There was also the fact that with a prohibitively high tariff on foreign goods, Southerners could be forced to pay Northern merchants inflated prices for domestic goods that had once been available at a lower cost. In addition to these grievances, the South also argued that money being collected in the common treasury of the United States was used, disproportionately, to the advantage of the North.

South Carolina was the state most aggrieved by the Tariff of 1828, also known as the "Tariff of Abominations," and acted accordingly on the issue. Vice President Calhoun anonymously published a pamphlet entitled *The South Carolina Exposition and Protest*, which examined the powers delegated to Congress by the Constitution and declared that a state could nullify a law of Congress that it deemed to be unconstitutional. President Andrew Jackson and Massachusetts Senator Daniel Webster, among others, reacted strongly to the doctrine of nullification, pronouncing it as rebellion to the authority of the federal government.

Controversy over the "Tariff of Abominations" finally reached its climax in 1832, when Congress passed a revised tariff with the support of President Jackson. Southerners thought that this new tariff was still too high, and continued in their opposition. In November, South Carolina's legislature called a special state convention and passed an Ordinance of Nullification, declaring the tariffs of 1828 and 1832 to be unconstitutional and, therefore, not legally binding on the State of South Carolina. Andrew Jackson was incensed by the South Carolina convention and issued a stern warning to the state. "Tell them that they can talk and write resolutions and print threats to their hearts' content," Jackson said. "But if one drop of blood be shed there in defiance of the laws of the United States, I will hang the first man of them I can get my hands on, to the first tree I can find."[14] Jackson later threatened to blockade the city of Charleston and invade the state with federal troops in order to enforce the tariff.

Jackson's uncompromising stance on the issue was answered equally by the South Carolinians, who made it quite clear that any attempt to force compliance with the Tariffs of 1828 and 1832 would result South Carolina's immediate secession. Had the crisis of 1832 actually resulted in the secession of South Carolina and an attempt by Andrew Jackson to invade the state, we may have seen the outbreak of a North/South war nearly thirty years prior to the actual event. In the end, however, the crisis was averted by a series of compromise measures that allowed both sides to claim victory. In 1833, the year of the great Senate debate between Webster and Calhoun on the nature of the Union, Congress passed a reduced tariff, the brainchild of John C. Calhoun and Henry Clay, effectively forestalling further steps toward secession on the part of South Carolina. Congress also passed a law known as the Force Bill, which attempted to justify the President's threat of forceful measures to require South Carolina's adherence to the original tariffs. South Carolina responded by rescinding its nullification of the Tariffs of 1828 and 1832, accepting the Tariff of 1833, and nullifying the Force Bill.

Texas and the Mexican War

The sectional debate flared again when Texas applied – on three occasions – to join the Union, prompting Massachusetts to pass a resolution threatening secession as late as 1844:

> *Resolved*...the project of the annexation of Texas, unless arrested on the threshold, may drive these States into dissolution of the Union.[15]

Resurgent nationalism in the face of mounting hostility with Mexico eventually prevailed over Northern objections and Texas was finally invited to join the Union in 1845. Texas accepted the invitation and conflict with Mexico then became inevitable, as Mexicans refused to recognize the southern border of Texas and were determined to halt the westward expansion of the United States.

The Mexican War began in May 1846, and ended with the Treaty of Guadalupe Hidalgo in 1848. It was during this war with Mexico that nearly every major commander in the forthcoming war between North and South first tasted combat and gained the experience that would follow them to the immortal battlefields of the War of Secession. Robert E. Lee, Thomas J. "Stonewall" Jackson, and Ulysses S. Grant were among those future leaders who were first made soldiers during the conflict with Mexico. Of more interest to our present discussion, however, is the fact that, while the shooting war with Mexico had scarcely begun in 1846, a sectional battle was well underway in Congress concerning the outcome of that war. David Wilmot, a Democratic congressman from Pennsylvania, proposed legislation to the effect that slavery should be banned from any territory that was gained from Mexico. This proposal became known as the "Wilmot Proviso". Southerners were outraged at this proposal, seeing it as yet another in a mounting series of increasingly aggressive moves by Northerners to limit Southern power in Washington while increasing their own. It was the threat of this very sort of conflict that had led elder statesmen like John C. Calhoun to vote against the Mexican War, not for fear that the Union would not prevail, but for fear that its fabric might not withstand the strain of victory.

California – The "Test Question"

Following America's triumph in the war with Mexico, there came yet another spark to set the sectional fuse burning on its way to disaster. Gold was discovered in California in 1848, and a torrential flood of settlers headed West looking for a parcel of land to stake a claim and a bit of gold dust to secure their fortunes. As a result, California's population increased enormously in a very short period of time. The state formally applied for admission to the Union under an anti-slavery constitution in 1850, and, as there was no slave state with which to match its admission, sectional conflict was unavoidable.

The California question proved to be a sectional Pandora's box, and a great debate soon raged in Congress, with Henry Clay of Kentucky stepping forward once again in his persona of "The Great Compromiser," proposing legislation that was designed to defuse the California crisis. Clay's proposal, called the Omnibus Act, was as follows: 1) California was to be admitted to the Union as a free state; 2) The disposition of slavery in the Utah and New Mexico territories was to be decided by "popular sovereignty," an idea most often associated with Senator Stephen Douglas of Illinois, holding that the people of a territory should decide the slavery question for themselves; 3) Prohibition of the slave trade in Washington D.C.; 4) The settlement of Texas' western boundaries and federal assumption of that state's debts; and 5) The passage of a more stringent fugitive slave law. Northerners tended to favor Clay's compromise suggestions, but some leading Southerners, such as Jefferson Davis of Mississippi and John C. Calhoun, sought to settle the California dispute by reverting to the provisions of the Missouri Compromise and extending its 36-30 boundary line all the way to the Pacific Ocean. They proposed this idea to the Senate, where it was rejected by a vote of twenty-four to thirty-two, a vote cast largely along sectional lines.[16]

The Senate debate on Clay's proposed compromise measures involved two familiar 19th Century orators: Calhoun of South Carolina, and Webster of Massachusetts. Calhoun, now near the end of his life, was too frail to speak and could hardly stand on his own. Nevertheless, he believed the California issue to be "the test question" as to whether sectional animosity could be resolved and the Union preserved, and the strength of this belief brought him once again to the floor of the Senate in spite of this rapidly deteriorating condition. On March 4, 1850, Calhoun took his place in the Senate chambers and a friend read his speech concerning the Clay compromise measures to the assembly. In his speech, Calhoun outlined three major Southern concerns: 1) The South's exclusion from the common territories, which left that vast amount of land open for creating future *Northern* states; 2) An "undue burden of taxation imposed upon the South," the proceeds of which were then spent disproportionately in the North; and 3) "a system of political measures by which the original character of the government has been radically changed."[17]

Calhoun developed his three points and implored the Northern states to share the blessings of the Union equally with the South and to restore the balance of power. In return, Calhoun promised that "discontent will cease, harmony and kind feelings between the sections will be restored, and every apprehension of danger to the Union removed". Calhoun also promised that the South stood ready to act in defense of its interests if the Northern states would not agree to share the territories equally or address the issues of protective tariffs and the balance of power:

> It is time, senators, that there should be an open and manly avowal on all sides as to what is intended to be done. If the question is not now settled, it is uncertain whether it ever can hereafter be; and we, as the representatives of the States of this Union regarded as governments, should come to a distinct understanding as to our respective views, in order to ascertain whether the great questions at issue can be settled or not. If you who represent the

stronger portion, can not agree to settle them on the broad principle of justice and duty, say so; and let the States we both represent
agree to separate and part in peace.

If you are unwilling we should part in peace, tell us so; and we
shall know what to do when you reduce the question to submission or resistance. If you remain silent, you will compel us to infer
by your acts what you intend. In that case California will become
the test question. If you admit her under all the difficulties that
oppose her admission, you compel us to infer that you intend to
exclude us from the whole of the acquired Territories, with the intention of destroying irretrievably the equilibrium between the
two sections. We should be blind not to perceive in that case that
your real objects are power and aggrandizement, and infatuated,
not to act accordingly.[18]

Daniel Webster rebutted Calhoun's March 4, 1850 speech on March 7;
and while Webster did make several conciliatory gestures toward the
South in his speech, he ended with a sharp rebuke of Calhoun's suggestion that North and South should "agree to separate and part in
peace," should the North continue to oppose Southern expansion into
the territories:

I hear with distress and anguish the word "secession," especially
when it falls from the lips of those who are patriotic, and known
to the country, and known all over the world, for their political
services. Secession! Peaceable secession! Sir, your eyes and mine
are never destined to see that miracle. The dismemberment of this
vast country without convulsion! The breaking up of the fountains
of the great deep without ruffing the surface! Who is so foolish, I
beg every body's pardon, as to expect to see any such thing?

No, Sir! No, Sir! There will be no secession! Gentlemen are not serious when they talk of secession...[19]

Ironically, Senator Webster spoke with open animosity of principles
that leading men of his state had once proclaimed from the housetops.
And while Webster was certainly mistaken when he declared that,
"Gentlemen are not serious when they talk of secession," he was,
nonetheless, accurate when he predicted that no one present at the
time would see the "miracle" of peaceable secession. Both Webster
and Calhoun had made predictions that would come to pass within a

mere decade's time, but neither of the old political adversaries would witness the storm that finally broke upon the country. Webster himself was dead within two years of making his "Seventh of March" speech and would not see secession, peaceable or otherwise, come to pass. For his part, Calhoun did not live to see the month of April.

But the secessions of 1860-1861 and the bloody struggle that followed were still a decade away. This was 1850 and the country still had one last compromise left in it. Henry Clay's Omnibus Act was defeated as a whole, but its principle parts prevailed. California became a state; the issue of slavery in the remaining territories was left to "popular sovereignty" for the time being; the slave trade was outlawed in Washington DC; the Texas border dispute was resolved; and the South got a stronger fugitive slave law.

And the stage was set for disaster. For although the Compromise of 1850 ended the immediate threat to the Union, it also served to challenge the measuring stick that had lent so much stability to territorial disputes in the past: the Missouri Compromise of 1820 and the 36-30 line that it prescribed as the northernmost boundary of slave-holding land. California's admission did not directly negate the old 36-30 line because the Missouri Compromise had applied only to the territory acquired under the Louisiana Purchase; however, it did bar any future extension of that line, and it would have permitted the citizens of Utah – which is entirely above 36-30 – to create a new slave state, had they chosen to do so. As it happens, there were slaves in Utah but the practice of slavery was never widespread there.

"Bleeding Kansas"

For a number of years, fear of renewing controversy over the introduction of slavery into the remaining territories, as well as disagreement over various proposals for a transcontinental railroad, resulted in a delay in organizing a government for that region known as "the Kansas-Nebraska Territory". Then, in 1854, Senator Stephen Douglas of Illinois introduced a bill to organize the territory into two distinct portions: Kansas and Nebraska, to settle the issue of slavery in those territories by "popular sovereignty," and to officially withdraw the old 36-30 boundary line set by the Missouri Compromise. Douglas, working together with Jefferson Davis, persuaded President Franklin Pierce to support the Kansas-Nebraska Act, and the President, in turn, rallied the support of the Democratic Party. With this broad backing, the bill became law in May of 1854.

Various Northern elements immediately railed against the South on grounds that Southerners had supported the Kansas-Nebraska Act in order to spread slavery across the continent. This was an interesting stance on the part of Northerners, for while they opposed the spread of slavery, they had already facilitated it by agreeing to the terms of the Compromise of 1850, under which both Utah and New Mexico could have opted to permit slavery. Northerners might have taken some heart where those two states were concerned because Southern expansion into them was unlikely; however, Kansas was another matter entirely. They knew that it would be a relatively simple matter for Southerners to cross over into Kansas from Missouri and vote it a slave state now that they could do so legally. Thus Kansas-Nebraska had just made the possibility of a new future slave state a very real one.

These events opened the sectional rift once again, and into it poured vast numbers of emigrants from both North and South, all determined to outdo each other in the newly organized territories, thus swaying "popular sovereignty" in their section's favor. Abolitionist clergyman Henry Ward Beecher secured a place for himself in history at this tumultuous time by raising funds to buy Sharpe's rifles (called Beecher's Bibles) in order to equip Northern emigrants headed for Kansas in their crusade to oppose the extension of slavery. Southerners had also brought weapons with them to Kansas though, and incidents of violence between the two sides were inevitable.

The most widely celebrated incident of violence in Kansas occurred in May of 1856, when a group of pro-slavery Missourians dubbed "border ruffians" sacked the "free-town" of Lawrence, Kansas. Militant abolitionist John Brown quickly organized a retaliatory strike, which resulted in the murder of five settlers near Dutch Henry Crossing along the Pottawatomie Creek. Armed clashes of this nature between pro and antislavery forces in the territory of "Bleeding Kansas" continued right up through the beginning of the war in 1861.

The Formation of the Republican Party

It was during this era of mounting tensions that a prophecy once made by John Quincy Adams concerning the rise of a political party that would be "terrible to the whole Union, but portentously terrible to the South," was finally fulfilled. Following the adoption of the Kansas-Nebraska Act in 1854, various anti-slavery elements in the North, accusing the South of destroying the Missouri Compromise and calling for the repeal of the Kansas-Nebraska Act, defected from their previous political affiliations and banded together to comprise the new Republican Party.

The political scene at this time was in a state of upheaval, with the Democratic party slowly fragmenting over the issue of "popular sovereignty," and the old Whig party almost entirely disintegrated. In the midst of this political turmoil, the Republicans entered the political contest of 1856 with vigor, running John C. Fremont and William L. Dayton as President and Vice Presidential candidates. The Republican Party managed an impressive display that year, capturing forty-five percent of the Northern vote, thirty-three percent of the overall popular vote, carrying eleven out of sixteen free states, and securing a favorable showing in Congress as well. Although the Republicans did lose the 1856 presidential race to Democrat James Buchanan, they had proven themselves to be a rising force in American politics, and certainly the party to be reckoned with in the North. By 1860, just six short years after their formation, Republicans had grown so strong that they captured the presidency, despite the fact that Abraham Lincoln actually received a minority percentage of the overall popular vote, and not one electoral vote from any Southern state.

In the South, the formation and success of the Republican Party were taken as evidence that "radical" elements of the North were finally on the verge of taking over the government and forcing upon them, in the words of Calhoun, the "question of submission or resistance". Republican triumph was Northern triumph, and Northern triumph meant Southern exclusion from the territories, the general government, and the treasury; as well as the plundering of the South via taxation. For these reasons, the triumph of the Republican Party in 1860 proved to be the ultimate death-knell of the Union. Southerners finally declared that they had had enough of sectional animosity, and resolved to look to their own futures in a separate Southern confederacy.

South Carolina seceded on December 20, 1860, and was quickly followed by Mississippi, Florida, Alabama, Georgia, Louisiana, and

Texas. By February 1861, all seven had proclaimed themselves out of the Union. The sectional conflicts of nearly a century had finally taken their inevitable toll. In the words of South Carolina: "It is now too late to reform or restore the Government of the United States. All confidence in the North is lost in the South. The faithlessness of half a century has opened a gulf of separation between them which no promises or engagements can fill."

Lincoln and the Northern Attitude on Slavery and Racial Equality

Many Americans today have the mistaken notion that Abraham Lincoln was an abolitionist and a crusader for racial equality. In truth, he was neither. While he disagreed with slavery, he was not intent upon ending slavery in the states where it already existed in 1861. His primary concern was that the institution not spread to new territory.

Consider Lincoln's letter to Alexander Stephens on December 22, 1860. Lincoln asked:

> Do the people of the South really entertain fears that a Republican administration would, directly or indirectly, interfere with their slaves, or with them, about their slaves? If they do, I wish to assure you, as once a friend, and still, I hope, not an enemy, that there is no cause for such fears.
>
> The South would be in no more danger in this respect than it was in the days of Washington.[20]

In his first inaugural address as President, Lincoln stated:

> I have no purpose, directly or indirectly, to interfere with the institution of slavery in the States where it exists. I believe I have no lawful right to do so, and I have no inclination to do so.

Having said this, Lincoln then went on to publicly endorse a proposed constitutional amendment that would have protected slavery in perpetuity in those states where it already existed at the time of his inauguration. Named for its author James Corwin of Ohio, the Corwin Amendment – or "Ghost Amendment" as it sometimes known – successfully passed both houses of Congress, and was even ratified by the legislatures of Ohio and Maryland before the outbreak of war between North and South. The proposed amendment read as follows:

> No amendment shall be made to the Constitution which will authorize or give to Congress the power to abolish or interfere, within any State, with the domestic institutions thereof, including that of persons held to labor or service by the laws of said State.

In his first inaugural, Lincoln remarked:

> I understand a proposed amendment to the Constitution – which amendment, however, I have not seen – has passed Congress, to the effect that the Federal Government shall never interfere with the domestic institutions of the States, including that of persons held to service. To avoid misconstruction of what I have said, I depart from my purpose not to speak of particular amendments so far as to say that, holding such a provision to now be implied constitutional law, I have no objection to its being made express and irrevocable.

Without the advent of war, the Corwin Amendment might well have gone on to become the 13th Amendment to the United States Constitution, and – oddly enough – Abraham Lincoln's legacy would then have been equated with the perpetuation of slavery rather than with emancipation.

No, Lincoln was certainly no abolitionist. Indeed, he was not altogether certain that emancipation would improve the condition of slaves, and confessed that the problem was beyond his ability to resolve. The following words to that effect are taken from a speech he made during one of his debates with Stephen Douglas while a candidate for the Senate:

> Before proceeding, let me say I think I have no prejudice against the Southern people. They are just what we would be in their situation. If slavery did not now exist among them, they would not introduce it. If it did now exist among us, we should not instantly give it up. This I believe of the masses North and South. Doubtless there are individuals on both sides who would not hold slaves under any circumstances; and others who would gladly introduce slavery anew, if it were out of existence...

> When the Southern people tell us they are no more responsible for the origin of slavery than we, I acknowledge the fact. When it is said that the institution exists, and that it is very difficult to get rid of it in any satisfactory way, I can understand and appreciate the saying. I surely will not blame them for not doing what I should not know how to do myself. If all earthly power were given me, I should not know what to do as to the existing institution.[22]

Now consider Lincoln's opinion on the issue of racial equality (as taken from the same speech):

> What then? Free them all, and keep them among us as underlings? Is it quite certain that this betters their condition? I think I would not hold one in slavery at any rate; yet the point is not clear enough to make me denounce people upon. What next? Free them and make them politically and socially our equals? My own feelings will not admit of this; and if mine would, we well know that those of the great mass of white people will not. Whether this feeling accords with justice and sound judgment is not the sole of the question, if indeed, it is any part of it. A universal feeling, whether well or ill-fashioned, cannot be safely disregarded. We cannot make them equals.

And here are some additional quotes from Lincoln, taken from various debates with Stephen Douglas:

Charleston, Illinois, September 18, 1858:

> I will say then that I am not, nor ever have been, in favor of bringing about in any way the social and political equality of the white and black races – that I am not, nor ever have been, in favor of making voters or jurors of Negroes, nor of qualifying them to hold office, nor to intermarry with white people; and I will say in addition to this that there is a physical difference between the white and black races which I believe will forever forbid the two races living together on terms of social and political equality. And inasmuch as they cannot so live, while they do remain together there must be the position of superior and inferior, and I as much as any other man am in favor of having the superior position assigned to the white race.[23]

During this same speech, Lincoln referred to an Illinois state statute that forbade interracial marriage, and stated that he would give Stephen Douglas his "most solemn pledge that I will to the very last stand by the law of this State".

Speaking at Ottawa, Illinois on August 21, 1858, Lincoln remarked:

> I have no purpose to introduce political and social equality between the white and the black races. There is a physical difference between the two, which, in my judgment, will probably forever

forbid their living together upon the footing of perfect equality; and inasmuch as it becomes a necessity that there must be a difference, I, as well as Judge Douglas, am in favor of the race to which I belong having the superior position.[24]

There are some who believe that Lincoln was just being a good politician when he made these remarks about black equality in that he preached one viewpoint in southern Illinois and another in northern Illinois, but Lincoln actually refuted this idea himself. Speaking in regard to Stephen Douglas during the Galesburg, Illinois debate on October 7, 1858, Lincoln declared that his views on racial inequality were perfectly consistent and accurate:

> When the judge [Douglas] says, in speaking on this subject, that I make speeches of one sort for the people of the northern end of the State, and of a different sort for the southern people, he assumes that I do not understand that my speeches will be put in print and read north and south...I have all the while maintained that in so far as it should be insisted that there was an equality between the white and black races that should produce a perfect social and political equality, it was an impossibility.[25]

Lincoln's views were perfectly consistent with the time in which he lived. Blacks might not have been enslaved in the Northern states, but this should not be construed to mean that they were considered equal citizens – far from it. Many Northern states had laws on their statute books that forbade free blacks from moving into their territory; and, as late as the year 1865, nineteen Northern states denied blacks the right to vote.[26] Eric Foner of Columbia University, who is certainly no apologist for the South, has commented that the "greatest obstacle" to the development of the Abolitionist Movement did not come from the South but from Northern "indifference": "Both major political parties, Whigs and Democrats," Foner comments, "basically agreed to keep this out of politics. You just were not allowed to raise this question in a public forum."[27] Margaret Washington, Associate Professor of History at Cornell University, also makes it clear that racial equality was hardly a watchword in the North. Speaking of the fact that some gradual emancipation laws kept blacks in slavery in the North, "well into the antebellum era," Washington comments that the status of free blacks still amounted to that of second-class citizens. Says Washington: *"The whole idea of Jim Crow and segregation of the races really origi-*

nates in the North."[28] [Emphasis mine]

Suffice it to say that, as Abraham Lincoln admitted as late as 1858, the political and social ramifications of emancipation in America presented a formidable barrier to abolishing slavery. European countries had a far easier time emancipating their slaves because the slaves they held were located in their far-flung colonies and not at home where, once freed, they could impose themselves upon society. America was not in that same situation. American slaves lived in the American homeland; consequently, many Americans, both North and South, were afraid of what might happen if slaves were freed and attempted to live among them. This consideration created strong opposition to emancipation even in the Northern states, for as long as slaves remained in bondage they would be kept in subjection, *and* they would remain in the South. A number of those Northerners who did favor emancipation also thought that freed blacks should be deported or else given their own state to inhabit, rather than being integrated into American society.

Another difference between Europe and America was that, in the case of European slavery, emancipation came about gradually, and ended, not in violence, but with compensation to slaveholders for the loss of their property, a prospect that American abolitionists denounced. Indeed, although it certainly sounds counterintuitive to the modern mindset, abolitionist societies were partially to blame for America's failure to peacefully resolve the slavery issue. Militant abolitionists denounced the Constitution, calling it "a covenant with death and an agreement with Hell," and called for Northern secession on the basis of "No Union with slaveholders! Away with this foul thing!" Some favored arming Southern slaves and turning them against their masters, as John Brown attempted to do during his ill-fated raid on the arsenal at Harper's Ferry, Virginia (now West Virginia) in 1859. Southerners increasingly came to fear an armed slave revolt instigated by militant abolitionists and quietly condoned by Northerners through their silence. Brown's raid sent an electric current of that fear throughout the South, and, in the words of the *Richmond Enquirer*, "advanced the cause of Disunion more than any other event that has happened since the formation of the Government":

> The, heretofore, most determined friends of the Union may now be heard saying, 'if under the form of a Confederacy, our peace is

disturbed, our State invaded, its peaceful citizens cruelly murdered, and all the horrors of servile war forced upon us, by those who should be our warmest friends…and the people of the North sustain the outrage, then let disunion come'.[29]

During his March 7, 1850 speech to the Senate, Daniel Webster referred to the abolition societies, commenting that he felt they were undermining their own stated purpose with their militant tactics. "I do not think them useful," Webster stated. "I think their operations have produced nothing good or valuable. I cannot but see what mischiefs their interference with the South has produced." To illustrate his point, Webster described the debates on gradual emancipation that took place in the Virginia House of Delegates in 1832, and argued that militant abolitionists had "created great agitation in the North against Southern slavery," and with unfortunate results:

> The bonds of the slave were bound more firmly than before, their rivets were more strongly fastened. Public opinion, which in Virginia had begun to be exhibited against slavery, and was opening out for the discussion of the question, drew back and shut itself up in its castle. I wish to know whether any body in Virginia can now talk openly as Mr. Randolph, Governor McDowell, and others talked in 1832, and sent their remarks to the press? We all know the fact, and we all know the cause; and every thing that these agitating people have done has been, not to enlarge, but to restrain, not to set free, but to bind faster the slave population of the South.[30]

Voices from the Past

As appalling as the history of slavery is to those of us living today, and in spite of the role it played in America's sectional controversy, it was not the central cause of the war between North and South. To demonstrate that contention, I provide the following quotations from various prominent individuals who participated in the war, beginning with those from the North. Note what each person claims to be fighting for, or at least feels is the focal point of the conflict:

Union General George B. McClellan:

> Help me to dodge the nigger – we want nothing to do with him. *I am fighting to preserve the integrity of the Union and the power*

of the Govt – on no other issue.[31] [Emphasis in the original]

Thaddeus Stevens (as cited previously):

Abolition – Yes! Abolish everything on the face of the earth but this Union.

Abraham Lincoln to Kentucky Governor Magoffin on the latter's request to have Federal troops removed from Kentucky:

I most cordially sympathize with your Excellency, in the wish to preserve the peace of my own native State, Kentucky; but it is with regret I search, and can not find, in your not very short letter, any declaration, or intimation, that you entertain any desire for the preservation of the Federal Union.[32]

Lincoln to Horace Greeley [Editor of the *New York Tribune* and a prominent abolitionist]:

I would save the Union. I would save it the shortest way under the Constitution. The sooner the national authority can be restored; the nearer the Union will be "the Union as it was." If there be those who would not save the Union, unless they could at the same time save slavery, I do not agree with them. If there be those who would not save the Union unless they could at the same time destroy slavery, I do not agree with them. My paramount object in this struggle is to save the Union, and is not either to save or to destroy slavery. If I could save the Union without freeing any slave, I would do it, and if I could save it by freeing all the slaves I would do it; and if I could save it by freeing some and leaving others alone I would also do that. What I do about slavery, about the colored race, I do because I believe it helps to save the Union; and what I forbear, I forbear because I do not believe it would help to save the Union. I shall do less whenever I believe what I am doing hurts the cause, and I shall do more whenever I shall believe doing more will help the cause.[33]

Lincoln's famous 1864 letter to Mrs. Bixby on the loss of her five sons fighting for the Union army:

I cannot refrain from tendering to you the consolation that may be found in the thanks of the Republic they died to save.[34]

Under increasing pressure from abolitionists to adopt emancipation,

Lincoln at first refused, stating:

> We didn't go into the war to put down slavery, but to put the flag back; and to act differently at this moment would, I have no doubt, not only weaken our cause, but smack of bad faith…[35]

Lincoln actually countermanded emancipation orders issued by Union generals Fremont and Hunter in Missouri early in the war. General Fremont's wife later traveled to Washington to speak with Lincoln about his actions, and recorded the President as explaining that he had acted against her husband because:

> It was a war for a great national idea, the Union …General Fremont should not have dragged the Negro into it.[36]

Thurlow Weed, a Northern diplomat operating in Europe, from a letter to Secretary Seward as to whether the European powers would recognize the Confederate government:

> If ours was avowedly a War for Emancipation, this Government [France] would sympathize with and aid us.[37]

Now let's take a look at some quotes from the memoirs of the two most famous Union generals, Grant and Sherman, in order to see what they felt that they and their enemies were fighting to achieve.

Ulysses S. Grant, from *Memoirs and Selected Letters*:

In defense of Union General Butler (following the war), and what the North was fighting for:

> I desire to rectify all injustice that I may have done to individuals, particularly to officers who were gallantly serving their country during the trying period of the war for the preservation of the Union.[38]

On Northern justification for the war:

> The Constitution was not framed with a view to any such rebellion as that of 1861-65. While it did not authorize rebellion it made no provision against it. Yet the right to resist or suppress rebellion is as inherent as the right to self-defence, and as natural as the right of an individual to preserve his life when in jeopardy.[39]

Excerpts from General William T. Sherman's *Memoirs*:

To General Halleck on the South in general and the nature of the war:

> Obedience to law, absolute – yea, even abject – is the lesson that this war, under Providence, will teach the free and enlightened American citizen. As a nation, we shall be better for it.[40]

To the Mayor and councilmen of Confederate Atlanta on the nature of the war and what was necessary to end it:

> We must have peace, not only at Atlanta, but in all America. To secure this, we must stop the war that now desolates our once happy and favored country. To stop war, we must defeat the rebel armies which are arrayed against the laws and Constitution that all must respect and obey...

> Once admit the Union, once more acknowledge the authority of the national Government, and, instead of devoting your houses and streets and roads to the dread uses of war, I and this army become at once your protectors and supporters, shielding you from danger, let it come from what quarter it may.[41]

Resolution of the United States Congress drafted in 1861 following the First Battle of Manassas, stating the purpose of the war:

> *Resolved*, That the war is not waged on our part, in any spirit of oppression, or for any purpose of conquest, or for interfering with the rights, or established institutions of these States [the Confederate states], but to defend, and maintain the supremacy of the Constitution, and to preserve the Union, with all the dignity and rights of the several States unimpaired.[42]

This resolution is particularly meaningful when you consider that Congress had recently passed the Corwin Amenment, an "unamendable" amendment that would have preserved slavery in perpetuity had the states approved it.

And having heard from Union sources, let's hear from Southerners on the subject:

Excerpt from Jefferson Davis' inaugural address as provisional President of the Confederacy:

> Our present political position has been achieved in a manner unprecedented in the history of nations. It illustrates the American

idea that governments rest on the consent of the governed, and that it is the right of the people to alter or abolish them at will whenever they become destructive of the ends for which they were established.[43]

From General Robert E. Lee:

From General Orders, No. 102, a proclamation to the Army of Northern Virginia issued in November of 1863:

A cruel enemy seeks to reduce our fathers and our mothers, our wives and our children, to abject slavery; to strip them of their property, and drive them from their homes. Upon you these helpless ones rely to avert these terrible calamities, and secure them the blessing of liberty and safety. Your past history gives them the assurance that their trust will not be in vain. Let every man remember that all he holds dear depends upon the faithful discharge of his duty, and resolve to fight, and, if need be, to die, in defense of a cause so sacred, and worthy the name won by this army on so many bloody fields.[44]

From General Orders, No. 7, a proclamation to the Army of Northern Virginia issued in January of 1864:

Soldiers! You tread, with no unequal steps, the road by which your fathers marched through suffering, privation, and blood, to independence!

Continue to emulate in the future, as you have in the past, their valor in arms, their patient endurance of hardships, their high resolve to be free...[45]

To General Pendleton, just prior to surrendering the Army of Northern Virginia:

We had, I was satisfied, sacred principles to maintain and rights to defend, for which we were in duty bound to do our best, even if we perished in the endeavour.[46]

To Philip Worsley of Oxford, England, after the war, upon Lee's receipt of a translation of Homer's *Iliad*, which Worsley had dedicated to Lee and inscribed with an original poem in praise of the Southern general:

The undeserved compliment in prose and verse, on the first leaves of the volume, I received as your tribute to the merit of my countrymen, who struggled for constitutional government.[47]

From comments after the war on the "sole object" of the Southern armies:

Our sole object [was] the establishment of our independence and the attainment of an honorable peace.[48]

General Thomas J. "Stonewall" Jackson, writing to his wife Anna:

How I do wish for peace, but only upon the condition of our national independence![49]

General Albert Sidney Johnston to Governor Pettus of Mississippi, on what the South wished to achieve:

If the enemy does not attack, the North embarrassed at home, menaced by war by England, will shrink foiled from the conflict, and the freedom of the South will be forever established.[50]

General P.G.T. Beauregard to the editors of the Richmond *Whig*:

The *acme* of my ambition is, after having cast my *mite* in defence of our sacred cause, and assisted to the best of my ability in securing our rights and independence as a nation.[51] [Emphasis in the original]

General John B. Gordon, in an address to the citizens of York, Pennsylvania during the Gettysburg campaign:

Our Southern homes have been pillaged, sacked, and burned: our mothers, wives, and little ones, driven forth amid the brutal insults of your soldiers. Is it any wonder that we fight with desperation? A natural revenge would prompt us to retaliate in kind, but we scorn to war on women and children. We are fighting for the God-given rights of liberty and independence, as handed down to us in the Constitution by our fathers. So fear not: if a torch is applied to a single dwelling, or an insult offered to a female of your town by a soldier of this command, point out to me the man, and you shall have his life.[52]

General John Bell Hood to General Sherman, following the Atlanta campaign, in response to a letter from Sherman blaming the South for the war:

You say we insulted your flag. The truth is, we fired upon it, and those who fought under it, when you came to our doors upon the mission of subjugation.[53]

Varina Howell Davis (Mrs. Jefferson Davis, writing here in her post-war biography of her husband) describing Northern war measures. I add this here because it shows that Southerners viewed the war in a consistent manner from beginning to end:

> Our people were unwilling to yield an inch to the aggressions of the North, for they no longer loved the Union as it had been distorted by our enemies, and as sincerely detested it as the abolitionists had before secession, though even then our people did not characterize it as "a compact with h---."[Hell] The time had passed when a compromise of our rights would have been willingly made, that we might fight under the banner our fathers so manfully aided to make the ensign of freedom to all nations.[54]

Consider also the response of the border state governors to Lincoln's call for troops in April, 1861. All but two of these states – Kentucky and Missouri – officially joined the Confederacy at a later time. Notice what these men seemed to think the war was about:[55]

Virginia (Governor Lechter):

> Your object is to subjugate the Southern states, and a requisition made upon me for such an object – an object, in my judgment, not within the purview of the Constitution or the act of 1795 – will not be complied with. You have chosen to inaugurate civil war, and having done so, we will meet it with a spirit as determined as the administration has exhibited toward the south.

Kentucky (Governor Magoffin):

> Your dispatch is received. I say emphatically that Kentucky will furnish no troops for the wicked purpose of subduing her sister Southern states.

Tennessee (Governor Harris):

> Tennessee will not furnish a single man for coercion, but fifty thousand, if necessary, for the defense of our rights, or those of our Southern brethren.

North Carolina (Governor Ellis):

> I regard the levy of troops made by the administration for the purpose of subjugating the states of the South as in violation of the Constitution, and a usurpation of power. I can be no party to this wicked violation of the laws of the country, and to this war upon the liberties of a free people. You can get no troops from North Carolina.

Arkansas (Governor Rector):

> In answer to your requisition for troops from Arkansas to subjugate the Southern states, I have to say that none will be furnished. The demand is only adding insult to injury. The people of this Commonwealth are freemen, not slaves, and will defend to the last extremity their honor, lives, and property against Northern mendacity and usurpation.

Missouri (Governor Jackson):

> Your dispatch of the 15th instant, making a call on Missouri for four regiments of men for immediate service, has been received. There can be, I apprehend, no doubt but the men are intended to form a part of the President's army to make war upon the people of the seceded states. Your requisition, in my judgment, is illegal, unconstitutional, and revolutionary in its object, inhuman and diabolical, and cannot be complied with. Not one man will the State of Missouri furnish to carry on such an unholy crusade.

In his 1990 introduction to Jefferson Davis' *Rise and Fall of the Confederate Government*, James McPherson argues that the ex-Confederate President defended his fallen country's legacy with the idea that Southerners were fighting for state sovereignty, an idea that McPherson terms "neo-Confederate orthodoxy" and, more sardonically, "the virgin-birth theory of secession". "After 1865," says McPherson, "it became unfashionable in the South to admit having fought to keep four million people in slavery".[56] McPherson aside, from the quotes we have just seen, it is rather obvious that Confederates seemed to think they were primarily fighting for their freedom and sovereignty, both before and after the war; and the quotes from Northerners corroborate that idea. The war was fought over the essential question of secession, not slavery.

In 1995, McPherson wrote a book entitled: *What They Fought For 1861-1865*, (later expanded upon in *For Cause and Comrades: Why Men Fought in the Civil War*). Interestingly enough, in *What They Fought For*, McPherson brings a bit more depth to his 1990 statement that the South "seceded and fought to keep four million people in slavery". The following are two examples taken from McPherson's book:

> Over and over again in Confederate letters, one finds sentences like these: "It is better to spend our all in defending our country than to be subjugated and have it taken away from us."

> One of the questions often asked a Civil War historian is, "Why did the North fight?" Southern motives seem easier to understand. Confederates fought for independence, for their property and way of life, for their very survival as a nation.[57]

The phrase "for their property and way of life" is likely made in at least partial reference to the institution of slavery; however, I find it interesting that, after having perused several thousand letters written by Union and Confederate soldiers in the field, McPherson lists the issues of independence and national identity as two out of three reasons for why the South fought in the war (with independence appearing first). He even states that Southern reasons for fighting "seem easier to understand," which is an incredible thing to say if you believe that the South fought to preserve slavery. Few modern Americans would find such a cause even remotely comprehensible, to say nothing of "easier to understand".

What about the Emancipation Proclamation?

As we have seen, Lincoln initially had no desire to "drag the Negro into the war"; however, pressures brought to bear by abolitionists and the military alike finally swayed the Union President. Britain and France seemed on the verge of recognizing the Confederacy, and it was correctly thought that these countries might hesitate if emancipation could lend a more humanitarian appearance to the Northern war effort. Also, as his advisors reasoned, with much of the Confederacy's upper class white male population in the army, tending affairs at home fell mainly to their servants. If Lincoln could somehow persuade those slaves to flee, he knew that he might hopelessly cripple the Confederate war effort.

Motivated by these considerations, Lincoln drafted an emancipation proclamation but held it in check until such time as a Union army might secure a victory in the field. The opportunity finally presented itself in September of 1862, when General McClellan's Army of the Potomac halted Robert E. Lee's invasion of the North. While McClellan failed to drive Lee from the field, he nonetheless presented an insurmountable obstacle, and Lee was forced to retreat back into Virginia to rebuild and strengthen his army. Judging this to be as good as a victory, Lincoln moved forward with his Emancipation Proclamation on September 22, 1862 (see Appendix F for the full text).

Did this proclamation change the nature of the conflict from a war to "preserve the Union" to a war for the abolition of slavery? Not in the least. In issuing this proclamation, Lincoln merely continued to do what he thought was necessary to "preserve the Union," and the document itself is very clear on that score. Consider the following:

1. The proclamation was military in nature. Several times through-out the document, Lincoln clearly stated that his proclamation was issued as a "war measure" designed to "suppress said rebellion". Nowhere within its text did Lincoln make reference to any motive other than that of "preserving the Union".

2. The proclamation was conditional in effect. The reader will note that Lincoln gave the Southern states from September of 1862 until January 1, 1863, in order to return to the Union before the proclamation went into effect. Any states "not then in rebellion" would not be affected by the proclamation. This document was not a final or sweeping abolition of the institution of slavery.

3. The proclamation was limited in scope. Only the regions specifically designated as "being in rebellion against the United States" were affected by it. Slaves in the Border States, and in those areas of the Confederacy that were controlled by Union armies, were not granted freedom. It would take the passage of the 13th Amendment to accomplish this following Lincoln's death and the war's end.

The idea that Lincoln, like some 19th Century Moses, led American slaves out of bondage is, as Allan Nevins, says, "ludicrously false". As the *London Spectator* observed at the time, the core principle of the proclamation was, "not that a human being cannot justly own another, but that he cannot own him unless he is loyal to the United States".[58]

Alexander Stephens and the "Cornerstone"

In modern times, we Americans like to think of ourselves as contending for great moral causes. For that reason, I believe we have latched onto the issue of slavery and elevated its importance in the North/South conflict because, while we can understand fighting over a moral issue, we no longer really identify with conquering territory and "empire building". Therefore, we look for some greater issue at stake in the terrible destruction and loss of life that took place from 1861-1865 than "preserving the Union," and abolishing slavery largely fits the bill; but to avail ourselves of this justification, we have to alter the truth of history.

The first seven states to secede from the Union did so in part due to the Republican Party's determination to prevent slavery from spreading to any additional territories; however, the territory dispute was mainly concerned with economics and the balance of power in Washington, as opposed to slavery itself. The institution was not threatened at that time in those states where it already existed. Remember that Congress had just passed the Corwin Amendment, which would have guaranteed the existence of American slavery in perpetuity.

Furthermore, without slavery, North and South would still have had their differences on other issues, such as the tariff, which, as we have seen, was nearly sufficient to start a war all by itself in 1833. Indeed, economic issues played a much larger role in eventually bringing about Southern secession than is generally known. Confederate Vice President Alexander Stephens argued that Republicans were motivated to oppose secession for just such reasons. Puzzling over Republican determination to neither allow slavery's extension nor release existing slave states from the Union, Stephens concluded that, "Their philanthropy yields to their interest":

> Notwithstanding their professions of humanity, they are disinclined to give up the benefits they derive from slave labor...The idea of enforcing the laws, has but one object, and that is a collection of the taxes, raised by slave labor to swell the fund necessary to meet their heavy appropriations. The spoils is what they are after – though they come from the labor of the slave.

For readers who wish to learn more about the economic issues involved in secession, I would recommend reading the secession ordinances of the Southern states (they can be found online), and consulting Charles Adams' excellent book: *When in the Course of Human Events: Arguing the Case for Southern Secession.*

As for the last four states to secede: Virginia, Tennessee, North Carolina, and Arkansas, slavery played no direct role in their decisions. They, too, were slaveholding states, and they sympathized with the concerns of their Deep South brethren, but they seceded only after the clash at Fort Sumter and Lincoln's call for troops. They refused to make war against the seceded states, and the prospect of being forced to do so drove them from the Union when nothing else had. As for Fort Sumter and the start of the war itself, slavery was nowhere involved in the issue. Note once again Lincoln's reluctance to address slavery at all in the conflict; note his support of the Corwin Amendment; and note Congress' resolution indicating that the war was not fought for the purpose of "interfering with the rights, *or established institutions* of these States," but "to defend and maintain the supremacy of the Constitution".

In waging war against the South, Abraham Lincoln was not involved in some great humanitarian crusade. He was fighting a political war for the dream of American Empire; and, as he himself admitted, what he did about slavery and the black race he did because he believed it helped to "save the Union". As much as many of his apologists would like to pretend otherwise, Lincoln's war cannot be glorified on the basis of emancipation; it was an old fashioned contest for power in which emancipated slaves were as much pawns as the soldiers in the field.

Before concluding, let me briefly touch upon a famous quotation by Alexander Stephens, a quote that has often been used to vilify the Confederate cause as inherently racist. Speaking in Savannah, Georgia, on March 21, 1861, Stephens listed various improvements the Confederate Constitution boasted over the U.S. Constitution, including the following:

> Our new government is founded upon exactly the opposite idea; its foundations are laid, its corner-stone rests, upon the great truth that the Negro is not equal to the white man; that slavery – subordination to the superior race – is his natural and normal condition.

Stephens himself explained this statement in his *Constitutional View of the Late War Between the States*, commenting as follows:

> In the corner-stone metaphor, I did but repeat what Judge Baldwin of the Supreme Court of the United States, had said of the Federal Government itself, in the case of Johnson vs. Thompkins. In that case, he declared that "the foundations of this Government are laid, and rest on the rights of property in slaves, and the whole fabric must fall by disturbing the corner-stone."
>
> It was disturbed, as we have seen, and the only intended differences between the old "edifice" and the "new," in this respect, was to fix this corner-stone more firmly in its proper place in the latter, than it had been in the former. This is the substance of that speech; and there is no conflict between the sentiments expressed in both upon the same subject matter.[59]

In his "Cornerstone" speech, Stephens was arguing that forces of consolidation had been hard at work in the American Republic, and that "agitation" over the status of slavery was evidence of this. He points out that the U.S. Constitution could not have been established without compromises where slavery was concerned – which is a well recognized fact – and that the Confederate Constitution clarified those issues, thus fixing that "cornerstone" of the Confederate States more firmly than that of the United States. And, before it can be alleged, this is not an example of an ex-Confederate backpedaling to cover his tracks following an unsuccessful war to preserve slavery. In the same two-volume work cited above, Stephens reiterated his favorable opinion of slavery, and made no apology for the language of his "Cornerstone" speech, or any other position that he held prior to, or during, the war. I would also remind the reader that, as we have seen in the words of Abraham Lincoln, the idea espoused in the Cornerstone Speech that "the Negro is not equal to the white man" and was best kept in subjection, was a concept embraced by both North and South in the 1860s. It was not unique to the Confederacy.

Position Four:

The United States & Confederate States could not have peacefully Co-existed

The United States and the Confederate States could never have lived together in peace. If the South had separated, we would have been continuous conflict, and perhaps even war, between the two countries. Lincoln was right to prevent the separation of the South in order to prevent some future calamity between the two countries.

In arguing against secession in his first inaugural address, Lincoln proclaimed:

> Physically speaking, we can not separate. We can not remove our respective sections from each other nor build an impassable wall between them. A husband and wife may be divorced and go out of the presence and beyond the reach of each other, but the different parts of our country can not do this. They can not but remain face to face, and intercourse, either amicable or hostile, must continue between them...Suppose you go to war, you can not fight always; and when, after much loss on both sides and no gain on either, you cease fighting, the identical old questions, as to terms of intercourse, are again upon you.

Nothing is inevitable in human relationships. Human beings make choices as to how they will relate to one another. Nations choose how they will interact with other nations. If the United States and the Confederate States had chosen to live together in peace, they could have done so, just as we peacefully co-exist with Canada and Mexico today. We have disagreements with these countries from time to time, but these disagreements have not resulted in open hostilities for many years now.

The United States co-existed with many nations at the time of secession. It navigated the high seas with them, engaged in trade with them, and was able to resolve most problems without resorting to war. Why should they have been incapable of this with regard to the South, especially given the fact that there was already a common history and bond between the two countries? North and South had fought common foes side-by-side. They revered the same core principles, embraced the same form of representative government, and honored the same heroes. As much distrust and antagonism as existed between them at the time of secession, there was much that each understood and appreciated about the other. They benefited from a political and social reality that would have made them less alien to one another than either was to the other nations of the world. Additionally, with separation achieved, the most volatile of the issues between them would have been resolved by the mere fact that they were no longer vying for control of the same government.

Timothy Pickering, a New England Federalist who had served in Washington's cabinet, suggested just such a mutual separation several times in the early 1800s, believing that it would prove beneficial to both sections of the Union, as he stated in a letter to George Cabot, dated January 29, 1804:

> I do not believe in the practicability of a long-continued union. A Northern confederacy would unite congenial characters, and present a fairer prospect of public happiness; while the Southern States, having a similarity of habits, might be left "to manage their own affairs in their own way". If a separation were to take place, our mutual wants would render a friendly and commercial intercourse inevitable.[1]

Some may object to the idea of peaceful separation here by pointing out the fact that the even the founders themselves feared that violence would result if the United States ever separated from one another, citing the example set by Europe's perpetual conflicts. And while it is true that the European powers had fought continuously among one another, we should consider the fact that they were largely ruled by authoritarian regimes at the time. Later, when they adopted representative governments, such as those in the American states, they no longer resorted to war so readily. Doubtless, our founders would have been intrigued by that development had they witnessed it. By the 1860s, representative government was well established on these shores, and was revered both in the North and the South. Thus, given this and the fact that representative governments are not inclined to resort to war – at least not nearly so easily as nations ruled by monarchs or dictators – the United and Confederate States might have separated and lived in peace just as the once adversarial European nations do today. Ironically, Europe has served as an example to both the founders' generation and our own, although for dramatically different reasons.

And consider another thought here where the issue of perpetually hostile relations among the states is concerned; for as much as Lincoln detested the thought of losing eleven states of the Union, merely losing those states was not his only consideration:

It was not written in stone that the North would win the war. In fact, it was actually a very close thing. The Southern states nearly won their independence. General Grant wrote in his memoirs that the North was tired of fighting and might have simply let the South go had the war dragged on for another year. Suppose for a moment that the South *had* won. What sort of peace and relationship would have been established between the two countries after such a protracted and violent contest? It is safe to say that there would have been tremendous lingering hostility between the two countries, setting the stage for renewed conflict in the future. And what if General Lee had refused to surrender after retreating from Richmond, and had chosen to engage in guerrilla warfare instead, as he considered doing? Perhaps then we would have faced a Vietnam on our own shores, featuring assassination, perpetuated martial law, and reprisal upon reprisal. What sort of country would we have now in the wake of that hideous scenario? We nearly lost our freedoms as it was, due to Lincoln's dictatorship; a guerrilla situation and continued fratricidal warfare might have toppled representative government altogether on these shores.

Speculation is only speculation, but these scenarios are plausible given the circumstances, and serve to illustrate that Lincoln risked many outcomes in his decisions, not merely the prospect of losing eleven states for the Union. And, in making his decisions, he did not have the benefit of our hindsight. It is clear from accounts that the war did not proceed as he hoped and thought it would. It lasted far longer and grew far more violent than he had anticipated. In truth, there is much to suggest that the United and Confederate States might have peacefully separated and co-existed had it not been for the will of one man in 1861.

Position Five:

The United States of America is too important in World Affairs to permit Secession

If Lincoln had not resorted to force quickly, the seceded states would have been lost forever. Lincoln was a man of vision, and understood that the United States of America had a vital role to play on the world stage. For that reason, the country had to be held together. This is also a reason why we should deny secession today. The USA still has a vital role to play in world affairs.

Whenever I hear this argument, I always have to ask why it would have been unbearable for the United States to have lost the seceded Southern states in 1861? Why should the Northern states have found the absence of their old political foes so bothersome? If all of the slave states had left the Union, what harm would have resulted? There would have been no more debate over slavery in the territories, no more fugitive slave law to enforce, and no more agitation over the tariff. In other words, the Northern states would have enjoyed full and unfettered control of the Union. As one Missouri newspaper put it in 1861: "Let them go, we shall then have internal improvements and a protective tariff."[1]

Indeed, by forcing the Southern states back into the Union, the Northern states accomplished little more than to ensure that they would continue to battle the South for control of the government in the future. At the time of the war, some believed that, with the issue of slavery resolved, the old antagonism between the rival sections would fade and nationalism would prevail; however, as we can see in the contentious state of politics today, this assumption was in error. Slavery was but one issue. The Northern and Southern states represented – and, nearly a century and a half after the war's end, continue to represent – two different peoples, two very distinct cultures, no matter how many traits they share in common. Had the Northern states considered this aspect of the secession equation more seriously, as men like Timothy Pickering once had, they might have realized that the departure of the Southern states would have benefited both sections. Both resulting Unions would have boasted far less contentious central governments, to say nothing of the fact that a certain disastrous war could have been avoided and many lives saved.

Second, it is not necessarily true that the seceded states would have been lost forever. Prior to Lincoln's coercive actions in regard to Fort Sumter and his call for 75,000 troops, there were only seven states in the Confederacy. The other four states that would later join had not done so yet because they did not feel it was necessary. Had Lincoln not resorted to force as his first choice in dealing with the crisis, there is no reason to assume that the states of the upper South would have been lost to the Union immediately, if ever. There is also the possibility that, with time and patience, compromise might have been attained, and officials from those upper states might have prevailed upon their Deep South brethren to return to the Union. Resorting to war, however, virtually eliminated any prospect of a future peaceful reconciliation.

The Road to World Superpower

There are also those who would have us believe that Lincoln could not let the Southern states go because the United States of America was destined to become a world power and force for good that would have been weakened by the loss of the South. We saw that Don Feder, writing in the *Boston Herald*, thought that the United States would have become "a basket case" had the South seceded. Others seem to feel the same way. Even Webb Garrison, who criticizes Lincoln harshly in his writings, concludes his book *Lincoln's Little War* with the following:

> At least one significant factor in contemporary American life is not in question. Here and throughout much of the world, the United States is frequently billed as the only "superpower" on earth. Regardless of whether this is good or bad in the long run, the United States would not be a superpower if fifty strong and separate states made all the significant decisions.[2]

During the 2000 Presidential race, George W. Bush and Vice President Al Gore debated the Clinton administration's practice of what Bush called "nation-building," meaning that the U.S. was actively involving itself in the structuring of other countries throughout the globe. For his part, Gore defended this policy as a rightful exportation of American values; but I had to ask at the time: what right do we have to export our values and force them upon others, even if we think that our way is best? Is this not merely another form of Manifest Destiny, carried out on a global stage? We have prospered greatly in this country because of our freedoms, and we would like to see other countries embrace those same freedoms and prosper as well, but what right do we have to force our system on them? Is it possible to be an authoritarian freedom fighter? Would we tolerate other countries interfering in our affairs to the extent that we interfere in theirs, even if they did so with the best of intentions?

Oddly enough, after arguing against nation-building practices in 2000, George W. Bush is now actively engaging in it in Iraq and elsewhere. It seems that, quite often, how one feels power should be used tends to change when one finally acquires power. For this reason, I am not as prepared as Garrison is to shrug off the question of whether superpower status is a good thing in and of itself. Massing power for its own sake is never a good thing; history is rather clear on that subject.

"Look at the world wars," the nationalists like to say. "They never would have been won if the United States hadn't been involved, or if the Southern states had seceded. America would have been too weak to win." This argument presupposes two things: 1) The United States would virtually have ceased to exist, or would have been rendered impotent, if the South had seceded; and 2) world history would not have been any different after Southern secession.

In regard to the first proposition, I would like to point out again that the United States got along just fine without the Southern states, even to the point of fielding enormous armies and carrying on a sustained war. The remaining states of the Union were quite populous and prosperous, and continued immigration and industrialization was only increasing that growth. Continuing down the same road, the United States would still have become a major world power without the South. In fact, there are some in this country who feel that the Southern states are actually a hindrance to America's progress.

For example, Mark Strauss, senior editor of *Foreign Policy* magazine, published an article on March 13, 2001, entitled: *Let's Ditch Dixie, The Case for Northern Secession*. In this article, Strauss lamented Southern involvement in the government and gave several examples of why he feels the country would be better off without the Southern states. "North and South can no longer claim to be one nation," Strauss said, pointing to the contentious 2000 presidential election for proof of this sectional schism. After suggesting a peaceful separation of the two sections, and rejoicing in the fact that such a separation held the promise of eliminating twenty-four hour commercials for Dale Earnhardt merchandise, Strauss said that separation would be better for the South too, as the North could then provide something equivalent to foreign aid:

> Peace Corps volunteers could teach the necessary skills that would allow Southerners to pull themselves out of poverty and illiteracy while simultaneously promoting a better understanding of American values.[3]

Here, Strauss is only too clear in stating, although perhaps a bit tongue-in-cheek, that he believes that America has a destiny to fulfill and that this destiny is currently hindered by the Southern states and their backward peoples. Note that Strauss basically says that Southerners do not even understand "American values," which, from the tone of his writing, can be summarized as telling others what to do from a position of self-righteous preeminence. But this was precisely how Lincoln and the Republicans acted in their day. America was what they said it was; anyone who disagreed was a hindrance at best, a traitor at worst.

And what about those two world wars? What would have become of them had the United States lost eleven members? In regard to World War I, could the Union that fielded such great armies without Southern assistance in the 1860s have not participated in the contest had it wished to? There is no reason to think that it could not have. And what if the United States had not intervened in the war? By the time American troops departed for Europe in 1917, the belligerent nations were on the brink of exhaustion, and there is some belief today that the conflict would have ended by mutual treaty had America not intervened.

As it happened, American participation in World War I allowed the Allies to achieve a clear victory, a victory that resulted in the punishing peace terms and "nation-building" imposed upon the defeated powers by the Treaty of Versailles. There is much evidence to suggest that Germany's dramatic political and economic hardships following its defeat in World War I contributed heavily to the cause of World War II. Hitler's rise to power was naturally facilitated by Germany's desperate situation. The German people felt themselves under siege by enemies within and without, and were eager to regain some sense of security and national pride. Hitler bolstered this siege mentality among the defeated and destitute German people and used it to consolidate the power he needed to achieve his Third Reich.

Without Hitler, a second war in Europe so soon after the first would not have been likely. The nations involved in the first war had suffered tremendously; none of their peoples wished to fight such a conflict again. The desperate actions of Britain's Prime Minister Chamberlain, as well as other European leaders, with regard to the appeasement of Hitler during the 1930s, demonstrates that war would not have taken place at that time without Hitler's determination to have it. There were even those in the west, including Chamberlain, who felt it was in their best interest to foster a re-strengthened Germany in order to use that country as a buffer state against expansion by Stalinist Russia. Without Versailles, and/or without Hitler, the world might have taken such an alternate route.

Am I blaming the United States for Hitler? Certainly not. President Woodrow Wilson attempted to dissuade the other Allied powers from punishing Germany too harshly but was overruled, thus the United States should not be blamed for the consequences of Versailles. My point is simply that nationalistic fervor sometimes blinds us to considering alternatives. A different history would not necessary have been a worse history. It could even have been a better history. No one knows for certain.

At the risk of digressing here, let me ask the reader to consider one last thought. The history of the world, including our own American Revolution, has largely been the story of bloody conflict over power and influence. If North and South had separated peacefully, resolved their border issues with time and deliberation, and then proceeded to peacefully co-exist, would this not have shown the world a better way: namely that people can disagree and conduct their own affairs without resorting to violence and bloodshed? What did Lincoln show the world by going to war against the South to "preserve the Union" except to reaffirm the age-old idea that might makes right and those who are powerful can rule those who are not? Under which example is the cause of freedom best served, and by which creed do we seek to identify ourselves today?

Yes, the United States of America has been a great defender of freedom in the world; but those who believe that the United States government had to defeat the Southern secession movement in order to accomplish this should scrutinize their ideology a bit more closely. They are essentially arguing that only through despotism could the United States defend freedom; only by first putting out our own guiding light could we help the rest of the world find its way.

Position Six:

The Founders opposed Secession and hoped for Consolidation

The Founding Fathers actually opposed secession from the American Union, and hoped that the United States government would become consolidated and strong.

In his first inaugural address on March 4, 1801, Thomas Jefferson stated:

> If there be any among us who would wish to dissolve this Union or to change its republican form, let them stand undisturbed as monuments of the safety with which error of opinion may be tolerated where reason is left free to combat it.

Writing to William Cabell Rives on December 23, 1832, James Madison said:

> It is high time that the claim to secede at will should be put down by the public opinion; and I shall be glad to see the task commenced by one who understands the subject.[1]

The founders also spoke to some degree of the "consolidation" of the government. For instance, in its letter to the states upon completion of the Constitution, the Philadelphia Convention expressed the following opinion:

> In all our deliberations on this subject, we kept steadily in our view that which appeared to us the greatest interest of every true American – the consolidation of the Union, in which is involved our prosperity, felicity, safety – perhaps our National existence.[2]

Do these examples serve to unravel everything that we have seen thus far in regard to the nature of the Union and the legality and morality of secession? Nationalists today seem to think so, but let's take some time to examine these ideas a bit more closely. As it happens, the founders did speak of their objections to the "dissolution" of the Union, but there are some qualifications that should be noted on that score:

As mentioned previously, the dissolution of the Union was feared because it was felt that several confederacies of states might end up warring like European countries, leading to the establishment of despotism and non-republican forms of government. Jefferson, for instance, feared that the continent could become, "an arena of gladiators".[3] Consequently, the founders felt that a single Union of all the states – one in which the government operated under limited, constitutional guidelines – was the best guarantee of republican liberty in North America. Yet, note that they did not attempt to force such a Union on the states. Each state freely decided for itself whether or not it would join the Union.

The arguments employed by the founders to combat the dissolution of the Union were mostly emotional and philosophical. They did not usually try to employ legal arguments. For instance, George Washington spent a great deal of time in his Farewell Address trying to persuade the American people to maintain their Union. If you read that address, however, you will quickly come to realize that Washington made no legal argument against the secession of one or more states, or even dissolving the entire Union of states. Washington did not tell Americans why they *could not* dissolve the Union, he told them why they *should not* dissolve it. As John Quincy Adams once stated, "the indissoluble union between the several States of this confederated nation is, after all, not in the right but in the heart."[5]

It should be remembered that the founders, by their own actions, showed that they considered liberty more precious than unity. When their Union under the British flag proved detrimental to their liberties, they rejected it. When their Union under the Articles of Confederation proved insufficient, they rejected it. When they formed the Constitution and argued for its adoption, they did so because of their belief that such a government, properly administered, would be the best safeguard of their liberties. What they did for the cause of Union was due to their concern for the safety of liberty and self-determination.

In Thomas Jefferson's first inaugural, he stated that the idea of dissolving the Union or changing its republican form was an "error of opinion" that could be combated by reason, but he certainly did not condone preserving the Union by force of arms. He simply saw no cause at that time that justified a separation of the states. However, writing in his draft of the 1798 Kentucky Resolutions, Jefferson did see a cause that might have resulted in the justifiable dissolution of the Union. In protesting the Alien and Sedition Acts on the behalf of the State of Kentucky, Jefferson wrote: "The several States composing the United States of America, are not united on the principle of unlimited submission to their General Government," and gave the following warning:

> These and successive acts of the same character, unless arrested at the threshold, [will] necessarily drive these States into revolution and blood, and will furnish new calumnies against republican government, and new pretexts for those who wish it to be believed that man cannot be governed but by a rod of iron.[6]

In his *Draft Declaration and Protest of the Commonwealth of Virginia*, written in 1825, Jefferson clearly stated that secession was a right retained by the states, and that the breakup of the Union was not the worst fate which could befall the United States:

> Whilst the General Assembly thus declares the rights retained by the States, rights which they have never yielded, and which this State will never voluntarily yield, they do not mean to raise the banner of disaffection, or separation from their sister States, co-parties with themselves to this Compact. They know and value too highly the blessings of their Union...They would, indeed, consider such a rupture as among the greatest calamities which could befall them; but not the greatest. There is yet one greater, submission to a government of unlimited powers.[7]

James Madison, for his quote on secession "at will" also held the opinion that certain causes justified separation. In a letter to Nicholas P. Trist, dated May 1832, Madison commented on the tariff crisis with South Carolina and said:

> The idea that a Constitution which has been so fruitful of blessings, and a Union admitted to be the only guardian of the peace, liberty and happiness of the people of the States comprising it

should be broken up and scattered to the winds *without greater than any existing causes* is more painful than words can express.[8] [Emphasis mine]

In the letter to William Cabell Rives that was quoted above, Madison reiterated the nature of the constitutional compact with regard to secession:

> The fallacy which draws a different conclusion from them lies in confounding a single *party*, with the *parties* to the Constitutional compact of the United States. The latter having made the compact may do with it what they will with it. The former as only one of the parties, owes fidelity to it, till released by consent, *or absolved by an intolerable abuse of the power created.*[9] [Emphasis on "party" and "parties" is original]

Also, in his draft of the Virginia Resolutions of 1798, Madison stated the nature upon which the Union rested while pledging Virginia's love of the Union:

> RESOLVED…That this Assembly most solemnly declares a warm attachment to the Union of the States, to maintain which, it pledges all its powers; and that for this end, it is their duty, to watch over and oppose every infraction of those principles, *which constitute the only basis of that union, because faithful observance of them, can alone secure its existence* and the public happiness. [10] [Emphasis mine]

To accurately gauge the thoughts of men like Jefferson and Madison with regard to secession, it is absolutely necessary to understand that they thought of a Union as valid only if it protected the liberty and harmony of the people. Anything else was, to varying degrees, despotism. In constructing the Constitution, the founders' intention was to create a lasting Union, and they did everything in their power to achieve this; however, their own actions testify as to their beliefs regarding the perpetuity of governments. If a government no longer protected the liberties of the people or contributed to their happiness, it had lost the justification for its own existence and could justly be altered or abolished. Simply because the founders intended that the government of the Constitution should endure does not mean that the Lincoln government had the right to force itself upon a people that no longer consented to it.

Consider the analogy of a sinking ship. Do the captain and crew of a sinking ship have any right to hold the passengers on board just because the ship's builders never meant for it to sink? A sinking ship has lost the ability to sustain its passengers, and thus, in forfeiting its purpose, deserves to be abandoned so that the passengers might take a chance to save their lives. If they stay aboard, they will certainly perish; and those passengers who do choose to stay aboard and perish should not restrain those who desire to escape. Admittedly, the analogy is imperfect, but it does speak forcefully to the central question we are considering here. The Constitution's "builders" certainly never meant for it to "sink," but this does not mean that they intended for us all to cling to it until we drown, either. People must sometimes make their liberties and other interests secure by abolishing old governments and establishing new ones. The founders certainly understood this principle and practiced it themselves.

Consider again the words of the Declaration of Independence:

> *Prudence, indeed, will dictate that governments long established should not be changed for light and transient causes;* and accordingly all experience hath shown that mankind are more disposed to suffer, while evils are sufferable, than to right themselves by abolishing the forms to which they are accustomed. *But when a long train of abuses and usurpations, pursuing invariably the same object evinces a design to reduce them under absolute despotism,* it is their right, it is their duty, to throw off such government, and to provide new guards for their future security. [Emphasis mine]

In regard to Madison's statements about the "parties" to the compact having the right to do with it as they will, we should hold Madison to his previous statements as we did with Webster. According to Madison, and as agreed to by others that we have examined, the "parties" to the Constitution did not ratify it as one corporate act, but individually. Each state acted for itself. Individual states were the parties, and, accordingly, they should have the right to do with the Constitution and the Union what they will. Madison was backpedaling a bit from his previous stance in 1833 because he feared the consequences of the Union breaking up, and little wonder, since Andrew Jackson was threatening armed intervention against South Carolina at the time. It should also be noted here that Madison believed the Constitution allowed the federal government full authority to impose tariffs, and thus, in his opinion, Washington was not guilty of usurping unconstitutional power in that instance, as South Carolina argued.

Lastly, we should take care to correctly evaluate the attitudes and actions of the founders where the issue of "consolidation" is concerned. We have seen that some of them favored a much stronger form of government than was adopted, with some even advocating the abolition of state governments. These thinkers would have been more in line with modern nationalists in that they preferred for the federal government to be endowed with absolute, unchallenged power. Yet this is far from what actually happened. The federal government was not given absolute power; it was given specified and limited powers, much to the disappointment of men like Hamilton, and even Madison, both of whom would have liked to have made it stronger.

Then what do we make of the letter from the Constitutional Convention that was quoted above and referenced the idea of "consolidating" the government? The answer to the question is once again a product of drawing distinctions between the modern sense of a word and the idea that it conveyed to the founders. In modern times, we seem to have lost sight of the fact that consolidating a government does not necessarily mean investing *all* power in that government. The founders understood that it was possible to consolidate *more* power into the government, as opposed to consolidating *all* power into it. Consider James Madison's remarks to Virginia's ratifying convention on June 6, 1788. Speaking of the construction of the proposed federal government, Madison said:

> Thus it is of a complicated nature, and this complication, I trust, will be found to exclude the evils of absolute consolidation, as well as of a mere confederacy. If Virginia were separated from all the states, her power and authority would extend to all cases: in like manner were all powers vested in the general government, it would be a consolidated government; but the powers of the federal government are enumerated; it can only operate in certain cases: it has legislative powers on defined and limited objects, beyond which it cannot extend its jurisdiction.[11]

Here we have an example of the "Father of the Constitution" himself clearly arguing that the consolidation of powers in the federal government is partial, not absolute. And as for his remark about the government not being a "mere confederacy," I think it wise to reiterate that Madison believed a "mere confederacy" was a government established by the various state legislatures as though it were a simple treaty amongst them (i.e., The Articles of Confederation). As we have seen on several occasions, Madison did refer to the Constitution as being a "compact" and forming a "confederacy," but he was also careful to point out that the new government was "established by the thirteen states of America, not through an act of their legislatures, but by the people at large". To properly appreciate Madison's views, it is essential that this distinction be understood.

Now Madison's words again, this time in a letter to Henry Lee, dated June 25, 1824. Here Madison explains precisely what the founders meant by the term "consolidation" in their 1787 letter to the states:

> Not to look farther for an example, take the word "consolidate" in the Address of the Convention prefixed to the Constitution. It there and then meant to give strength and solidarity to the Union of the States. In its current and controversial application it means a destruction of the States, by transfusing their powers into the government of the Union.[12]

Thomas Jefferson, writing to Supreme Court Justice William Johnson on June 12, 1823, addressed the matter of consolidation in similar terms:

> I have been blamed for saying that a prevalence of the doctrines of consolidation would one day call for reformation or revolution. I answer by asking if a single State of the Union would have agreed to the constitution, had it given all powers to the General Government? If the whole opposition did not proceed from the jealousy and fear of every State, of being subjected to the other States in matters merely its own? And if there is any reason to believe the States more disposed now than then, to acquiesce in this general surrender of all their rights and powers to a consolidated government, one and undivided?[13]

How has this concept of consolidation and authority changed over time? I doubt it will astonish anyone if I say that human beings have a tendency to be arrogant, hypocritical and opportunistic. Consider the Puritans. They left the Old World for the New in order to escape religious persecution and worship God as they saw fit; but once they were out from under their old oppressors, it was not long before they began to persecute others for exercising different religious beliefs. The situation has not been all that different with the government of the United States. Having embraced the concept that all men have an inherent right to a government of their consent, Americans separated from England and established their own government. But with time, those in positions of power began to rewrite our core principles. Before long, this country that had been founded by an act of political separation was itself declared to be "indivisible". Those who advocated limited governmental authority had done so when they were under someone else's authority; but once they had established their own authority over others, suddenly the concept of limited authority no longer suited their needs – it actively hindered them. Some of the founders were later guilty of this.

However, once again, what is most important to remember is not what some hoped would be achieved, but what actually *was* achieved: a government with strictly limited powers and states with considerable reserved rights and status. Despite the designs of nationalists like Hamilton and Lincoln, the core nature of our Constitution and government remains the same. The United States of America is a confederated republic, not a consolidated national entity.

Position Seven:

The Southern States entered into an unconstitutional Confederation

The seceded states entered into a confederation, which the Constitution clearly forbids.

Article I, Section 10 of the Constitution reads, in part: "No State shall enter into any Treaty, Alliance or Confederation..." James Madison referred to this prohibition as "a part of the existing Articles of Union; and for reasons which need no explanation, is copied into the new Constitution." Madison was referring to Article VI of the Articles of Confederation, which states: "No two or more states shall enter into any treaty, confederation or alliance whatever between them, without the consent of the united states in congress assembled, specifying accurately the purposes for which the same is to be entered into, and how long it shall continue."

This prohibition makes a fundamental assumption that renders it inapplicable to seceded states: it presupposes that the states in question are members of the Union and subject to the Constitution's authority. If a state is not in the Union, the Constitution's authority cannot extend to it. Thus the Southern states did not violate Article I, Section 10 in 1861 because they did not confederate with one another until after each had separately seceded from the Union. They were no longer members of the Union when the Confederate States of America was formed.

Position Eight:

Secession is a Question for the Supreme Court

Lincoln and the Southern states should have resolved the issue of secession by referring it to the Supreme Court, where all constitutional matters should rightfully be decided. And if the issue of secession were to arise again today, the Supreme Court should certainly decide the matter.

John Marshall and the Federalists

As we have seen throughout our various discussions, the Constitution that empowers the federal government does not forbid states from leaving the Union, nor does it say that the Union is perpetual, nor does it say that the states have relinquished their sovereignty or may not withdraw their delegations of sovereign power. Consequently, secession falls within the sphere of powers reserved to the states and their people; and, as states do not require court sanction to exercise their reserved powers, the Supreme Court cannot properly hinder any state from withdrawing from the Union. The Court could legitimately rule in matters arising as a result of secession: border disputes, apportionment of the national debt, and other such entangling issues, but the issue of secession itself unquestionably lies with the individual states and their people. After all, upon what basis would the court rule against secession? The Constitution never once addresses the issue, never even implies anything with regard to it.

Nevertheless, one of the marked successes of the nationalists is that they have been able to subvert the sovereignty of the states and the people by instilling in Americans the notion that any question may be referred to the federal courts, and that those courts, particularly the Supreme Court, should rightfully have the ultimate say in any dispute. This trend began with John Marshall's verdict in the 1803 case of

Marbury vs. Madison, in which Marshall advanced the notion that the Supreme Court had the right to rule acts of Congress unconstitutional. Marshall later extended this doctrine to cover acts of state legislatures and the verdicts of state courts. Like Lincoln and Webster, Marshall thought the Constitution represented a consolidated national system based upon the people, and used the concept of "implied powers" to enormously expand the scope of federal authority. Marshall summarized his ideal as follows:

> Let the end be legitimate, let it be within the scope of the Constitution, and all means which are appropriate, which are plainly adapted to that end, which are not prohibited, but consistent with the letter and spirit of the Constitution, are constitutional.[1]

Taken at face value, Marshall's attitude seems to defend the integrity of the Constitution and solvency of the Union, and that was indeed the heart of his justifications for his actions. Above all, Marshall and his Federalist colleagues feared an impotent federal government, one unable to further their vision for a consolidated national system. For this reason, they determined that the states had to be thoroughly suppressed beneath the thumb of federal oversight, and the sooner the better, lest the country fly apart at the seams.

Marshall and his colleagues endured heated criticism of their actions at the time from men like Madison and Jefferson, but they persevered and largely triumphed. Today, their doctrines are accepted as constitutional gospel, as though they were never controversial at all. Using such doctrines as "implied powers," and the "general welfare," and by twisting certain provisions such as the Commerce Clause, nationalists have built on Marshall's foundation and have, for the most part, achieved their supreme federal dream.

The Judicial Power

The "judicial power," the Constitution informs us in Article III (see Appendix C), extends to "all Cases, in Law and Equity, arising under this Constitution" and all laws made by the United States in certain specified situations. The 11th Amendment was later adopted to modify these powers so that they "shall not be construed to extend to any suit in law or equity, commenced or prosecuted against one of the United States by citizens of another State, or by citizens or subjects of any foreign state".

The provisions of Article III clearly apply only to those laws made under the Constitution and to those situations affecting national matters, such as US government personnel and disputes between states. Nothing here can be construed to extend the powers of the federal judiciary, including the United States Supreme Court, to any other matter. So, no, the federal courts do not have absolute authority over any and all matters. If they did, why were state and local courts not abolished by the Constitution? There would simply have been no need for them. Every court might as well have been a federal court, every case a federal case.

Our glimpse into the Constitution and the thinking of the founders has clearly indicated that the states and the people of the states have certain reserved powers; therefore, logically, the dominion of the federal courts must have an end. The judiciary must answer to a higher power than itself; there simply *must* be matters in which states and individuals cannot be brought before the federal bar, otherwise there is no situation in which they cannot be potentially overruled and stripped of their powers. If the federal courts are ultimately supreme in all matters, then the states and their people have only allotted areas of jurisdiction and privilege subject to federal oversight and revocable in pursuit of the "national interest," whatever that is determined to be at the time.

An absolutely powerful federal judiciary is not what the Constitution describes and not what the founders intended. Indeed, it flies in the face of the very notion of limited government; for, what limits can there be upon a government empowered to empower itself? Why would the Constitution be so carefully crafted with specific delegations of authority and sweeping prohibitory clauses against the usurpation of other authority (the 9th and 10th Amendments), if the government it is designed to limit is free to interpret it so liberally?

Writing in Federalist 81, Alexander Hamilton commented on the powers of the federal judiciary in response to criticisms that the Supreme Court would become all-powerful. Hamilton stated that this objection to the Court was founded on "false reasoning" and "misconceived fact," and provided the following rebuttal:

> In the first place, there is not a syllable in the plan under consid-

eration which *directly* empowers the national courts to construe the laws according to the spirit of the Constitution, or which gives them any greater latitude in this respect than may be claimed by the courts of every State. I admit, however, that the Constitution ought to be the standard of construction for the laws, and that wherever there is an evident opposition, the laws ought to give place to the Constitution.

As Hamilton stated, there is no provision in the Constitution that empowers the national courts to make value judgments as to how the spirit of the Constitution applies to a given issue, contrary to John Marshall's insistence to the contrary. Nevertheless, Hamilton went on to argue that laws should be passed in deference to the Constitution in order to uphold the integrity of the document. Further, in Federalist 80, he had already argued that the Supreme Court should be superior to the state courts in order to ensure that the states did not violate constitutional prohibitions on their powers, and also because:

> The mere necessity of uniformity in the interpretation of the national laws, decides the question. Thirteen independent courts of final jurisdiction over the same causes, arising upon the same laws, is a hydra in government, from which nothing but contradiction and confusion can proceed.

A Constitutional Blind Spot

This issue of the scope of the federal courts is perhaps the Constitution's greatest failing. The founders left certain aspects of the Constitution open to broad interpretation and gave us no definitive means of resolving conflicts that might arise in those areas. Marshall's doctrine of Judicial Review was an attempt to step into that vacuum, and it is constitutionally consistent at least in part. As we have seen, Article III empowers the Supreme Court with legitimate authority over all "cases in law and equity arising under this Constitution", and Article VI states that the Constitution is the "supreme Law of the Land...any Thing in the Constitution or Laws of any State to the Contrary not with-standing". As a result, it follows that the Court should have authority to rule in situations where violations of some clear constitutional provision are alleged to have occurred.

However, what if the question before the court is not *how* the Constitution applies to a given matter, but *if* the Constitution applies to it at all? Or what if a verdict of the court somehow changes the fundamental relationship of the federal government to the states and individual Americans? Now the question has undergone a fundamental change. We are no longer considering an overt – or, as Hamilton put it, "evident" – violation of a constitutional provision or prohibition. In this case, we are dealing with the question of what are the delegated powers of the federal government and what are the reserved powers of the states and the people, of whether the federal courts, by involving themselves in a given matter, are somehow changing the Constitution and the framework of our country by fiat, as opposed to utilizing the amendment process. This is where Marshall's concept of Judicial Review breaks down, and even becomes an affront to the notion of limited government. No government is limited that is responsible for limiting itself, and that is precisely the power that Marshall sought for the court: the authority to be its own authority.

Also, consider how the steady politicization of the federal courts has affected our society at large, given this steady expansion of judicial power:

This issue came to light in a particularly noteworthy way following the 2000 General Election. When the matter of recounting votes was thrown into the courts, suddenly the media was filled with stories of how "Judge so-and-so" votes, or who appointed him, and whether he was a Republican or Democrat; but, interestingly enough, what was not being discussed was the fact that we were openly admitting that our court systems have become politicized, and that Lady Justice was no longer blind but actually on the take.

The politicization of our courts is now all but openly admitted as such, and some politicians and special interest leaders take considerable pride in their efforts to tip the scales of justice in their agenda's favor. Consider any typical Senate hearing on the appointment of a federal judge or Supreme Court justice. Senators parade before the television cameras asking candidates how they feel on various litmus test political issues. Judicial appointments come down, not to whether the judge understands the Constitution and has a history of upholding the law, but to whether he passes the political litmus test of the dominant party! Thus, our sacred liberties under the law have slowly been supplanted by the advancement of political agendas operating in the halls of justice. Due to the efforts of the nationalists, we have lost the concept of federalism and the separation of powers. Anything and everything is now subject to being read into the federal Constitution, and politics reigns supreme.

In the 'National Interest'?

Aside from the matter of simple partisan maneuvering though, we should also examine the specific idea that the Supreme Court should intervene in situations where the "national interest" and "general welfare" are involved. Once again, this premise suffers from the fact that it tramples the notion of limited government by permitting the Court to intervene in virtually any matter whatsoever, and on the most subjective of justifications. Consider James Madison's remarks to Spencer Roane on September 2, 1819, in regard to the Marshall court's decision in the case of *McCulloch vs. Maryland*:

> But what is of most importance is the high sanction given to a latitude in expounding the Constitution which seems to break down the landmarks intended by a specification of the Powers of Congress, and to substitute for a definite connection between means and ends, a Legislative discretion as to the former to which no practical limit can be assigned. In the great system of Political Economy having for its general object the national welfare, everything is related immediately or remotely to every other thing; and consequently a Power over any one thing, if not limited by some obvious and precise affinity, may amount to a Power over every other...The British Parliament in collecting a revenue from the commerce of America found no difficulty in calling it either a tax for the regulation of trade, or a regulation of trade with a view to the tax, as it suited the argument or the policy of the moment.[2]

As Madison points out here, if the court claims to be acting in the "national welfare," then there is theoretically nothing beyond its power, due to the fact that practically every aspect of our society can be indirectly connected with every other aspect. And if the court has made itself the sole determiner of the extent of its own power, how can its definition of the "national welfare," or any other arbitrary assumption of power be challenged? The term "general welfare" is yet another example, and a particularly famous one, of a concept that has been misconstrued and abused by partisan political design, by the courts and by Congress as well. The phrase itself appears twice in the Constitution, once in the preamble:

> We the People of the United States, in Order to form a more perfect Union, establish Justice, insure domestic Tranquility, provide for the common defence, promote the general Welfare, and secure the Blessings of Liberty to ourselves and our Posterity, do ordain and establish this Constitution for the United States of America.

And once in Article I, Section 8:

> The Congress shall have Power To lay and collect Taxes, Duties, Imposts and Excises, to pay the Debts and provide for the common Defence and general Welfare of the United States; but all Duties, Imposts and Excises shall be uniform throughout the United States...

Where it appears in the preamble, the phrase "to promote the general welfare" should not be read as an actual provision of the Constitution, but rather, as part of the Constitution's overall statement of purpose. It was one of the goals that the Constitution was meant to achieve, not a blank check provision for the federal government to do anything at all. Once again, such an idea defies the very notion of limited government. How can the government be limited if it may do whatever it pleases? And if the founders did mean for "the general welfare" to be a sweeping provision for boundless federal empowerment, why did they then muddy their own legalistic waters by stating that the federal government had only those powers specifically delegated to it by the Constitution and no more?

As for the general welfare reference in Article I, Section 8, some claim that this surely gives Congress the right to legislate as it sees fit, and it has often done so for this very reason. We can attribute the existence of the modern welfare state, along with other interesting things, to this clause, but it is by no means a recent point of controversy. James Madison commented on this very matter in a letter to Edmund Pendleton on January 21, 1792:

> If Congress can do whatever in their discretion can be done by money, and will promote the General Welfare, the Government is no longer a limited one, possessing enumerated powers, but an indefinite one, subject to particular exceptions.

Madison commented on this general welfare issue on two other notable occasions as well. The following two quotes are somewhat lengthy, but they are essentially reading on the subject at hand. The first Madison quote comes from Federalist 41:

> It has been urged and echoed, that the power "to lay and collect taxes, duties, imposts, and excises, to pay the debts, and provide for the common defense and general welfare of the United States," amounts to an unlimited commission to exercise every power which may be alleged to be necessary for the common defense or general welfare. ...
>
> For what purpose could the enumeration of particular powers be inserted, if these and all others were meant to be included in the preceding general power? Nothing is more natural nor common than first to use a general phrase, and then to explain and qualify it by a recital of particulars. But the idea of an enumeration of particulars which neither explain nor qualify the general meaning, and can have no other effect than to confound and mislead, is an absurdity, which, as we are reduced to the dilemma of charging either on the authors of the objection or on the authors of the Constitution, we must take the liberty of supposing, had not its origin with the latter. It is for error to escape its own condemnation! [Emphasis mine]

The second Madison quote comes from his March 3, 1817, veto of a congressional measure designed to fund roads and other internal improvements:

> To refer the power in question to the clause "to provide for common defense and general welfare" would be contrary to the established and consistent rules of interpretation...Such a view of the Constitution would have the effect of giving to Congress a general power of legislation instead of the defined and limited one hitherto understood to belong to them, the terms "common defense and general welfare" embracing every object and act within the purview of a legislative trust. It would have the effect of subjecting both the Constitution and laws of the several States in all cases not specifically exempted to be superseded by laws of Congress...
>
> But seeing that such a power is not expressly given by the Constitution, and believing that it can not be deduced from any part of it

without an inadmissible latitude of construction and reliance on insufficient precedents; believing also that the permanent success of the Constitution depends on a definite partition of powers between the General and the State Governments, and that no adequate landmarks would be left by the constructive extension of the powers of Congress as proposed in the bill, I have no option but to withhold my signature from it...

Writing to Thomas Jefferson on June 27, 1823, Madison returned to the issue of judicial abuses of the Constitution in particular, and referred to the previously quoted letter to Spencer Roane. In one section of his letter, Madison identified the underlying partisan nature of judicial usurpation:

> The Court, by some of its decisions, still more by extrajudicial reasonings and dicta, has manifested a propensity to enlarge the general authority in derogation of the local, and to amplify its own jurisdiction, which has justly incurred the public censure. But the abuse of a trust does not disprove its existence. And if no remedy of the abuse be practicable under the forms of the Constitution, I should prefer a resort to the Nation for an amendment of the Tribunal itself, to continual appeals from its controverted decisions to that Ultimate Arbiter.[3]

Jefferson, who found John Marshall's actions to be "very irregular and very censurable," spoke even more harshly of the Supreme Court in a letter to Thomas Ritchie, dated December 25, 1820:

> The judiciary of the United States is the subtle corps of sappers and miners constantly working under ground to undermine the foundations of our confederated fabric. They are construing our constitution from a co-ordination of a general and special government to a general and supreme one alone. This will lay all things at their feet...We shall see if they are bold enough to take the daring stride their five lawyers have lately taken. If they do, then, with the editor of our book, in his address to the public, I will say, that "against this every man should raise his voice," and more, should uplift his arm.[4]

Nationalists respond to this allegation of judicial usurpation in several ways, one of which is to emphasize Marshall's argument that there must be an "ultimate arbiter" in cases where disputes arise.

Thomas Jefferson acknowledged that argument and responded to it as follows:

> But the Chief Justice says, "there must be an ultimate arbiter somewhere." True, there must; but does that prove it is either party? The ultimate arbiter is the people of the Union, assembled by their deputies in convention, at the call of Congress, or of two-thirds of the States. Let them decide to which they mean to give authority claimed by two of their organs. And it has been the peculiar wisdom and felicity of our constitution, to have provided this peaceable appeal, where that of other nations is at once to force.[5]

A 'Living' Constitution?

Another way that some try to defend the activist federal court system is to argue that we have moved on from the pure Constitution that the founders gave us. The Constitution has no fixed meaning, they say; instead, it is a "living document," and is thus open to constant reinterpretation. Consider the words of former Vice President Al Gore who, during the 2000 election campaign, stated that the Constitution "was intended by our founders to be interpreted in the light of the constantly evolving experience of the American people". Gore expanded on this idea during an interview with Jim Lehrer of PBS's "NewsHour" program, during which he stated that the Constitution is "a living and breathing document" that has been reinterpreted over the years "in light of the subsequent experience in American life." Gore went on to say that what he called a "strict constructionist, narrow-minded" view of the Constitution "harkening back to a literalist reading from 200 years ago" is "a mistake."[6]

The concept that we have a "living Constitution" is perhaps the most dangerous notion in modern American politics. Essentially, it means that the Constitution has no definite meaning. If this is the case, then we the states and the people have no rights at all – to say nothing about that "unalienable rights" verbiage in the old Declaration of Independence. The federal government could, at any time, suddenly decide to "reinterpret" the meaning of a given constitutional passage and remove our rights as though they had never existed – out of concern for "the general welfare" or "the national interest," of course.

Indeed, there are a number of serious, fundamental flaws inherent in this "living Constitution" doctrine:

For one, the founders clearly intended that the provisions of the Constitution have a stable, definable meaning. Once again, they were establishing a limited government. It makes no sense to claim you are establishing a limited government when you provide that government with a sweeping fiat power to interpret its role in whatever light is expedient at the moment. The writers of the *Federalist Papers* went to great pains to explain to doubters that the federal government could not overstep its proper role under the Constitution because of its carefully restricted scope of power. But how could they promise this if the Constitution was a "living document," capable of being interpreted in a variety of ways? Also, even more than Federal incursion, the founders feared state usurpation of the Federal role in those days. If the Constitution was not a meaningful document in terms of its provisions, though, how could they be certain that the states would respect their role in its plan? Could the states not also reinterpret the Constitution to their own benefit?

Another inherent difficulty with this "living Constitution" model is that it essentially does away with the need for an amendment process. If we can interpret the Constitution as we like, and read all sorts of new things in between its stately lines, why go through a formal process of changing it? Thus the amendment process by itself is unassailable proof that the founders meant for the Constitution to be interpreted strictly and concretely. The provision would be entirely superfluous otherwise.

And for one last evidence against this "living Constitution" notion, I would ask the reader to consider the oath that our public officials take to uphold the Constitution. If the Constitution derives its meaning from the eye of the beholder instead of some set standard, what is there to uphold in it? If our justices and other public officials are pledging to uphold a Constitution that means only what they say it does, are they not merely pledging to uphold their own opinions and agendas? Consider also how this dovetails with the language of Article VI, in which we are told that the Constitution and all laws made pursuant to it are the Supreme Law of the Land. Ask yourself this: if the Constitution itself is the Supreme Law of the Land, are the Supreme Court justices and our other political leaders not subject to it?

And, if so, how can they be subject to it when it means only what they say it means? If the Constitution is open to such a cycle of interpretation and re-interpretation, then it is actually the opinion of the politicians, especially that of the Supreme Court justices, that is supreme, and not the words of the Constitution.

In his book, *Harvest of Rage: Why Oklahoma City is Only the Beginning*, journalist Joel Dyer offers us many insights into heartland America's growing antipathy toward the federal government. In one section of his book, Dyer addresses the idea of "Original Intent," and states that many militia and other "right wing" groups are mistaken when they complain that the federal government has violated the original intent of the founders by enacting legislation and taking other actions that are not authorized by the Constitution. Dyer then offers us the "living Constitution" argument from a rather unusual angle, which is the idea that our modern government has decided that the original intent of the Constitution was that "its original intent could be discarded in favor of creating a government that was totally different from the one described in the document." "This argument is enough to make your head spin," Dyer tells us, "but that's essentially what happened." Dyer then goes to inform us that's just the way things are now, and, as Lincoln might have put it, it is done and we will just have to get along as best we can:

> In 1976, Congress passed the National Emergency Termination Act. [Franklin] Roosevelt's emergency powers would no longer be considered as such. Instead, they had been written into permanency, forever changing the status of the Constitution. But again, I must point out that this action was done with the blessing of all three branches of government. Like it or not, it's legal.[7]

With all due respect to Mr. Dyer, this argument betrays a remarkable lack of understanding of basic constitutional concepts. As we have seen time and again, the founders intended for us to have a Constitution empowering a strictly limited federal government, one that could only be given additional grants of power by a formal amendment process. If they had intended for us to simply add to the Constitution as we pleased, they would never have prescribed any certain means of doing it. Again, I remind the reader that not only did they prescribe a certain means of amending the Constitution, but they also required an oath to uphold the document, including the form of government it describes and the means for changing it. That our founders intended a limited government is beyond question. It is fact.

Further, once again with all due respect to Mr. Dyer, like it or not if the actions of Congress – or the courts – are not in conformity to the requirements of the Constitution, they are invalid, in other words, illegal. If our government has decided to simply ignore the Constitution by construing original intent to mean whatever they think it should, then we might as well be honest with ourselves, toss the document out altogether and use the theme song from Batman as our Supreme Law.

It is my sincere hope that Americans will understand precisely how dangerous such notions are to our liberty. The "living Constitution," and the supposed right to intervene in the "best interest of the nation" in spite of the guaranteed rights of the states and the people, are all doctrines that overthrow the very core premise of what it means to have a limited government and a supreme law which all must obey. Instead, the politicians themselves become the law, and you and I have only those rights they choose to allow us, meaning, in essence, a slate of privileges existing at their whim.

Texas v. White

Some who argue that secession is unconstitutional point to the United States Supreme Court's ruling in the 1868 case of *Texas v. White*. In this case, the State of Texas sued to recover a number of treasury bonds that were issued by the state during the War of Secession, while Texas was a member of the Confederate States of America. In response, two of the defendants, George White and John Chiles, challenged the state's right to sue in federal court, claiming, among other things, that Texas, due to her participation in the Confederacy and the fact that she was under martial law during Reconstruction, was not properly considered a State of the American Union and had no right to file suit in federal court.[8]

This assertion compelled the court to examine the question of secession and the status of Texas as a State of the Union. Ultimately, the court, stacked with Lincoln appointees – most notably Chief Justice Salmon Chase, who had been Lincoln's Secretary of the Treasury until 1864 – ruled by a margin of five-to-three that secession was unconstitutional and that Texas had never ceased being a State of the Union.

Chief Justice Chase authored the majority opinion, the highlights of which I would now like to examine:

"The Union of the States never was a purely artificial and arbitrary relation," says Chase:

> It began among the Colonies, and grew out of common origin, mutual sympathies, kindred principles, similar interests, and geographical relations. It was confirmed and strengthened by the necessities of war, and received definite form, and character, and sanction from the Articles of Confederation. By these the Union was solemnly declared to 'be perpetual.' And when these Articles were found to be inadequate to the exigencies of the country, the Constitution was ordained 'to form a more perfect Union.' It is difficult to convey the idea of indissoluble unity more clearly than by these words. What can be indissoluble if a perpetual Union, made more perfect, is not?

Not surprisingly, Chase subscribed to the continuous Union ideology of Lincoln and Webster, arguing that the Union began in colonial times and evolved – fundamentally altered but, nevertheless, intact – through various stages, finally being perfected by the Constitution. Yet, we have seen abundant evidence demonstrating that the states asserted themselves to be separate, sovereign entities, that they acknowledged no Union or other obligation amongst themselves until the time of the Articles, and that the Union under the Articles was eventually broken when nine states abandoned it in favor of the Constitution, thus leaving the remaining states to do as they pleased.

Also, note that Chief Justice Chase was forced to refer back to the language of the Articles of Confederation – a document that had been legally null and void for nearly a century by 1868 – to support his legal case for a perpetual Union. Here we have nothing less than the Chief Justice of the United States Supreme Court resurrecting a legally dead document in order to argue that one of its provisions was still legally binding nearly a hundred years after the entire document was laid to rest. Lazarus, come forth!

The continuous Union theory is a nationalist fantasy. We have already seen some legal, logical and historical problems that it creates for its adherents, and this is yet another glaring complication. The Articles of Confederation created a political Union and various legal obligations that ceased to be meaningful – in total – in the year 1788. Chase arguing that one of its provisions was still applicable in 1868 would be rather like the British government trying to collect overdue taxes from the United States of America today based on provisions of the Stamp Act of 1765 – another dead law. Indeed, the only way in which the perpetual Union provision could still have been applicable in 1868 would have been if the founders had transferred it to the Constitution, but they did not – a fact which is quite telling all by itself.

This leads to another problem for Chase. He argues: "What can be indissoluble if a perpetual Union, made more perfect, is not?" But how can a *perpetual* Union be made more perfect in that regard? A perpetual union *is* an indissoluble union. How do you improve upon that? Can you make it even more indissoluble? As it happens, the founders omitted the perpetual Union clause from their 'perfected' Constitution, and for this reason I must ask: how can a perpetual Union be made more perfectly indissoluble when the very language that made it indissoluble in the first place is removed? The idea is ludicrous, and yet it perfectly illustrates the lengths to which the nationalists must reach in attempting to prove their case. It should be an embarrassment to the high court that such a thoroughly ridiculous argument was ever made by a sitting chief justice.

Chase continues:

> But the perpetuity and indissolubility of the Union, by no means implies the loss of distinct and individual existence, or of the right of self-government by the States. Under the Articles of Confederation each State retained its sovereignty, freedom, and independence, and every power, jurisdiction, and right not expressly delegated to the United States. Under the Constitution, though the powers of the States were much restricted, still, all powers not delegated to the United States, nor prohibited to the States, are reserved to the States respectively, or to the people. And we have already had occasion to remark at this term, that the people of each State compose a State, having its own government, and endowed with all the functions essential to separate and independent existence,' and that 'without the States in union, there could be no such political body as the United States.' Not only, therefore, can there be no loss of separate and independent autonomy to the States, through their union under the Constitution, but it may be

not unreasonably said that the preservation of the States, and the maintenance of their governments, are as much within the design and care of the Constitution as the preservation of the Union and the maintenance of the National government.

As we saw in Part II, Position Six: *The Southern States might have formed non-Republican Governments*, the Constitution does guarantee a Republican form of government to each state "in this Union", and does promise that the Union shall protect each state from invasion and, upon request, from domestic violence. Thus, to an extent, what Chase is saying is true; however, he takes his conclusions too far. The guarantees to the states are benefits of their being part of the Union, not requirements to remain part of it. Chase is confusing two entirely different ideas here.

> The Constitution, in all its provisions, looks to an indestructible Union, composed of indestructible States. When, therefore, Texas became one of the United States, she entered into an indissoluble relation. All the obligations of perpetual union, and all the guaranties of republican government in the Union, attached at once to the State.

Where are these "obligations of perpetual union" found in the Constitution? Nowhere. There is not, as Alexander Hamilton might have put it, "a particle of language" in the entire document that even suggests such a notion, much less anything that actually mandates it. Chase implied as much himself when he referred back to the Articles of Confederation. Guarantees "of republican government in the Union," yes, but obligations to remain a part of that Union? No.

Also, it should be considered here that if the states are "indestructible," as the Constitution looks to their preservation, then the nationalists have another problem: namely, the fact that Abraham Lincoln's war overthrew the elected governments of the Confederate states and the expressed will of their people. A further problem crops up due to the fact that, in 1867, Congress passed the Reconstruction Acts, by which it stripped the former Confederate states of their representation in Congress and placed them under martial law, essentially destroying them as states. Indeed, Associate Justice Robert Grier, in his dissenting opinion on *Texas v. White*, argued that the majority's contention that Texas had remained a State of the Union through the war and reconstruction was essentially "a legal fiction". In developing his point, Grier stated:

> Is Texas a State, now represented by members chosen by the people of that State and received on the floor of Congress? Has she two senators to represent her as a State in the Senate of the United States? Has her voice been heard in the late election of President? Is she not now held and governed as a conquered province by military force? The act of Congress of March 2d, 1867, declares Texas to be a 'rebel State,' and provides for its government until a legal and republican State government could be legally established. It constituted Louisiana and Texas the fifth military district, and made it subject, not to the civil authority, but to the 'military authorities of the United States'...
>
> I do not consider myself bound to express any opinion judicially as to the constitutional right of Texas to exercise the rights and privileges of a State of this Union, or the power of Congress to govern her as a conquered province, to subject her to military domination, and keep her in pupilage. I can only submit to the fact as decided by the political position of the government; and I am not disposed to join in any essay to prove Texas to be a State of the Union, when Congress have decided that she is not. It is a question of fact, I repeat, and of fact only. Politically, Texas is not a State in this Union. Whether rightfully out of it or not is a question not before the court.

Grier was correct; the issue of secession itself aside, the war and reconstruction had reduced Texas, and all of the former Confederate states save Tennessee, to the status of a conquered province by 1868. Chief Justice Chase's "indestructible states" had, in fact, been destroyed politically, their republican governments overthrown and the will of their people thwarted. Secession did not kill republican government in Texas; Lincoln's war and Congress's reconstruction did that. Even Chase admitted that a majority of the people of Texas had voted in favor of secession. Yet, he continued to assert that the United States government was justified in its actions, based upon the idea that Texas had broken her obligations to the Union and had to be restored to loyalty:

> During this condition of civil war, the rights of the State as a

member, and of her people as citizens of the Union, were suspended. The government and the citizens of the State, refusing to recognize their constitutional obligations, assumed the character of enemies, and incurred the consequences of rebellion.

These new relations imposed new duties upon the United States. The first was that of suppressing the rebellion. The next was that of re-establishing the broken relations of the State with the Union. The first of these duties having been performed, the next necessarily engaged the attention of the National government.

Once again: where there is no authority, there can be no rebellion. Texas's secession violated no laws or any other obligations under the Constitution, therefore, the federal government had no right to accuse the state of "rebellion" or to wage war against it to re-establish "broken relations". The Constitution does not speak to any of these things; just as Lincoln and the Congress were, Chase was forced to create new constitutional doctrines to defend the invasion and overthrow of the Confederate states' governments.

And now more from Chase:

The act which consummated her admission into the Union was something more than a compact; it was the incorporation of a new member into the political body. And it was final. The union between Texas and the other States was as complete, as perpetual, and as indissoluble as the union between the original States. There was no place for reconsideration, or revocation, except through revolution, or through consent of the States.

As we have seen repeatedly, the Constitution of the United States of America *is* a compact between the member states of the Union. Even Daniel Webster himself eventually admitted as much. Where it refers to itself, it plainly states that it was established "between the states," and the states that ratified it spoke to that fact as well. Several of them even underscored the fact that they retained the right to withdraw their delegations of power to the Union, and none of them ever surrendered their ultimate sovereignty in acceding to the Constitution.

Interestingly, in the above excerpt, Chief Justice Chase tells us that states could legitimately separate from the Union by obtaining the consent of the other states. But I thought the Union was "indissoluble", and even more perfectly so under the Constitution (where no such language ever appears) than it was under the Articles of Confederation (where it was stated outright)? Chase took his doctrine of an indissoluble Union from the Articles, but if we look to the Articles, they merely say that the Union "shall be perpetual". They grant no exceptions to that perpetuity, no escape clause. So how is it then that states can separate from our current, even more perfectly "indissoluble" Union, which admits of no such mechanism? Chase's own logic and legal reasoning would seem to deny the assertion, and the judge himself never bothers to account for it.

In the final analysis, *Texas v. White* was little more than a Lincoln-appointed court reaffirming Lincoln logic and a Lincoln-sanctioned view of history; in other words, the victor adjudicating his right to the spoils. Indeed, as a former member of Lincoln's cabinet, Salmon Chase had been actively involved in prosecuting the war against the Confederate states, and could hardly pretend to be an unbiased party. This, combined with the evidence we have reviewed concerning the nature of the Union and the Constitution – and especially the fact that Chase was forced to import an essential supporting doctrine into the Constitution from elsewhere – should be sufficient to at least cast doubt on the constitutional validity of the majority decision.

Put simply, *Texas v. White* is bad law. It rests on historical error, faulty logic and, in Justice Grier's words, "legal fiction". Should the issue of secession arise again – as I believe it ultimately must – the court would do well to reconsider this case, and the opponents of secession as a constitutional right would do well to look elsewhere for evidence in their favor.

Part Four:

The Lincoln Legacy and
Modern Secession Movements

"We cannot undo the past; that is forever gone; but the future is in our hands."

– Robert E. Lee

"America has undergone a cultural and social revolution. We are not the same country that we were in 1970 or even 1980. We are not the same people."

– Patrick J. Buchanan, *The Death of the West*

The War for the American Ideal

A Contest Years in the Making

In the introduction to his widely acclaimed book *Founding Brothers*, Joseph Ellis comments that the United States of America was not founded upon a few words written by Thomas Jefferson, but rather, upon a disagreement about what those words meant. Ellis states:

> The subsequent political history of the United States then became an oscillation between new versions of the old tension, which broke out in violence only on the occasion of the Civil War. In its most familiar form, dominant in the nineteenth century, the tension assumes a constitutional appearance as a conflict between state and federal sovereignty. The source of the disagreement goes much deeper, however, involving conflicting attitudes toward government itself, competing versions of citizenship, differing postures toward the twin goals of freedom and equality.[1]

The conflict Ellis describes found its champions in the Hamiltonian – or nationalist – and Jeffersonian – or individualist – schools of political ideology. Both sides laid claim to the legacy of the American Revolution and argued that the proper destiny of the Republic lay along the path prescribed by their particular worldview. The Hamiltonians longed for the federal government to rise supreme above the states, effectively reducing them to political subdivisions of itself. They saw the government as a tool for activism on both the foreign and domestic fronts. They were the architects of American empire, the forerunners of those who later gave us the New Deal and the Great Society. The Jeffersonians, on the other hand, longed to maintain the separation of powers, ensuring that the federal government did not grow so strong as to absorb the states and overthrow the limitations of the Constitution. They saw government as largely a hindrance to human potential and a menace to local interests. They became the states' righters and defenders of the constitutional compact, the forerunners of many modern conservatives and libertarians.

For many years the government was strongly divided between these schools of thought. Back and forth the contest raged, until the matter finally came to a head in 1860. Seven Southern states that were displeased with the course of the Union decided to break from it and form their own confederation. This was surely a Jeffersonian ideal at heart, the ultimate assertion of states rights and self-determination. Abraham Lincoln, however, advocating what was surely the Hamiltonian ideal of nationhood and empire, declared that those states had no right to leave the Union, and threatened the ultimate assertion of that proposition: war to ensure unity by force. Four more Southern states objected to the idea of coercing the first seven to remain in the Union, and they, too, seceded.

And so the war came – as Lincoln put it – and in the end, the Jeffersonians were defeated by military force. From that time forth, the country embraced the nationalist concept of consolidated nationhood as though it had never been in doubt from the beginning; and the government began openly and vigorously operating in line with that principle. It was not a complete conversion to be sure; that would not occur until the Supreme Court's determined campaign of usurpation in the 20th Century, combined with the socialistic scheming of FDR's "New Deal" and Lyndon Johnson's "Great Society". Nevertheless, it was most assuredly the turning of the tide in a fervent, long running struggle to define America.

Nationalist commentary on this subject, in both the past and present, is interesting to say the least. They view the limited government prescribed by the Constitution as merely an outline, one that successfully overcame the qualms of the Anti-federalists and paved the road to a supreme federal system, which, or so they argue, was always both necessary and inevitable. Once the government was established, it could be "perfected," mostly via partisan interpretation of certain vague aspects of the Constitution's language, and the insertion of several "essential" supporting doctrines. Men of vision would detour around the legal roadblocks of the strict constructionists and lead the United States on her way to what she was meant to be, or else protect her from her enemies. Washington, Hamilton, and Marshall were primary among those men during the early years of the Republic. Men like Abraham Lincoln, Franklin Delano Roosevelt, Woodrow Wilson and Lyndon Johnson would follow.

In the opinion of the nationalists, those who opposed the work of such men stood in the way of "progress" because they lacked "vision" or did not understand what was "necessary" for the government to function properly. Men like Patrick Henry, Thomas Jefferson, James Madison and George Mason are the culpable parties here, although Jefferson and Madison have escaped the vilification usually reserved for Anti-federalists like Henry and Mason, and modern limited government advocates such as Ronald Reagan. After all, Jefferson and Madison were essential to the success of the Revolution and the beginning of the government, even if they should have moved over to the passenger seat and allowed Hamilton and Marshall to drive once things finally got rolling.

Jeffersonians protested then, and still protest to this day, that strict construction was essential to the preservation of liberty and the harmonious preservation of the Union. The government must be kept in check, they argued. Once encroachments on the reserved powers of the states and the people began, they would be nearly impossible to halt without violence. In the eyes of the Hamiltonians, however, talk of guarding against federal usurpation was fatally shortsighted, and even selfish. The United States had a destiny to fulfill. The proper task at hand was thus to strengthen and expand the role of America's central government, not restrict it.

Today's political heirs of Hamilton and Lincoln often employ similar justifications for their actions. For them, expanding government's powers is merely part of doing "what's right for America," and those who stand in their way stand in the very path of progress, the corporate good and our natural destiny. The term "general welfare" has been used to extrapolate the existence of an American "social contract" to which we are all automatic, unconscious signatories. Volunteerism and private organizations are insufficient to the furtherance of the Great Society. Government must be involved; further, it must lead and dominate. Laws must be passed to ensure that all Americans participate in the designs of the nationalist planners because "we're all in this together". People must be forced to do what is right and best for themselves and for the country, as the nationalists see it. They sell their ideology to the American public at large by calling it "patriotism" or "fair play" and by promising to share the spoils of their conquest and see to it that the "winners of life's lottery" are made to "pay their fair share," whatever that is.

Lincoln's war gave the nationalists their first watershed victory, their greatest enduring triumph. But even then they were impeded by the vastness of the country, the sluggishness of communications, and a population that was still very much regionally oriented. The 20th Century changed all that, though. Bolstered by our Copernican revolution in finance, transportation, television, computers, satellite communications, and the Internet, nationalists eventually found the tools of control to do what had been physically and technologically impossible in the past: to influence the life of every individual American – down to the smallest detail – from Washington D.C. And so it appears that Manifest Destiny never really died at all; it simply turned inward for a while. We gave up on the idea of trying to conquer new territories in favor of trying to conquer one another, vying for the right to claim the American Ideal and the power to build the ideal America.

What is probably the single best illustration of the foundational schism between the Jeffersonian and Hamiltonian schools of thought may be found in the following excerpt from a letter by Thomas Jefferson to Benjamin Rush, in which Jefferson describes a visit from Hamilton. During his visit, Hamilton took notice of several portraits that Jefferson had on display and asked who the men in the portraits were:

> I told him they [Isaac Newton, Francis Bacon, and John Locke] were my trinity of the three greatest men the world had ever produced, naming them. He paused for some time: "the greatest man," said he, "that ever lived, was Julius Caesar." Mr. [John] Adams was honest as a politician as well as a man; Hamilton honest as a man, but, as a politician, believing in the necessity of force or corruption to govern men.[2]

Today, the war between the forces of control and freedom continues. Oddly, both sides claim many of the same principles and heroes; but at their core, they could not be more different.

The Perplexing Lincoln Legacy

It is safe to say that Alexander Hamilton and John Marshall – perhaps even George Washington – would have held Abraham Lincoln in great esteem. Lincoln's presidency was a triumphant realization of the authoritarian ideal of employing forceful means against others in order to achieve what you believe to be in the best interest of everyone. And this leads us into what I believe is one of the most perplexing aspects of Lincoln's enduring legacy. For as much as Americans tend to reject authoritarianism, and as far removed as that philosophy is from the foundational ideals that enabled the American Revolution to take place and the United States to come together, most Americans still tend to feel that Lincoln saved – or even embodied – the American Ideal.

This startling contradiction in our thinking was recently exemplified by an op-ed piece that appeared on July 5, 2004. Writing in "Americans increasingly unwilling to surrender civil liberties," Cynthia Tucker, editorial page editor for the Atlanta *Journal-Constitution*, referred to examples of what she termed a "wave of neo-McCarthyism" in which those who oppose US government policies in the War on Terror have often been condemned as traitors.[1] Tucker stated that the Bush Administration has used the war as an opportunity "to curtail civil liberties and conduct the people's business in secret." Amazingly enough, however, Tucker then praised Abraham Lincoln, stating that Lincoln's administration was superior to the current one because Lincoln's vision of America was one in which "common people would be allowed to criticize the president without fear of persecution," in which an accused individual would have the chance to "face his accuser in court," and in which no individual, "no matter how rich or powerful, would be above the law".[2]

Throughout our discussions relating to the war, we have seen that Abraham Lincoln and those who served his cause repeatedly and knowingly violated all three rights to which Ms. Tucker referred in her article. Many who disagreed with the policies of the Lincoln administration and dared to speak out were imprisoned or otherwise silenced; many were held on the most spurious of charges and denied access to the civil courts; and Lincoln himself repeatedly, knowingly placed himself above the law.

An even more recent example of Lincoln's curious political longevity comes courtesy of former Vice President Al Gore. Speaking during a Martin Luther King Day celebration on January 16, 2006, Gore unleashed a scathing attack on the Bush administration for disregarding the Constitution's limits on Executive power and privacy laws passed by Congress. Incredibly, after accusing President Bush of "breaking the law, repeatedly and insistently," and stating that, "A president who breaks the law is a threat to the very structure of our government. Our founding fathers were adamant that they had established a government of laws and not men," Gore went on to praise Abraham Lincoln for his democratic vision:

> When Lincoln declared at the time of our greatest crisis that the ultimate question being decided in the Civil War was, in his memorable phrase, "whether that nation, or any nation so conceived, and so dedicated, can long endure," he was not only saving our union, he was recognizing the fact that democracies are rare in history. And when they fail, as did Athens and the Roman Republic upon whose designs our founders drew heavily, what emerges in their place is another strongman regime.[3]

In practice, Lincoln was no defender of republican ideals at all; he was an authoritarian. To use Gore's phrase, Lincoln was the strongest American "strongman" ever. He did not save the Union of our Founding Fathers; he supplanted it with one made in his own ideological image. He did not do what he had to do; he did what he chose to do.

Admittedly, Lincoln was a shrewd politician and a supremely clever wordsmith. He stands with Reagan and Kennedy in the foremost ranks of communicator presidents, due to his ability to capture ideas in such a way as to make them resonate with ordinary people; thus he may be considered America's "great communicator" of the 19th Century. However, while this distinction qualifies Lincoln as an effective politician, it does not make him a great man, worthy of emulation. The distinguishing characteristic of truly great men is that their ideas endure the tests of time and scrutiny, and do not serve merely as means to self-serving ends. And while many of Lincoln's words endure, his core ideas and flowery speech were, for the most part, empty even in his own day, and were certainly self-serving.

No, with all due respect to Mario Cuomo and others, Lincoln was no giant, intellectual or otherwise. As we have seen in some of his most important speeches, Lincoln's arguments were neither profound nor particularly sophisticated. His knowledge of the Republic's early history and the making of its constitution was seriously flawed, if what he said on those subjects can be taken at face value, which is doubtful due to his habit of twisting facts. His stubbornness and manipulative tactics made a train wreck of a crisis that might have been resolved peacefully, needlessly plunging the country into the most disastrous period in its history. His legacy is primarily based upon distortions of history and truth perpetuated by those who share Lincoln's emotional, mystical attachment to the word "Union," or those who favor a consolidated national government that extends its influences to all areas of American life.

H.L. Menken was correct when he said that Lincoln himself never even remotely approached his own grandiose verbiage, and it is well past time we Americans confront the little man behind the big curtain. If we are to preserve this Union and our freedom – truly preserve them – we as a people must divorce ourselves from the unworthy Lincoln legacy once and for all.

Modern Secession Movements

A Changing Country, a Growing Backlash

History is a continuously evolving story, one great book, if you will, the pages of which are turned by the winds of change. And just as the winds of this world constantly reshape the surface of the earth, eroding even the greatest mountains in time, so the winds of change that blow through history are constantly reshaping the peoples and nations of humanity. No nation is so great that it stands in defiance of time, and the United States of America is no exception.

For better or worse, this country is changing, and it is changing very rapidly. We are seeing tectonic shifts in culture, politics, and creed, shifts that are alienating entire segments of our population from one another. Until recently, we were somewhat able to conceal the growing divides in our midst and put on a respectable face for the rest of the world; the pot was always boiling, but we were able to keep a lid on it. This is no longer the case. Americans are markedly divided in their affections and undeniably at odds over cultural and ideological issues; and we can no longer afford to pretend otherwise merely because the words "one nation, indivisible" sound so good when recited over stadium speakers. Indeed, I believe the question of the hour is not whether this country can be divided, but how much longer it can be held together without conflict.

In my introduction, I provided some excerpts from articles, letters and websites that grant us insights into why we find ourselves at this divisive juncture in our history; however, the following excerpt from a letter published on the Internet following Election 2004 strikes even more to the core of the matter in common terms. Writing in "Dear Liberal Friend," J.D. Tucille comments:

> I feel your pain. You just suffered through an election in which your side lost and a politician you despise was returned to the White House at the head of a triumphant band of congressional allies. Now you fear that the "enemy" administration will use the power of the state to shove its alien values down your throat.

> Of course I sympathize. As a libertarian, I've spent all my life suffering through disappointing election returns. Each turn of the po-

litical wheel brings new laws and bureaucracies that exist to impose values on me that I utterly reject. The difference between me and you is that I never have high hopes on election eve, so I feel resignation instead of despair. Oh. Another difference is that some of the alien values shoved down my throat in the past were yours. Whoops! I guess now you know how it feels.[1]

Contrary to popular rhetoric, we Americans are not one people. We are not of one mind. We do not speak with one voice. We are tremendously diverse. We have numerous cultures and sub-cultures among us. We hold to different worldviews and value systems born of underlying differences in race, religion, philosophy, education and life experience. To some extent, this has always been true; we have always been a diverse people. Once again, however, the 20th Century brought about certain developments, particularly in communications and the introduction of mass marketing. These advances brought us closer together by letting us see the country and the world in real-time, and simultaneously pushed us further apart because we did not often like what we saw, and we differed on what needed to be done to change things.

The 20th Century also saw the beginning of another significant change in the United States: the immigration of millions of persons of non-European descent, and the introduction of new cultural factors with unprecedented ramifications. Indeed, the face of America is changing along with the face of the average American. In his book *The Death of the West*, Patrick J. Buchanan, former candidate for President of the United States, documents the demographic changes occurring in America today and paints us an interesting picture of the future:

> In 1960, only sixteen million Americans did not trace their ancestors to Europe. Today, the number is eighty million…No nation in history has gone through a demographic change of this magnitude in so short a time, and remained the same nation … Uncontrolled immigration threatens to deconstruct the nation we grew up in and convert America into a conglomeration of peoples with almost nothing in common – not history, heroes, language, culture, faith, or ancestors. Balkanization beckons.[2]

Whatever your position on foreign immigration, it is evident that the United States of America is being fundamentally transformed at its most basic level: the individual American. We are already seeing the effects of this trend widely manifested in cultural elements; and the political process, while it lags somewhat behind due to an entrenched political infrastructure, is rapidly following. We are poised to witness startling changes over the next twenty years, changes we might not have thought possible only a short time ago. Already this country has changed in ways that amaze even younger persons such as myself, those now in their early thirties.

What distant shore these political, cultural and ideological steering currents may ultimately cast us upon is difficult to tell. But history demonstrates with some consistency that peoples who become greatly dissimilar to one another, as modern Americans are now becoming, are not likely to endure for long under the same form of government without conflict. If events continue along their present course, we will likely find ourselves at one of three possible destinations: authoritarian consolidation, balkanization, or decentralization. We will hold the national puzzle together by force, split into various sections and go our separate ways, or agree to live-and-let-live.

When the Laws are Silent

In addition to the general nationalist agenda – in either its liberal or conservative guise – there is one additional element that commonly inflates the powers of government and tramples freedom: an old fashioned crisis, real or imagined. Franklin Roosevelt used the Great Depression and World War II as a means of expanding the powers of government to unprecedented heights. The result was the beginning of the modern social welfare state, the confiscation of privately held valuables, Japanese internment camps, and a host of other wide-reaching, authoritarian endeavors. Roosevelt was able to operate by using the precedents set by Lincoln; and now, our current federal government is operating on the precedents set by both Lincoln and Roosevelt on the pretext of responding to the heightened threat of terrorism against the United States.

The "War on Terror," as it has become known, is a nebulous, apparently open-ended affair under which our leaders are expanding the federal government's authority to realms that might have astonished Lincoln and Roosevelt, all in the name of "security". There is certainly no question that we face a greater threat of terrorism on our shores now than ever before, but in combating it we seem ready to throw away everything we claim to be defending. Part of this new Lincolnesque reality is the "enemy combatant" designation. Enemy combatants, the Bush administration tells us, are those individuals whom the administration regards as potential terrorists. Those designated as enemy combatants, so says the administration, may be imprisoned without charge and held without trial – even American citizens. As of this writing (spring 2006) the Bush administration's "enemy combatant" doctrine is currently working its way through the federal court system courtesy of one Jose Padilla, an American citizen and former Chicago gang member, who was arrested by federal authorities in 2002 on suspicion of plotting to blow up buildings and set off a radioactive "dirty" bomb.

In March of 2005, a federal judge in South Carolina ruled that Padilla could not be held indefinitely without charge; however, on September 9, a three-judge panel of the 4th U.S. Circuit Court of Appeals overruled that decision. "The exceedingly important question before us," wrote Judge Michael Luttig of the Court of Appeals, "is whether the President of the United States possesses the authority to detain militarily a citizen of this country who is closely associated with al Qaeda, an entity with which the United States is at war. We conclude that the President does possess such authority." Padilla's attorney, Andrew Patel, saw the matter somewhat differently. "It's a matter of how paranoid you are," Patel said. "What it could mean is that the president conceivably could sign a piece of paper when he has hearsay information that somebody has done something he doesn't like and send them to jail — without a hearing (or) a trial."[3]

It may surprise Judge Luttig to learn this, but not only do American citizens have certain enumerated and inviolable rights, but the Office of the President is empowered – and thus limited – by Article II of the United States Constitution, not the courts. Therefore, it makes no difference what the 4th Circuit Court of Appeals thinks the President *should* be able to do; what ultimately matters is what the Constitution says he may do. And nowhere in the Constitution do we find any reference whatsoever to "enemy combatants," or to the President having any power to designate an American citizen as such, or to hold said citizen indefinitely without charging him, trying him, or permitting him legal counsel. According to Article III, Section III of the Constitution, if a citizen is guilty of making war against the United States, he is guilty of treason, and he may be tried and punished for the crime of treason, provided that he is formally charged, speedily and publicly tried before a jury, and represented by counsel – period. He cannot be arbitrarily stripped of the privileges of his citizenship, treated as a non-entity, and filed away under 'E' for Enemy Combatant in some federal prison.

Now, as you read this, please understand that I am not arguing the case for Jose Padilla's innocence. He may very well be guilty, of this alleged crime or something equally sinister. What I am arguing here is that Judge Michael Luttig, 4th U.S. Circuit Court of Appeals, got it wrong. Horribly wrong. The exceedingly important question before his court was not whether Mr. Padilla is in league with al Qaeda, or whether he is a threat to the United States, but whether or not the United States is a country of laws. The simple fact of the matter is that the President cannot hold an American citizen indefinitely without either charge or trial.

"So what is the President to do then?" some will ask. "Nothing? Should he just turn a suspected terrorist loose on the streets again and take the chance of him going through with his alleged plans to cause murder and mayhem? Is it not worth granting the president the benefit of the doubt if it takes a potential mass murderer off the streets?"

I find questions like this fundamentally disturbing. On the one hand, it alarms me that Americans are so willing to sell out their own hard-won freedoms; and on the other, it concerns me that the President of the United States and the 4th Circuit judges, all of whom have sworn an oath to uphold the Constitution, either think so little of the document, or are so ignorant of it, that they have overlooked a legitimate, constitutional means for dealing with the Padilla situation – outside of charging him with treason and having a trial, that is.

The constitutional solution here is very simple and could be implemented easily. If the President feels, but cannot necessarily prove, that an American citizen is, or was, involved in making war against the United States in cahoots with a foreign enemy, and does not want to free him to walk the streets again, he can appeal to Congress to suspend the privilege of the writ of habeas corpus for that person, as provided for in Article I, Section 9 of the Constitution. If Congress agrees, it can grant the suspension and the President will be able to honor his obligation to uphold the Constitution and respect the rights of American citizens, while keeping a potentially dangerous person off the streets at the same time. This pattern could be repeated with other suspected terrorists, up to and including the issuance of a general grant of power to the President to suspend habeas corpus in whatever cases where he should deem it necessary, although Congress should retain oversight in order to maintain accountability.

Unfortunately, respect for the Constitution as our Supreme Law has eroded to the point where this legitimate solution has, apparently, not even occurred to the administration, the 4th Circuit judges, or to many of the everyday people who are dependent upon the sanctity of the Constitution for their freedoms and very way of life. Whatever you think of Jose Padilla personally, Andrew Patel has it right. We are teetering on the brink of a dangerous plunge. Remember John Merryman!

As of this writing, it appears that Padilla may finally get his day in court; however, the Bush administration has not reversed its stance on the treatment of so-called enemy combatants. Thus we are likely to see the Padilla situation repeated at some point in the future; and the legal precedents in this matter are not particularly promising.

A host of other infringements on civil liberties appear to await us in the near future as well. One such potential infringement is the proposed national ID card, which you would be required to produce upon demand, and which could be linked to any number of databases tracking and storing data about virtually any aspect of your life. Would such a system really help deter terrorism or apprehend known terrorists? Congressman Ron Paul (R-TX) comments:

> Those who are willing to allow the government to establish a Soviet-style internal passport system because they think it will make us safer are terribly mistaken. Subjecting every citizen to surveillance and "screening points" will actually make us less safe, not in the least because it will divert resources away from tracking and apprehending terrorists and deploy them against innocent Americans![4]

Additionally, let me invite you to consider the advent of what is being called "secret law". For an example, consider the case of former Idaho congresswoman Helen Chenoweth-Hage, who was attempting to board a flight at the Boise airport in October 2004, when she was stopped and asked to submit to a pat-down search. Ms. Chenoweth-Hage was apparently stopped because she had a one-way ticket, which is now a type of screening criteria the Transportation Security Administration (TSA) uses to check for potential terror threats. So why did the TSA shake down a "66-year-old white grandmother they greeted by name"? The *Idaho Statesman* interviewed TSA representative Julian Gonzalez and was told that Mrs. Chenoweth-Hage was not allowed to fly because she would not submit to "additional screening" after being told that she could not look at the specific regulation allowing pat-down searches in such instances. When asked why TSA wouldn't let her see the regulation, Gonzalez replied: "Because we don't have to...That is called 'security sensitive information.' She's not allowed to see it, nor is anyone else."[5]

What would it be like to live in a society where you are legally bound by regulations you are not permitted to examine? How would you avoid violating such regulations, or even know if you had violated one of them already? And how would a violation of secret regulations be tried? In a secret court? Would your legal counsel be permitted to examine the regulation in question to ascertain whether it had truly been violated? Would you even be permitted counsel?

Some who read this may think that that the last question is absurd. Of course you would be permitted counsel! It would be un-American to deny a defendant counsel! But I would caution you to think about this: is a government that is prepared to confine you indefinitely without charge, or strip you of your constitutional rights altogether and essentially make you a non-person likely to be concerned about whether you have counsel? Once up until a very short time ago, it would have been considered un-American to create a national ID card, hold people accountable to secret laws, confine suspects indefinitely without charging them, or strip a citizen of their constitutional rights. Sadly, times have changed. We are now operating under the assumption that there is a large glass box in the Oval Office with a crown and a scepter inside and the words IN CASE OF EMERGENCY, BREAK GLASS stenciled on the front.

The fact of the matter is that the present administration has already attempted to deny counsel to so-called enemy combatants, and was called down by the Supreme Court for it (occasionally, the court does fulfill its legitimate role of upholding the Constitution, but let's keep that between us lest we embarrass the justices). On June 28, 2004, ruling in the case of *Hamdi v. Rumsfeld*, the Court determined that, "a citizen-detainee seeking to challenge his classification as an enemy combatant must receive notice of the factual basis for his classification, and a fair opportunity to rebut the Government's factual assertions before a neutral decision maker".[6] The Court further ruled:

> Moreover, as critical as the Government's interest may be in detaining those who actually pose an immediate threat to the national security of the United States during ongoing international conflict, history and common sense teach us that an unchecked system of detention carries the potential to become a means for oppression and abuse of others who do not present that sort of threat.[7]

As the Court stated in the above decision, the fact that an accused individual should be given a chance to hear and refute the charges against him or her seems all too commonsensical; and that commonsensical notion is clearly articulated in the text of our Constitution. But then we must remember that some of our leaders now consider the Constitution a stumbling block in their quest to do what they feel is "necessary". And, appropriately enough, that is exactly what the Constitution was intended to be: a stumbling block, a restraint upon the ambitious or zealous who would seek to harness the power of government for their own purposes. This is, again, why the founders went to such lengths to limit the power of the federal government, and why they inserted a requirement for our public officials to swear an oath to uphold those limitations. A system where the laws are "silent" – or, in former Chief Justice Rhenquist's preferred euphemism "muted" – is a system where you have no rights at all, and where you will find no appeal beyond the mercy of your accuser. The Constitution's strict plan of limited government was not meant to hinder us, but to protect us.

Reaping the Whirlwind

A backlash against this trend toward authoritarianism, both in terms of centrism and encroachments on civil liberties due to the "War on Terror," has already begun. And in the wake of Election 2004, we are now seeing that backlash spreading to both sides of the political aisle. Towns, cities, counties, and even a couple of states, have enacted legislation condemning the recent USA PATRIOT Act and reaffirming their commitment to civil liberties. Talk of states' rights is on the rise, even among liberals who normally champion federal intervention, and groups openly committed to secession or otherwise altering the relationship of the states to the federal government are emerging and gaining a following. Some of these groups, like the Free State Project, the Free West Alliance, and Christian Exodus, are encouraging those who are weary of the heavy hand of government to "vote with their feet" and move to certain states where government regulation is currently less onerous, and where they might have a greater personal impact on the system.

Legislation reserving the right of secession in the event of some sweeping federal assault on civil liberties was introduced in the legislatures of Montana – in 1994 – and Arizona – in 2000. In 2003, the Libertarian Party of Alaska proposed a citizen initiative allowing Alaskans to vote for secession. This attempt was struck down by the state attorney general, who erroneously argued that such an initiative would first require amending the US Constitution to allow for secession.

Also of interest is the fact that the federal government essentially paved the way for the secession of Hawaii in 1993, when it apologized to the native Hawaiian population for overthrowing the Hawaiian government in 1893. Passed by Congress and then signed by President Bill Clinton on November 23, 1993, the apology resolution concludes as follows:

> Resolved by the Senate and House of Representatives of the United States of America in Congress assembled,
>
> The Congress –
>
> (1) on the occasion of the 100th anniversary of the illegal overthrow of the Kingdom of Hawaii on January 17, 1893, acknowledges the historical significance of this event which resulted in the suppression of the inherent sovereignty of the Native Hawaiian people;
>
> (2) recognizes and commends efforts of reconciliation initiated by the State of Hawaii and the United Church of Christ with Native Hawaiians;

(3) apologizes to Native Hawaiians on behalf of the people of the United States for the overthrow of the Kingdom of Hawaii on January 17, 1893 with the participation of agents and citizens of the United States, and the deprivation of the rights of Native Hawaiians to self-determination;

(4) expresses its commitment to acknowledge the ramifications of the overthrow of the Kingdom of Hawaii, in order to provide a proper foundation for reconciliation between the United States and the Native Hawaiian people; and

(5) urges the President of the United States to also acknowledge the ramifications of the overthrow of the Kingdom of Hawaii and to support reconciliation efforts between the United States and the Native Hawaiian people.[8]

Notice how this resolution differentiates the United States from the "Native Hawaiian people". This may prove to be a significant legal factor in Hawaii's political future.

In addition to secession and other peaceful considerations, the growing backlash against the changing face of America and the expansion of its federal government has full potential to turn violent. In fact, it already has.

Several years prior to September 11, 2001, America experienced another day of infamy: April 19, 1995. It was on this date that the truck bomb assembled by Timothy McVeigh and Terry Nichols detonated outside the Alfred P. Murrah Federal Building in Oklahoma City. One hundred sixty-eight persons died in the destruction of the building. This attack was made in direct retaliation to the federal government's debacle two years to the day previously in Waco, Texas, where David Koresh and approximately 86 men, women and children, all of whom were members of Koresh's Branch Davidian cult, perished after a siege orchestrated by the FBI and ATF.

In *Harvest of Rage*, Joel Dyer points to numerous forces that seem to be pushing our society toward the brink of serious sustained internal violence. Dyer primarily focuses on the situation in America's heartland, where federal interference and mismanagement and a transformed national economy are leading to the collapse of the small family farm and destruction of the rural way of life. Some of those affected by these changes are directing their frustrations inward. "Farmers were – and likely still are – killing themselves at least three times as often as the general population," Dyer says.[9] Others are directing their animosity outward, most notably at the federal government, and the number of those who are doing so is rising. The Oklahoma bombing was "just the first shot" in America's "collective suicide," Dyer argues. He predicts that we will see escalating violence "until we come to understand, first, that the nation is holding a loaded gun to its head and, second, why so many among us are struggling to pull the trigger".[10] Dyer maintains that the answer to the struggles of America's rural population is somehow to be found in government social programs and what he terms a truly representative democracy; and while I disagree that government is the answer, I do wholeheartedly agree with him that we are fast approaching a violent confrontation.

Must It Happen?

If America was still operating by the original intent of the founders today, our country would indeed be a different – and I would argue, even better – place. More people would have greater control over their own affairs, as opposed to having the details of their lives administered by the hands of strangers and up for grabs in the next election, or for sale to the highest special interest bidder in the next congressional session. Indeed, a return to true principles of federalism is, in my opinion, the only alternative to having one agenda forced down all of our throats from Washington, or witnessing the eventual break-up the current Union. The devolution of federal power to the states might seem like a step backward to some, but consider the potential benefits.

Think about just the issue of abortion, for a moment. The Constitution does not give the federal government power over this issue in any way, shape, or form; however, in 1973, an activist Supreme Court usurped the issue, and now the entire country is forced to operate by the opinion of a majority of nine people concerning an issue that is likely the most divisive we have faced since Slavery. Abortion rears its ugly head at every corner. Politicians on Capitol Hill, abandoning any pretense of objectivity, do their best to ensure that the Supreme Court and lower federal courts are stacked with judges who think "correctly" about abortion.

But what if this issue was returned to the states? Think, for a moment, how much of the venom and posturing would disappear from national politics. Also, think of the fact that millions of Americans would have a chance to express their feelings on this very personal issue at the polls in their own states, as opposed to grinding their teeth in frustration every time it appears in the federal courts, and instead of doing their best to back such-and-such a candidate or activist judge for high office just to protect their interest in this one issue. Instead of one fiat law for the entire country, we could have up to fifty different legitimate methods of handling the matter; and if you found yourself in a state that did not handle it according to your beliefs, you would always have the option of relocating. Currently, you do not have that option; the Supreme Court has rendered one edict for the entire country, and the possibility always exists that it could reverse itself at any time to your potential detriment.

Think of the other divisive issues we face today, and consider the fact that where government goes politics must invariably follow. Consider education. A government school education is, in many ways, a political education. Politics determines such issues as funding, subject matter, testing standards, and even the social atmosphere of a school, in addition to whatever requirements the teachers unions impose. If you find yourself resentful that your tax money is being used to teach things you do not agree with – whether your child is in a public school or not – let me be the first to welcome you to the reality of politicized education. If you are concerned that your child's school is not being adequately funded, think about where that problem originates: in the legislature, both state and national. If you are angry because you have to find additional monies to afford to send your child to a private school, or to homeschool him or her, after you have already been taxed for an education system you have chosen not to use – or one that has failed you – consider how it happened.

Education is another example of an issue that simply does not belong in the federal scope, by constitutional right or even any pragmatic sense. Children are not statistics to be charted on some bureaucrat's graph. They are individuals. They learn differently and have different needs. Their education is their one chance at the foundational learning that will prepare them for success or failure in life, and such a vitally important aspect of their development should not be clay in partisan hands. It should be handled by those who know them best and can best attend to their needs, giving them every available opportunity for success. Ideally, this is the family. Parents know their children best. I believe it makes sense, at the very least, for control of public education to be handled at the lowest possible level. Even at the state level, parents and guardians would have far more influence in the education process than they currently do at the federal level. And individual states face many challenges that cannot be adequately addressed by one-size-fits-all federal policies like the so-called "No Child Left Behind" law. The State of Utah recently pulled out of the program for just that reason, and other states are contemplating similar action.

Abortion and education are just a couple of examples of issues where federal involvement is unconstitutional, inappropriate, and detrimental due to how these issues divide us into camps, set us against one another, and place the things we care about most in partisan hands. These issues, among many others, should be entirely devolved to the states and handled as their individual populations see fit.

Some may ask if this solution would not simply transfer the political wrangling from the national to the state level, and the answer is yes, it would. However, at the state level, you as an individual would enjoy far greater influence in the process, and likely far greater identity with your fellow voters, than if you had to compete at the national level with states and populations that have very little in common with you. And, again, if you found the situation in your state was not to your liking, you would have forty-nine others to choose from, a few of which would likely be closer to your beliefs on the issues that matter most to you. States could also exercise the option of further devolving control of such issues to the city or county level.

This was the wisdom of our founders in giving us a confederated republic instead of a consolidated nation state: the ability to sustain unity in diversity. And a return to such a system, to true federalism and separation of powers, could very well prevent our descent into consolidated authoritarianism, or keep us from flying apart at the seams.

Potentially Helpful Constitutional Amendments

I believe our unity as a country – and, most importantly, the preservation of our freedoms – would benefit from the adoption of new constitutional amendments designed to deal with various aspects of federal usurpation and federal/state conflict that have arisen over the years: a 21st Century bill of rights, if you will. Of particular concern here are the objectives of reigning in presidential powers and protecting the sanctity of civil government and individual liberties. The following list of potential amendments is by no means complete, but it would serve as a significant start in helping us to partially recapture the Constitution and government we were meant to have:

1.   Limitations on the War Power of the President

Article II, Section II, Clause 1 of the Constitution of the United States is amended as follows:

The President of the United States shall have authority to act as commander in chief of the militia and regular military forces of the United States when faced with an imminent or actual enemy attack, or upon a declaration of war by Congress; however, he may not employ the armed forces in any purely offensive, pre-emptive, "peace-keeping," or punitive operation on foreign soil without the consent of two-thirds of Congress.

2.   Protection of Citizen Rights and Prevention of Arbitrary Imprisonments

No citizen of the United States may be stripped of the rights pertaining to his citizenship without his earnest consent, nor be charged with any crime higher than treason against the United States, nor denied counsel, nor be subjected to cruel and unusual methods of interrogation. Nor may any citizen be held in confinement for any more than sixty days unless the President shall appeal to Congress to suspend the privilege to a writ of habeas corpus in the matter of that citizen. In all cases wherein the President requests a suspension, he shall be required to present evidence in favor of the suspension; however, he shall have discretion to hold Congress to secrecy as to the nature of the evidence. Congress shall have authority to review the status of any persons imprisoned by the Executive Branch, regardless of cause or citizenship, and shall have power to compel the release of such persons by simple majority vote, and to revoke any and all prior authorized suspensions of the writ of habeas corpus.

3.   Provision Against Martial Law

In accordance with Article IV, Section IV of this Constitution, in which the United States guarantee 'to each State in this Union a Republican Form of Government,' the government of the United States may not employ the militia, the regular armed forces, or any paramilitary or auxiliary units for the purpose of quarantine, law enforcement, or emergency management in any state without the consent of that state's legislature; or should the legislature not be in session, the governor. An exception shall be provided in those instances in which the government of a state is incapacitated by some calamity, and then only until civil government has been restored to operation and requests a withdrawal; and every effort shall be made to restore the civil government speedily and according to the normal course of elections as defined by the law in that state or this Constitution. Further exception shall be made in those instances where the armed forces of the United States are engaged in intercepting or repelling an enemy attack; however, the military shall not interfere with the operation of state or local civil government beyond the extent necessary to ensure the success of its mission.

4.   Sanctity of the Constitution

The Constitution of the United States, being the Supreme Law of this Union and the sole guarantor of the rights of the states and the people, shall not be suspended, in whole or in part, or made otherwise ineffective by any act of any branch of the federal government beyond the normal amendment process as described in Article V of this Constitution.

5.   Curbing the Power of Executive Orders

Executive orders issued by the President of the United States shall apply solely within the Executive department of the federal government, shall not exceed those powers expressly granted the President by Article II of this Constitution, and shall be inapplicable to the states and their citizens save only on those lands owned by the federal government.

6.   Tightening up Search and Seizure Requirements

Warrants shall be issued in all cases of search and/or seizure of private property, as provided by Amendment Four of this Constitution; however, in rare instances where rapid search and/or seizure may be required to prevent or respond to an act by which the public safety is imminently threatened, full disclosure shall afterwards be made to a civil court having proper jurisdiction, establishing whether the search and/or seizure was proper. If the court shall deem that it was improper or mistaken, a complete list of the premises and other properties searched shall be provided to the owner, and all seized items shall be restored in addition to any compensation the court may deem appropriate.

7.   Prohibition Against Invasion of Privacy

No citizen, professional domestic entity or business, or public entity of a state or local government may be compelled to surrender private information to the federal government without an order of the civil court having appropriate jurisdiction, nor may any person or entity who is compelled to surrender such data be forbidden from informing their clients, customers, or constituents of the court's order, unless the court shall stipulate such in the body of the order. For the purposes of this amendment, "private information" shall be defined as any physical or electronic data pertaining to any person or entity that has not given express permission for that data to be shared.

8.   The 'Ultimate Arbiter' Amendment

In order that the states and the people of this Union may preserve their rights, and so that disputes pertaining to the nature of those powers delegated to the United States may be amicably resolved, one half of the states of this Union – by action of their legislatures – may overturn or invalidate any act of the President, or the Congress, or any ruling of the Supreme Court, or any regulation of a federal agency that, in their estimation, exceeds those powers granted to the United States by this Constitution or constitutes an abuse of those powers.

9.   International Laws not a Consideration for U.S. Courts

The Constitution of the United States, all laws of Congress made in pursuance thereof, and any treaties made under the authority of the

United States shall be the sole authority of reference in the Supreme Court of the United States and all inferior federal courts.

10. Treaties to be Approved by the States

Article II, Section II, Clause II of the Constitution of the United States is amended as follows:

The President shall have Power, by and with the Advice of the Senate, to make Treaties; however, no Treaty shall be valid until it shall have been ratified by the legislatures of three-quarters of the States.

11. International Regulation and Taxes

Neither taxes nor regulatory laws imposed by any international body shall be made applicable to the states of this Union, or their people, without the consent of three-quarters of the States, such consent to be given by a majority of the popular vote in each State.

12. Re-defining the Commerce Clause

Article I, Section 8, Clause 3 of the Constitution of the United States is amended as follows:

Commerce between the several States of this Union, such as shall be regulated by Congress, shall extend only to actual exchanges of goods and services and related monies between persons and/or entities of differing states, and shall be inapplicable to transactions between persons and/or entities of the same state; nor shall use of electronic infrastructure housed in differing States, or general fees for such use, be considered interstate commerce provided that the transaction is conducted between persons and entities of the same state.

13. Inheritance Taxes Forbidden

Neither Congress nor any State or locality shall impose a tax upon monies or properties transferred to any individual by means of inheritance.

14. Individual and Domestic Law in the Purview of the States

Congress shall make no law – nor coerce the States for the purpose of implementing laws – regulating the private or public behavior of individuals; domestic institutions and civil unions; reproductive concerns; minor child rights and status; or private business contracts and practices, where interstate commerce is not involved – and then only in application to the actual commerce – or where any such interaction takes place with citizens or entities of foreign countries, or on federal properties.

Secession — American Style

Would a State Secede Today?

We Americans are a proud people, and proud of our heritage in particular; but the rapid cultural changes taking place in the United States today, combined with the increasing intrusion of the federal government, are steadily weakening the ties of affection that bind us together. As I have argued before, I believe this will result in one of three possible destinations for us: authoritarian consolidation in an effort to hold things together, the division of the Union to preserve state and regional self-determination, or a return to federalism and a proper separation of powers to maintain our unity while protecting our diversity.

Our government is currently headed along the path of consolidation, but when you consider the fact that there are decentralization movements in the works all across the globe – such as the breakup of the former Soviet Union, the devolution of power from the United Kingdom to Scotland, the near secession of Quebec from Canada in 1990s, and Alberta's rumblings of potential secession today – chances are that the United States may look very different in twenty years, perhaps even sooner. Consider that the American Revolution took shape very quickly, and started out as a protest against acts of the British Parliament, not as an independence movement. Who knows what current dissension efforts may become tomorrow, particularly if heavy-handed leaders attempt to widely or dramatically curtail civil liberties. Americans value their freedom, and while they may be slow to act against gradual legislative encroachments, overt attacks on civil liberties by an overconfident administration or dominant party are almost certain to stir their wrath. One test of these waters may soon come to us via an attempt to reinstate the Draft, due to the current over-extension of American forces across the globe in nation-building efforts. If this occurs, the American peoples' reaction, and the administration's response, may provide us with a glimpse into the future.

Pat Buchanan seems to fear balkanization; but, if America must undergo some type of fundamental change, I believe balkanization is preferable to authoritarian consolidation. Under a consolidated framework, there would be little that we recognize of the America that so many have laid down their lives to preserve for those of us living today. In states that broke away from such a system, however, there would be a chance to preserve something of that old American dream. If that day comes, and such a decision lies before us, we must ask ourselves which we value more: the title of "American," or the state of freedom that made that title precious to start with. I believe authoritarian consolidation and balkanization are both avoidable; however, history has shown us that governments, when they start down the path to consolidation, are reluctant to change course without turmoil.

Of course, it is also possible that the idea of dividing the Union may take hold as a mainstream political movement, leading to a constitutional amendment or convention and a peaceful, mutually acceptable realignment of the states. They might either break apart into separate confederations, or they could simply agree on one large confederation bound by a central government with severely limited authority, leading to the rise of conservative states, liberal states, libertarian states – a wide assortment of potential republican flavors. As with consolidation, balkanization need not be total. We may yet successfully balance unity in diversity.

How Would a State Secede?

One question that is usually asked about secession is whether a state could secede today without triggering another war. The answer to this question depends entirely upon the mindset of the American people and the President in office at the time. If we have a President who fancies himself another Lincoln, then we are likely in for a fight of some sort – if the state in question is determined to leave the Union. No President will want to be remembered as the one who presided over the breakup of the Union, even the departure of one just one or two states – which will be viewed by nationalists as the beginning of total disintegration and chaos, if not the end of the world – but the stance of the American people on the matter will decide the issue.

It is unlikely that another war would take place over secession, as long as the secession itself was attempted peacefully. Twenty-first century Americans are unlikely to tolerate the type of warmongering that 19th Century Americans did. They are simply less prone to resort to war altogether. In the past, war was a rather distant thing, something fathers, sons and brothers wrote home about; and those who were most distant from the sound of the guns were more prone to engage in it for the vicarious armchair glory it brought. In our modern times, however, strides in communications technology have brought the sights and sounds of war into our homes in real-time. War has become far less glorious, and far more gruesome; and ever since we have gained this new personal touch with conflict, we as a country have had less stomach for it.

Foreign wars generate enough debate and outcry as it is in our national councils; I believe that the prospect of engaging in a domestic one would strike Americans as nearly unconscionable. As many as would mourn the loss of a state or states from the Union, most modern Americans would likely prefer to part in peace than to see Americans shedding one another's blood, setting us once again at war, not merely with ourselves, but with our own exalted rhetoric of freedom. The world would surely notice and scorn such blatant hypocrisy.

Personally, I believe the federal government would resort to legal maneuvering to stop a secession movement today, as opposed to the use of military force, at least in the beginning. The State or Justice Department would likely request an injunction against any secession vote in a state, thereby forcing the matter into our politicized federal court system, where the federal government would undoubtedly win on the basis that secession is not "in the national interest". After that, what happens depends on how badly the state in question wants out of the Union, and what the American people are willing to let their government get by with.

And then there is the question of exactly how a state would go about seceding. There is no constitutional guideline for this sort of event, so how could it be handled? Here are a few thoughts on the matter, for what they are worth:

1. While I cannot argue that a state wanting to exit the Union must ask for permission to do so, I believe the state in question should request that the rest of the states acknowledge her right to leave and help her to do so in good faith. The state should declare her intention to leave and ask the other states to work with her to that end, or to resolve the differences that are triggering her desire to leave.

This declaration should be sent the legislatures of all the states, and also directed to the attention of the United States Senate, which is the traditional seat of the states – as states – in the federal government. In the Senate, the states are all equal. The Senate also embodies the greatest power of any branch of the federal government, considering that it approves presidential appointments, ratifies treaties, and can remove a president or justice from office. Specifically, it is the Senate's treaty making power that concerns this discussion. Any state leaving the Union would need to be dealt with as a foreign entity, and the Senate would be the only body of the federal government capable of officially treating with it in that capacity. The Senate could then either handle the matter itself or, perhaps even better, issue a call for a convention of the states.

2. Those individuals in the seceding state who wish to remain US citizens should be allowed to do so. They would continue to pay their taxes to the United States government and would continue to be subject to whatever benefits or obligations follow from that loyalty while obeying local law, just as US citizens living in foreign lands handle their affairs today. This means that they would still receive their Social Security, Medicare, etc. Those who wish to relinquish their citizenship would do so, and naturally, all those born in that state from the time of secession forward would be citizens of that new entity.

3. To mitigate the possible economic issues involved with secession, both with regard to the US government and the seceding state, I would suggest a ten-year plan. Citizens of the state would pay all applicable taxes to the state government, including those owed to the United States government (exempting, of course, those retaining their citizenship). The state would pass along whatever is owed to the United States government, holding back 10% for each year of the ten-year period. Consequently, in the first year, the state would retain 10% of the tax revenues collected and pay 90% to the United States government. The following year the state would retain 20% and forward 80%. And so forth until the transition was complete. These monies paid to the federal government could be used to help resolve any applicable economic issues, such as assigning the state a percentage of the national debt of the

United States.

4. Federal lands, such as national parkland, would need to be returned to the state or else ceded to neighboring states. Many such lands have been acquired unconstitutionally (i.e. without state consent), and this is a matter that needs to be set right regardless of any secession effort.

5. US citizens and those of the seceded state should be allowed free travel across borders, such as the member nations of the European Union allow today. Thus, if Montana seceded, North Dakotans would not need a passport to travel through Montana to Idaho.

These are a few suggestions as to how the most obvious issues of a state's secession from the Union might be peacefully, even amicably, handled. In all other matters, the US and the seceded state would simply deal with one another through the usual diplomatic channels that currently govern our dealings with any other nation in the world.

Conclusion

The history of our country bears witness to the fact that it was founded on the idea that all human beings have an unalienable right to a government of their consent, a government by which they can best secure and defend their liberties and happiness. Its Constitution was enacted with the view in mind that the rights of the people should be preserved and defended, that the government itself should be dedicated to this singular end, and that the ambitious should be restrained in their designs by equality with the people under the law.

In 1861, the Southern states, believing their rights violated, their liberties endangered, and their grievances unheard, determined themselves to be in a relationship of near servitude toward the Northern states and seceded from the Union upon the same set of principles their forefathers had invoked in 1776. Ultimately, whether the participants wore blue or gray, whether they referred to it as the "War for the Union" or the "War for Southern Independence," whether they called Abraham Lincoln or Jefferson Davis "President," and whether or not we agree on its causes and principles today, one fact stands absolutely clear: the war between North and South was truly a war for the American Ideal. For the North, the American Ideal centered on the continuance of a political-geographical Union; for the South, the American Ideal centered on government by consent.

Which side was right? Which view truly represented the American Ideal? Are we really "one nation, indivisible"? To answer this question, one must first establish what the American Ideal truly is; and to identify the American Ideal we need go no further than the words and deeds of that group of individuals without whom there would have been no United States of America at all, and this is what I have tried to do in the pages you have just read.

Which America would the founders have recognized and identified with, and which do we wish to be remembered for maintaining? A Union of force or consent? Truly, everything we have seen from those men who gave us the United States of America testifies over and over again to the fact what they said and did was devoted to the preservation of one treasure above all others: liberty. For liberty, they were willing to sacrifice unity with Great Britain; and when they finally created a Union amongst themselves, they did so because it promised to be the best means of defending the liberties they had won at such great cost. Separate the founders' words and deeds from the central aspect of liberty and you strip them of all their meaning. Separate the flag from the idea that raised her, and you have just another national banner. Separate government from the preservation of human freedom, and you have just another empire. Separate America from her primary devotion to liberty, and you rob her of all that makes her unique and special.

In the end, I would argue that both sides lost the war. The North might have won a military victory, and the South might have suffered a military defeat, but it was liberty that suffered the greatest blow of all. Despite Lincoln's rhetoric at the time, and that of his apologists today, there was nothing special that resulted from Northern victory in this war. Something special is something *different or distinct*. Lincoln and the North gave us nothing along those lines. All that was accomplished at Appomattox was to prove that a militarily stronger people can conquer a militarily weaker people, a truth we hardly needed to see proven again after thousands of years of previous examples, and certainly not here in the "land of the free".

We cannot celebrate both the ideals of Jefferson and those of Lincoln. Those ideals were in conflict in 1861, and they remain in conflict today. Since the end of the War of Secession, Americans have tried their best to reconcile this ideological contradiction and embrace both legacies, but the folly of this approach has become more apparent with time. If we celebrate the American Revolution, then we celebrate its ideals: the ideals of Jefferson, the concepts of liberty and government by consent. If we celebrate Lincoln's war, then we also celebrate its ideals: the ideals of government by force and unity at the expense of liberty. These two philosophies are mutually exclusive, and attempts to embrace them both as equals can only result in confusion and conflict. The effects of this conflict are still with us today; and, although the guns fell silent long ago, the battles are far from over. Military questions can be resolved by military means, but not questions of ideology, of right and wrong. The war answered only the question of which side could prevail on the battlefield; it did not answer the question of which was right.

The American Union was, and is, worth preserving, but its potential division should not be the worst of our fears. That dubious honor belongs to the potential for losing our freedom to despotism; and the fact that we may have more freedom than some other countries does not mean we should not be concerned about the freedoms we *are* losing. He who sails in a leaky boat should not brag to those in the water, for he may soon be joining them. We must bear in mind that, no matter how much we love our country, we love that country so much because of the great freedoms it has given us. We cannot afford to turn a blind eye to the excesses of state and the designs of the ambitious. Freedom does not usually perish quickly and catastrophically, but gradually, and often in the name of "protecting" or doing "what's right" for the nation. In truth, the greatest service that we can do for our country is to profess our loyalty to those foundational principles that made its existence possible, and upon which it rose to greatness. They who would defend liberty are true American patriots and worthy of the name.

As we look back on men like Lincoln and the issues of his day, and contemplate the idea of "one nation, indivisible," let us remember that these issues are not uniquely American. The human race has faced them, in various forms, since the dawn of creation, and will continue to face them for as long as the world remains. Do we live with the greatest freedom for the greatest number, deriving our rights from the hand of the Creator, or do we surrender to the rule of those who would set themselves above us, deriving our rights from the whims of politicians? The story of world history has mostly been a tale of empires in which a few elites have advanced themselves upon the servitude of the people, to one degree or another. But it gives us cause to hope when we reflect that, for the King Johns of the world, there are Runnymedes; for the Edward Longshankses, there are William Wallaces; for the George IIIs, there are Washingtons. These heroes of freedom may not always triumph, but their sacrifice is immortal in the memory of those who follow them, and it serves as an everlasting banner to which the friends of freedom gather with their hopes for the future.

Writing to Charles Marshall in 1870, Robert E. Lee, who was then close to the end of his life, reflected on lessons he had learned over the years and presented an optimistic epistle we would do well to keep in mind when confronted with these issues:

> My experience of men has neither disposed me to think worse of them nor indisposed me to serve them; nor, in spite of failures which I lament, of errors which I now see and acknowledge, or of the present aspect of affairs, do I despair of the future.

> The truth is this: The march of Providence is so slow and our desires so impatient; the work of progress so immense and our means of aiding it so feeble; the life of humanity is so long, that of the individual so brief, that we often see only the ebb of the advancing wave and are thus discouraged. It is history that teaches us to hope.

Appendix A:

The Declaration of Independence

In Congress, July 4, 1776.

When, in the Course of human events, it becomes necessary for one people to dissolve the political bands which have connected them with another, and to assume, among the Powers of the earth, the separate and equal station to which the Laws of Nature and of Nature's God entitle them, a decent respect to the opinions of mankind requires that they should declare the causes which impel them to the separation.

We hold these truths to be self-evident, that all men are created equal, that they are endowed by their Creator with certain unalienable Rights, that among these, are Life, Liberty, and the pursuit of Happiness. That, to secure these rights, Governments are instituted among Men, deriving their just Powers from the consent of the governed. That, whenever any form of Government becomes destructive of these ends, it is the Right of the people to alter or to abolish it, and to institute new Government, laying its foundation on such Principles, and organizing its Powers in such form, as to them shall seem most likely to effect their Safety and Happiness. Prudence, indeed, will dictate that Governments long established should not be changed for light and transient causes; and, accordingly, all experience hath shewn, that mankind are more disposed to suffer, while evils are sufferable, than to right themselves by abolishing the forms to which they are accustomed. But, when a long train of abuses and usurpations, pursuing invariably the same Object, evinces a design to reduce them under absolute Despotism, it is their right, it is their duty, to throw off such Government, and to provide new Guards for their future Security. Such has been the patient sufferance of these Colonies; and such is now the necessity which constrains them to alter their former Systems of Government. The history of the present King of Great Britain is a history of repeated injuries and usurpations, all having in direct object the establishment of an absolute Tyranny over these States. To prove this, let Facts be submitted to a candid world.

He has refused his Assent to Laws the most wholesome and necessary for the public good.

He has forbidden his Governors to pass Laws of immediate and pressing importance, unless suspended in their operation till his Assent should be obtained; and when so suspended, he has utterly neglected to attend to them.

He has refused to pass other Laws for the accommodation of large districts of People, unless those People would relinquish the right of Representation in the legislature; a right inestimable to them and formidable to tyrants only.

He has called together legislative bodies at places unusual, uncomfortable, and distant from the depository of their Public Records, for the sole Purpose of fatiguing them into compliance with his measures.

He has dissolved Representative Houses repeatedly, for opposing, with manly firmness, his invasions on the rights of the People.

He has refused for a long time, after such dissolutions, to cause others to be elected; whereby the Legislative Powers, incapable of Annihilation, have returned to the People at large for their exercise; the State remaining in the mean time exposed to all the dangers of invasion from without, and convulsions within.

He has endeavoured to prevent the Population of these States; for that purpose obstructing the Laws for Naturalization of Foreigners; refusing to pass others to encourage their migrations hither, and raising the conditions of new Appropriations of Lands.

He has obstructed the Administration of Justice, by refusing his Assent to Laws for establishing Judiciary Powers.

He has made Judges dependent on his Will alone, for the tenure of their offices, and the amount and payment of their salaries.

He has erected a multitude of New Offices, and sent hither swarms of Officers to harrass our People, and eat out their substance.

He has kept among us, in times of Peace, Standing Armies, without the Consent of our legislatures.

He has affected to render the Military independent of and superior to the Civil Power.

He has combined with others to subject us to a jurisdiction foreign to our constitution, and unacknowledged by our laws; giving his Assent to their Acts of pretended Legislation:

For quartering large bodies of armed troops among us:

For protecting them, by a mock Trial, from Punishment for any Murders which they should commit on the Inhabitants of these States:

For cutting off our Trade with all parts of the world:

For imposing Taxes on us without our Consent:

For depriving us, in many cases, of the benefits of Trial by Jury:

For transporting us beyond Seas to be tried for pretended offences:

For abolishing the free System of English Laws in a neighbouring province, establishing therein an Arbitrary government, and enlarging its Boundaries, so as to render it at once an example and fit instrument for introducing the same absolute rule into these Colonies:

For taking away our Charters, abolishing our most valuable Laws, and altering fundamentally the Forms of our Governments:

For suspending our own Legislatures, and declaring themselves invested with Power to legislate for us in all cases whatsoever.

He has abdicated Government here, by declaring us out of his protection, and waging War against us.

He has plundered our seas, ravaged our Coasts, burnt our towns, and destroyed the Lives of our People.

He is at this time transporting large Armies of foreign Mercenaries to compleat the works of death, desolation and tyranny, already begun with circumstances of Cruelty and perfidy scarcely paralleled in the most barbarous ages, and totally unworthy the Head of a civilized nation.

He has constrained our fellow Citizens, taken Captive on the high

Seas, to bear Arms against their Country, to become the executioners of their friends and Brethren, or to fall themselves by their Hands.

He has excited domestic insurrections amongst us, and has endeavoured to bring on the inhabitants of our frontiers, the merciless Indian Savages, whose known rule of warfare, is an undistinguished destruction of all ages, sexes and conditions.

In every stage of these Oppressions, We have Petitioned for Redress, in the most humble terms: Our repeated Petitions, have been answered only by repeated injury. A Prince, whose character is thus marked by every act which may define a Tyrant, is unfit to be the ruler of a free People.

Nor have We been wanting in attentions to our British brethren. We have warned them from time to time of attempts by their legislature to extend an unwarrantable jurisdiction over us. We have reminded them of the circumstances of our emigration and settlement here. We have appealed to their native justice and magnanimity, and we have conjured them by the ties of our common kindred, to disavow these usurpations, which, would inevitably interrupt our connexions and correspondence. They too have been deaf to the voice of justice and of consanguinity. We must, therefore, acquiesce in the necessity, which denounces our Separation, and hold them, as we hold the rest of mankind, Enemies in War, in Peace Friends.

We, therefore, the Representatives of the united States of America, in General Congress assembled, appealing to the Supreme Judge of the World for the rectitude of our intentions, Do, in the Name, and by Authority of the good People of these Colonies, solemnly PUBLISH and DECLARE, That these United Colonies are, and of Right, ought to be Free and Independent States; that they are Absolved from all Allegiance to the British Crown, and that all political connexion between them and the State of Great Britain, is and ought to be totally dissolved; and that, as Free and Independent States, they have full Power to levy War, conclude Peace, contract Alliances, establish Commerce, and to do all other Acts and Things which Independent States may of right do. And for the support of this Declaration, with a firm reliance on the protection of divine Providence, we mutually pledge to each other our Lives, our Fortunes, and our sacred Honour.

Appendix B:

The Articles of Confederation
Effective March 1, 1781

To all to whom these Presents shall come, We, the undersigned, Delegates of the States affixed to our names, send greeting:

Whereas the delegates of the United States of America, in Congress assembled, did, on the fifteenth day of November, in the year of our Lord one thousand seven hundred and seventy-seven, and in the second year of the Independence of America, agree to certain Articles of Confederation and Perpetual Union, between the states of New Hampshire, Massachusetts Bay, Rhode Island and Providence Plantations, Connecticut, New York, New Jersey, Pennsylvania, Delaware, Maryland, Virginia, North Carolina, South Carolina, and Georgia, in the words following, viz: –

Articles of Confederation and Perpetual Union, between the States of New Hampshire, Massachusetts Bay, Rhode Island and Providence Plantations, Connecticut, New York, New Jersey, Pennsylvania, Delaware, Maryland, Virginia, North Carolina, South Carolina, and Georgia.

I. The Stile of this Confederacy shall be "The United States of America".

II. Each state retains its sovereignty, freedom, and independence, and every Power, Jurisdiction and right, which is not by this confederation expressly delegated to the United States, in Congress assembled.

III. The said states hereby severally enter into a firm league of friendship with each other, for their common defence, the security of their Liberties, and their mutual and general welfare, binding themselves to assist each other, against all force offered to, or attacks made upon them, or any of them, on account of religion, sovereignty, trade, or any other pretence whatsoever.

IV. The better to secure and perpetuate mutual friendship and intercourse among the people of the different states in this union, the free inhabitants of each of these states, paupers, vagabonds and fugitives from justice excepted, shall be entitled to all privileges and immunities of free citizens in the several states; and the people of each state shall have free ingress and regress to and from any other state, and shall enjoy therein all the privileges of trade and commerce, subject to the same duties, impositions and restrictions as the inhabitants thereof respectively, provided that such restriction shall not extend so far as to prevent the removal of property imported into any state, to any other state, of which the Owner is an inhabitant; provided also that no imposition, duties or restriction shall be laid by any state, on the property of the united states, or either of them.

If any Person guilty of, or charged with treason, felony, or other high misdemeanor in any state, shall flee from Justice, and be found in any of the united states, he shall, upon demand of the Governor or executive power, of the state from which he fled, be delivered up and removed to the state having jurisdiction of his offence.

Full faith and credit shall he given in each of these states to the records, acts and judicial proceedings of the courts and magistrates of every other state.

If any person guilty of, or charged with, treason, felony, or other high misdemeanor in any State, shall flee from justice, and be found in any of the United States, he shall, upon demand of the Governor or executive power of the State from which he fled, be delivered up and removed to the State having jurisdiction of his offense. Full faith and credit shall be given in each of these States to the records, acts, and judicial proceedings of the courts and magistrates of every other State.

V. For the more convenient management of the general interests of the united states, delegates shall be annually appointed in such manner as the legislature of each state shall direct, to meet in Congress on the first Monday in November, in every year, with a power reserved to each state, to recall its delegates, or any of them, at any time within the year, and to send others in their stead, for the remainder of the Year.

No state shall be represented in Congress by less than two, nor by more than seven Members; and no person shall be capable of being a delegate for more than three years in any term of six years; nor shall any person, being a delegate, be capable of holding any office under the united states, for which he, or another for his benefit receives any salary, fees or emolument of any kind.

Each state shall maintain its own delegates in a meeting of the states, and while they act as members of the committee of the states.

In determining questions in the united states in Congress assembled, each state shall have one vote.

Freedom of speech and debate in Congress shall not be impeached or questioned in any Court, or place out of Congress, and the members of congress shall be protected in their persons from arrests and imprisonments, during the time of their going to and from, and attendance on congress, except for treason, felony, or breach of the peace.

VI. No state, without the Consent of the united states in congress assembled, shall send any embassy to, or receive any embassy from, or enter into any conference, agreement, alliance or treaty with any King prince or state; nor shall any person holding any office of profit or trust under the united states, or any of them, accept of any present, emolument, office or title of ally kind whatever from any king, prince or foreign state; nor shall the united states in congress assembled, or any of them, grant any title of nobility.

No two or more states shall enter into any treaty, confederation or alliance whatever between them, without the consent of the united states in congress assembled, specifying accurately the purposes for which the same is to be entered into, and how long it shall continue.

No state shall lay any imposts or duties, which may interfere with any stipulations in treaties, entered into by the united states in congress assembled, with any king, prince or state, in pursuance of any treaties already proposed by congress, to the courts of France and Spain.

No vessels of war shall be kept up in time of peace by any state, except such number only, as shall be deemed necessary by the united states in congress assembled, for the defence of such state, or its trade; nor shall any body of forces be kept up by any state, in time of peace, except such number only, as in the judgment of the united states, in congress assembled, shall be deemed requisite to garrison the forts necessary for the defence of such state; but every state shall always keep up a well regulated and disciplined militia, sufficiently armed and accoutred, and shall provide and constantly have ready for use, in public stores, a due number of field pieces and tents, and a proper quantity of arms, ammunition and camp equipage.

No state shall engage in any war without the consent of the united states in congress assembled, unless such state be actually invaded by enemies, or shall have received certain advice of a resolution being formed by some nation of Indians to invade such state, and the danger is so imminent as not to admit of a delay till the united states in congress assembled can be consulted: nor shall any state grant commissions to any ships or vessels of war, nor letters of marque or reprisal, except it be after a declaration of war by the united states in congress assembled, and then only against the kingdom or state and the subjects thereof, against which war has been so declared, and under such regulations as shall be established by the united states in congress assembled, unless such state be infested by pirates, in which case vessels of war may be fitted out for that occasion, and kept so long as the danger shall continue, or until the united states in congress assembled, shall determine otherwise.

VII. When land-forces are raised by any state for the common defence, all officers of or under the rank of colonel, shall be appointed by the legislature of each state respectively, by whom such forces shall be raised, or in such manner as such state shall direct, and all vacancies shall be filled up by the State which first made the appointment.

VIII. All charges of war, and all other expences that shall be incurred for the common defence or general welfare, and allowed by the united states in congress assembled, shall be defrayed out of a common treasury, which shall be supplied by the several states in proportion to the value of all land within each state, granted to or surveyed for any Person, as such land and the buildings and improvements thereon shall be estimated according to such mode as the united states in congress assembled, shall from time to time direct and appoint. The taxes for paying that proportion shall be laid and levied by the authority and direction of the legislatures of the several states within the time agreed upon by the united states in congress assembled.

IX. The united states in congress assembled, shall have the sole and exclusive right and power of determining on peace and war, except in the cases mentioned in the sixth article – of sending and receiving ambassadors – entering into treaties and alliances, provided that no treaty of commerce shall be made whereby the legislative power of the respective states shall be restrained from imposing such imposts and duties on foreigners, as their own people are subjected to, or from prohibiting the exportation or importation of any species of goods or commodities whatsoever – of establishing rules for deciding in all cases, what captures on land or water shall be legal, and in what manner prizes taken by land or naval forces in the service of the united states shall be divided or appropriated – of granting letters of marque and reprisal in times of peace – appointing courts for the trial of piracies and felonies committed on the high seas and establishing courts for receiving and determining finally appeals in all cases of captures, provided that no member of congress shall be appointed a judge of any of the said courts.

The united states in congress assembled shall also be the last resort on appeal in all disputes and differences now subsisting or that hereafter may arise between two or more states concerning boundary, jurisdiction or any other cause whatever; which authority shall always be exercised in the manner following. Whenever the legislative or executive authority or lawful agent of any state in controversy with another shall present a petition to congress stating the matter in question and praying for a hearing, notice thereof shall be given by order of congress to the legislative or executive authority of the other state in controversy, and a day assigned for the appearance of the parties by their lawful agents, who shall then be directed to appoint by joint consent, commissioners or judges to constitute a court for hearing and determining the matter in question: but if they cannot agree, congress shall name three persons out of each of the united states, and from the list of such persons each party shall alternately strike out one, the petitioners beginning, until the number shall be reduced to thirteen; and from that number not less than seven, nor more than nine names as congress shall direct, shall in the presence of congress be drawn out by lot, and the persons whose names shall be so drawn or any five of them, shall be commissioners or judges, to hear and finally determine the controversy, so always as a major part of the judges who shall hear the cause shall agree in the determination: and if either party shall neglect to attend at the day appointed, without showing reasons, which congress shall judge sufficient, or being present shall refuse to strike, the congress shall proceed to nominate three persons out of each state, and the secretary of congress shall strike in behalf of such party absent or refusing; and the judgment and sentence of the court to be appointed, in the manner before prescribed, shall be final and conclusive; and if any of the parties shall refuse to submit to the authority of such court, or to appear or defend their claim or cause, the court shall nevertheless proceed to pronounce sentence, or judgment, which shall in like manner be final and decisive, the judgment or sentence and other proceedings being in either case transmitted to congress, and lodged among the acts of congress for the security of the parties concerned: provided that every commissioner, before he sits in judgment, shall take an oath to be administered by one of the judges of the supreme or superior court of the state, where the cause shall be tried, "well and truly to hear and determine the matter in question, according to the best of his judgment, without favour, affection or hope of reward:" provided also, that no state shall be deprived of territory for the benefit of the united states.

All controversies concerning the private right of soil claimed under different grants of two or more states, whose jurisdictions as they may respect such lands, and the states which passed such grants are adjusted, the said grants or either of them being at the same time claimed to have originated antecedent to such settlement of jurisdiction, shall on the petition of either party to the congress of the united states, be finally determined as near as may be in the same manner as is before prescribed for deciding disputes respecting territorial jurisdiction between different states.

The united states in congress assembled shall also have the sole and exclusive right and power of regulating the alloy and value of coin struck by their own authority, or by that of the respective states – fixing the standard of weights and measures throughout the united states – regulating the trade and managing all affairs with the Indians, not members of any of the states, provided that the legislative right of any state within its own limits be not infringed or violated – establishing or regulating post-offices from one state to another, throughout all the united states, and exacting such postage on the papers passing thro' the same as may be requisite to defray the expences of the said office – appointing all officers of the land forces, in the service of the united states, excepting regimental officers – appointing all the officers of the naval forces, and commissioning all officers whatever in the service of the united states – making rules for the government and regulation of the said land and naval forces, and directing their operations.

The united states in congress assembled shall have authority to appoint a committee, to sit in the recess of congress, to be denominated "A Committee of the States," and to consist of one delegate from each state; and to appoint such other committees and civil officers as may be necessary for managing the general affairs of the united states under their direction – to appoint one of their number to preside, provided that no person be allowed to serve in the office of president more than one year in any term of three years; to ascertain the necessary sums of Money to be raised for the service of the united states, and to appropriate mid apply the same for defraying the public expences – to borrow money, or emit bills on the credit of the united states, transmitting every half year to the respective states an account of the sums of money so borrowed or emitted, – to build and equip a navy – to agree upon the number of land forces, and to make requisitions from each state for its quota, in proportion to the number of white inhabitants in such state; which requisition shall be binding, and thereupon the legislature of each state shall appoint the regimental officers, raise the men and cloath, arm and equip them in a soldier like manner, at the expence of the united states; and the officers and men so cloathed, armed and equipped shall march to the place appointed, and within the time agreed on by the united states in congress assembled: But if the united states in congress assembled shall, on consideration of circumstances judge proper that any state should not raise men, or should raise a smaller number than its quota, and that any other state should raise a greater number of men than the quota thereof, such extra number shall be raised, officered, cloathed, armed and equipped in the same manner as the quota of such state, unless the legislature of such state shall judge that such extra number cannot be safely spared out of the same, in which case they shall raise officer, cloath, arm and equip as many of such extra number as they judge can be sagely spared. And the officers and men so cloathed, armed and equipped, shall march to the place appointed, and within the time agreed on by the united states in congress assembled.

The united states in congress assembled shall never engage in a war, nor grant letters of marque and reprisal in time of peace, nor enter into any treaties or alliances, nor coin money, nor regulate the value thereof, nor ascertain the sums and expences necessary for the defence and welfare of the united states, or any of them, nor emit bills, nor borrow money on the credit of the united states, nor appropriate money, nor agree upon the number of vessels of war, to be built or purchased, or the number of land or sea forces to be raised, nor appoint a commander in chief of the army or navy, unless nine states assent to the same: nor shall a question on any other point, except for adjourning from day to day be determined, unless by the votes of a majority of the united states in congress assembled.

The congress of the united states shall have power to adjourn to any time within the year, and to any place within the united states, so that no period of adjournment be for a longer duration than the space of six Months, and shall publish the Journal of their proceedings monthly, except such parts thereof relating to treaties, alliances or military operations, as in their judgment require secrecy; and the yeas and nays of the delegates of each state on any question shall be entered on the Journal, when it is desired by any delegate; and the delegates of a state, or any of them, at his or their request shall be furnished with a transcript of the said Journal, except such parts as are above excepted, to lay before the legislatures of the several states.

X. The committee of the states, or any nine of them, shall be authorized to execute, in the recess of congress, such of the powers of congress as the united states in congress assembled, by the consent of nine states, shall from time to time think expedient to vest them with; provided that no power be delegated to the said committee, for the exercise of which, by the articles of confederation, the voice of nine states in the congress of the united states assembled is requisite.

XI. Canada acceding to this confederation, and joining in the measures of the united states, shall be admitted into, and entitled to all the advantages of this union: but no other colony shall be admitted into the same, unless such admission be agreed to by nine states.

XII. All bills of credit emitted, monies borrowed and debts contracted by, or under the authority of congress, before the assembling of the united states, in pursuance of the present confederation, shall be deemed and considered as a charge against the united states, for payment and satisfaction whereof the said united states, and the public faith are hereby solemnly pledged.

XIII. Every state shall abide by the determinations of the united states in congress assembled, on all questions which by this confederation are submitted to them. And the Articles of this confederation shall be inviolably observed by every state, and the union shall be perpetual; nor shall any alteration at any time hereinafter be made in any of them; unless such alteration be agreed to in a congress of the united states, and be afterwards confirmed by the legislatures of every state.

And Whereas it hath pleased the Great Governor of the World to incline the hearts of the legislatures we respectively represent in congress, to approve of, and to authorize us to ratify the said articles of confederation and perpetual union. Know Ye that we the undersigned delegates; by virtue of the power and authority to us given for that purpose, do by these presents, in the name and in behalf of our respective constituents, fully and entirely ratify and confirm each and every of the said articles of confederation and perpetual union, and all and singular the matters and things therein contained: And we do further solemnly plight and engage the faith of our respective constituents, that they shall abide by the determinations of the united states in congress assembled, on all questions, which by the said confederation are submitted to them. And that the articles thereof shall be inviolably observed by the states we respectively represent, and that the union shall be perpetual.

In Witness whereof we have hereunto set our hands in Congress. Done at Philadelphia in the state of Pennsylvania the ninth day of July, in the Year of our Lord one Thousand seven Hundred and Seventy-eight, and in the third year of the independence of America.

Appendix C:

The Constitution of the United States
Effective among nine states: June 21, 1788

We the People of the United States, in Order to form a more perfect Union, establish Justice, insure domestic Tranquility, provide for the common defence, promote the general Welfare, and secure the Blessings of Liberty to ourselves and our Posterity, do ordain and establish this Constitution for the United States of America.

Article I

Section 1. All legislative Powers herein granted shall be vested in a Congress of the United States, which shall consist of a Senate and House of Representatives.

Section 2. The House of Representatives shall be composed of Members chosen every second Year by the People of the several States, and the Electors in each State shall have the Qualifications requisite for Electors of the most numerous Branch of the State Legislature.

No Person shall be a Representative who shall not have attained to the age of twenty five Years, and been seven Years a Citizen of the United States, and who shall not, when elected, be an Inhabitant of that State in which he shall be chosen.

Representatives and direct Taxes shall be apportioned among the several States which may be included within this Union, according to their respective Numbers, which shall be determined by adding to the whole Number of free Persons, including those bound to Service for a Term of Years, and excluding Indians not taxed, three fifths of all other Persons. The actual Enumeration shall be made within three Years after the first Meeting of the Congress of the United States, and within every subsequent Term of ten Years, in such Manner as they shall by Law direct. The Number of Representatives shall not exceed one for every thirty Thousand, but each State shall have at Least one Representative; and until such enumeration shall be made, the State of New Hampshire shall be entitled to chuse three, Massachusetts eight, Rhode-Island and Providence Plantations one, Connecticut five, New-York six, New Jersey four, Pennsylvania eight, Delaware one, Maryland six, Virginia ten, North Carolina five, South Carolina five, and Georgia three.

When vacancies happen in the Representation from any State, the Executive Authority thereof shall issue Writs of Election to fill such Vacancies.

The House of Representatives shall chuse their Speaker and other Officers; and shall have the sole Power of Impeachment.

Section 3. The Senate of the United States shall be composed of two Senators from each State, chosen by the Legislature thereof, for six Years; and each Senator shall have one Vote.

Immediately after they shall be assembled in Consequence of the first Election, they shall be divided as equally as may be into three Classes. The Seats of the Senators of the first Class shall be vacated at the Expiration of the second Year, of the second Class at the Expiration of the fourth Year, and the third Class at the Expiration of the sixth Year, so that one third may be chosen every second Year; and if Vacancies happen by Resignation, or otherwise, during the Recess of the Legislature of any State, the Executive thereof may make temporary Appointments until the next Meeting of the Legislature, which shall then fill such Vacancies.

No Person shall be a Senator who shall not have attained to the Age of thirty Years, and been nine Years a Citizen of the United States and who shall not, when elected, be an Inhabitant of that State for which he shall be chosen.

The Vice President of the United States shall be President of the Senate, but shall have no Vote, unless they be equally divided.

The Senate shall chuse their other Officers, and also a President pro tempore, in the Absence of the Vice President, or when he shall exercise the Office of President of the United States.

The Senate shall have the sole Power to try all Impeachments. When sitting for that Purpose, they shall be on Oath or Affirmation. When the President of the United States is tried, the Chief Justice shall preside: And no Person shall be convicted without the Concurrence of two thirds of the Members present.

Judgment in Cases of Impeachment shall not extend further than to removal from Office, and disqualification to hold and enjoy any Office of Honor, Trust or Profit under the United States: but the Party convicted shall nevertheless be liable and subject to Indictment, Trial, Judgment and Punishment, according to Law.

Section 4. The Times, Places and Manner of holding Elections for Senators and Representatives, shall be prescribed in each State by the Legislature thereof; but the Congress may at any time by Law make or alter such Regulations, except as to the Places of chusing Senators.

The Congress shall assemble at least once in every Year, and such Meeting shall be on the first Monday in December, unless they shall by Law appoint a different Day.

Section 5. Each House shall be the Judge of the Elections, Returns and Qualifications of its own Members, and a Majority of each shall constitute a Quorum to do Business; but a smaller Number may adjourn from day to day, and may be authorized to compel the Attendance of absent Members, in such Manner, and under such Penalties as each House may provide.

Each House may determine the Rules of its Proceedings, punish its Members for disorderly Behaviour, and, with the Concurrence of two thirds, expel a Member.

Each House shall keep a Journal of its Proceedings, and from time to time publish the same, excepting such Parts as may in their Judgment require Secrecy; and the Yeas and Nays of the Members of either House on any question shall, at the Desire of one fifth of those Present, be entered on the Journal.

Neither House, during the Session of Congress, shall, without the Consent of the other, adjourn for more than three days, nor to any other Place than that in which the two Houses shall be sitting.

Section 6. The Senators and Representatives shall receive a Compensation for their Services, to be ascertained by Law, and paid out of the

Treasury of the United States. They shall in all Cases, except Treason, Felony and Breach of the Peace, be privileged from Arrest during their Attendance at the Session of their respective Houses, and in going to and returning from the same; and for any Speech or Debate in either House, they shall not be questioned in any other Place.

No Senator or Representative shall, during the Time for which he was elected, be appointed to any civil Office under the Authority of the United States, which shall have been created, or the Emoluments whereof shall have been increased during such time: and no Person holding any Office under the United States, shall be a Member of either House during his Continuance in Office.

Section 7. All Bills for raising Revenue shall originate in the House of Representatives; but the Senate may propose or concur with Amendments as on other Bills.

Every Bill which shall have passed the House of Representatives and the Senate, shall, before it become a Law, be presented to the President of the United States; if he approve he shall sign it, but if not he shall return it, with his Objections to that House in which it shall have originated, who shall enter the Objections at large on their Journal, and proceed to reconsider it. If after such Reconsideration two thirds of that House shall agree to pass the Bill, it shall be sent, together with the Objections, to the other House, by which it shall likewise be reconsidered, and if approved by two thirds of that House, it shall become a Law. But in all such Cases the Votes of both Houses shall be determined by Yeas and Nays, and the Names of the Persons voting for and against the Bill shall be entered on the Journal of each House respectively. If any Bill shall not be returned by the President within ten Days (Sundays excepted) after it shall have been presented to him, the Same shall be a Law, in like Manner as if he had signed it, unless the Congress by their Adjournment prevent its Return, in which Case it shall not be a Law.

Every Order, Resolution, or Vote to which the Concurrence of the Senate and House of Representatives may be necessary (except on a question of Adjournment) shall be presented to the President of the United States; and before the Same shall take Effect, shall be approved by him, or being disapproved by him, shall be re-passed by two thirds of the Senate and House of Representatives, according to the Rules and Limitations prescribed in the Case of a Bill.

Section 8. The Congress shall have Power To lay and collect Taxes, Duties, Imposts and Excises, to pay the Debts and provide for the common Defence and general Welfare of the United States; but all Duties, Imposts and Excises shall be uniform throughout the United States;

To borrow Money on the credit of the United States;

To regulate Commerce with foreign Nations, and among the several States, and with the Indian Tribes;

To establish an uniform Rule of Naturalization, and uniform Laws on the subject of Bankruptcies throughout the United States;

To coin Money, regulate the Value thereof, and of foreign Coin, and fix the Standard of Weights and Measures;

To provide for the Punishment of counterfeiting the Securities and current Coin of the United States;

To establish Post Offices and post Roads;

To promote the Progress of Science and useful Arts, by securing for limited Times to Authors and Inventors the exclusive Right to their respective Writings and Discoveries;

To constitute Tribunals inferior to the supreme Court;

To define and punish Piracies and Felonies committed on the high Seas, and Offences against the Law of Nations;

To declare War, grant Letters of Marque and Reprisal, and make Rules concerning Captures on Land and Water;

To raise and support Armies, but no Appropriation of Money to that Use shall be for a longer Term than two Years;

To provide and maintain a Navy;

To make Rules for the Government and Regulation of the land and naval Forces;

To provide for calling forth the Militia to execute the Laws of the Union, suppress Insurrections and repel Invasions;

To provide for organizing, arming, and disciplining, the Militia, and for governing such Part of them as may be employed in the Service of the United States, reserving to the States respectively, the Appointment of the Officers, and the Authority of training the Militia according to the discipline prescribed by Congress;

To exercise exclusive Legislation in all Cases whatsoever, over such District (not exceeding ten Miles square) as may, by Cession of particular States, and the Acceptance of Congress, become the Seat of the Government of the United States, and to exercise like Authority over all Places purchased by the Consent of the Legislature of the State in which the Same shall be, for the Erection of Forts, Magazines, Arsenals, dock-Yards, and other needful Buildings; – And

To make all Laws which shall be necessary and proper for carrying into Execution the foregoing Powers, and all other Powers vested by this Constitution in the Government of the United States, or in any Department or Officer thereof.

Section 9. The Migration or Importation of such Persons as any of the States now existing shall think proper to admit, shall not be prohibited by the Congress prior to the Year one thousand eight hundred and eight, but a Tax or duty may be imposed on such Importation, not exceeding ten dollars for each Person.

The Privilege of the Writ of Habeas Corpus shall not be suspended, unless when in Cases of Rebellion or Invasion the public Safety may require it.

No Bill of Attainder or ex post facto Law shall be passed.

No Capitation, or other direct, Tax shall be laid, unless in Proportion to the Census or Enumeration herein before directed to be taken.

No Tax or Duty shall be laid on Articles exported from any State.

No Preference shall be given by any Regulation of Commerce or Revenue to the Ports of one State over those of another: nor shall Vessels bound to, or from, one State, be obliged to enter, clear or pay Duties in another.

No Money shall be drawn from the Treasury, but in Consequence of Appropriations made by Law; and a regular Statement and Account of Receipts and Expenditures of all public Money shall be published from time to time.

No Title of Nobility shall be granted by the United States: And no Person holding any Office of Profit or Trust under them, shall, without the Consent of the Congress, accept of any present, Emolument, Office, or Title, of any kind whatever, from any King, Prince, or foreign State.

Section 10. No State shall enter into any Treaty, Alliance, or Confederation; grant Letters of Marque and Reprisal; coin Money; emit Bills of Credit; make any Thing but gold and silver Coin a Tender in Payment of Debts; pass any Bill of Attainder, ex post facto Law, or Law impairing the Obligation of Contracts, or grant any Title of Nobility.

No State shall, without the Consent of the Congress, lay any Imposts or Duties on Imports or Exports, except what may be absolutely necessary for executing its inspection Laws: and the net Produce of all Duties and Imposts, laid by any State on Imports or Exports, shall be for the Use of the Treasury of the United States; and all such Laws shall be subject to the Revision and Control of the Congress.

No State shall, without the Consent of Congress, lay any Duty of Tonnage, keep Troops, or Ships of War in time of Peace, enter into any Agreement or Compact with another State, or with a foreign Power, or engage in War, unless actually invaded, or in such imminent Danger as will not admit of delay.

Article II

Section 1. The executive Power shall be vested in a President of the United States of America. He shall hold his Office during the Term of four Years, and, together with the Vice President, chosen for the same Term, be elected, as follows:

Each State shall appoint, in such Manner as the Legislature thereof may direct, a Number of Electors, equal to the whole Number of Senators and Representatives to which the State may be entitled in the Congress: but no Senator or Representative, or Person holding an Office of Trust or Profit under the United States, shall be appointed an Elector.

The Electors shall meet in their respective States, and vote by Ballot for two Persons, of whom one at least shall not be an Inhabitant of the same State with themselves. And they shall make a List of all the Persons voted for, and of the Number of Votes for each; which List they shall sign and certify, and transmit sealed to the Seat of the Government of the United States, directed to the President of the Senate. The President of the Senate shall, in the Presence of the Senate and House of Representatives, open all the Certificates, and the Votes shall then be counted. The Person having the greatest Number of Votes shall be the President, if such Number be a Majority of the whole Number of Electors appointed; and if there be more than one who have such Majority, and have an equal Number of Votes, then the House of Representatives shall immediately chuse by Ballot one of them for President; and if no Person have a Majority, then from the five highest on the List the said House shall in like Manner chuse the President. But in chusing the President, the Votes shall be taken by States, the Representation from each State having one Vote; A quorum for this Purpose shall consist of a Member or Members from two thirds of the States, and a Majority of all the States shall be necessary to a Choice. In every Case, after the Choice of the President, the Person having the greatest Number of Votes of the Electors shall be the Vice President. But if there should remain two or more who have equal Votes, the Senate shall chuse from them by Ballot the Vice President.

The Congress may determine the Time of chusing the Electors, and the Day on which they shall give their Votes; which Day shall be the same throughout the United States.

No Person except a natural born Citizen, or a Citizen of the United States, at the time of the Adoption of this Constitution, shall be eligible to the Office of President; neither shall any Person be eligible to that Office who shall not have attained to the Age of thirty five Years, and been fourteen Years a Resident within the United States.

In Case of the Removal of the President from Office, or of his Death, Resignation, or Inability to discharge the Powers and Duties of the said Office, the Same shall devolve on the Vice President, and the Congress may by Law provide for the Case of Removal, Death, Resignation or Inability, both of the President and Vice President, declaring what Officer shall then act as President, and such Officer shall act accordingly, until the Disability be removed, or a President shall be elected.

The President shall, at stated Times, receive for his Services, a Compensation, which shall neither be increased nor diminished during the

Period for which he shall have been elected, and he shall not receive within that Period any other Emolument from the United States, or any of them.

Before he enter on the Execution of his Office, he shall take the following Oath or Affirmation: – "I do solemnly swear (or affirm) that I will faithfully execute the Office of President of the United States, and will to the best of my Ability, preserve, protect and defend the Constitution of the United States."

Section 2. The President shall be Commander in Chief of the Army and Navy of the United States, and of the Militia of the several States, when called into the actual Service of the United States; he may require the Opinion, in writing, of the principal Officer in each of the executive Departments, upon any Subject relating to the Duties of their respective Offices, and he shall have Power to grant Reprieves and Pardons for Offences against the United States, except in Cases of Impeachment.

He shall have Power, by and with the Advice and Consent of the Senate, to make Treaties, provided two thirds of the Senators present concur; and he shall nominate, and by and with the Advice and Consent of the Senate, shall appoint Ambassadors, other public Ministers and Consuls, Judges of the supreme Court, and all other Officers of the United States, whose Appointments are not herein otherwise provided for, and which shall be established by Law: but the Congress may by Law vest the Appointment of such inferior Officers, as they think proper, in the President alone, in the Courts of Law, or in the Heads of Departments.

The President shall have Power to fill up all Vacancies that may happen during the Recess of the Senate, by granting Commissions which shall expire at the End of their next Session.

Section 3. He shall from time to time give to the Congress Information of the State of the Union, and recommend to their Consideration such Measures as he shall judge necessary and expedient; he may, on extraordinary Occasions, convene both Houses, or either of them, and in Case of Disagreement between them, with Respect to the Time of Adjournment, he may adjourn them to such Time as he shall think proper; he shall receive Ambassadors and other public Ministers; he shall take Care that the Laws be faithfully executed, and shall Commission all the Officers of the United States.

Section 4. The President, Vice President and all civil Officers of the United States, shall be removed from Office on Impeachment for, and Conviction of, Treason, Bribery, or other high Crimes and Misdemeanors.

Article III

Section 1. The judicial Power of the United States, shall be vested in one supreme Court, and in such inferior Courts as the Congress may from time to time ordain and establish. The Judges, both of the supreme and inferior Courts, shall hold their Offices during good Behaviour, and shall, at stated Times, receive for their Services, a Compensation, which shall not be diminished during their Continuance in Office.

Section 2. The judicial Power shall extend to all Cases, in Law and Equity, arising under this Constitution, the Laws of the United States, and Treaties made, or which shall be made, under their Authority;– to all Cases affecting Ambassadors, other public Ministers and Consuls;– to all Cases of admiralty and maritime Jurisdiction;– to Controversies to which the United States shall be a Party;– to Controversies between two or more States;– between a State and Citizens of another State;– between Citizens of different States; – between Citizens of the same State claiming Lands under Grants of different States, and between a State, or the Citizens thereof, and foreign States, Citizens or Subjects.

In all Cases affecting Ambassadors, other public Ministers and Consuls, and those in which a State shall be Party, the supreme Court shall have original Jurisdiction. In all the other Cases before mentioned, the supreme Court shall have appellate Jurisdiction, both as to Law and Fact, with such Exceptions, and under such Regulations as the Congress shall make.

The Trial of all Crimes, except in Cases of Impeachment, shall be by Jury; and such Trial shall be held in the State where the said Crimes shall have been committed; but when not committed within any State, the Trial shall be at such Place or Places as the Congress may by Law have directed.

Section 3. Treason against the United States, shall consist only in levying War against them, or in adhering to their Enemies, giving them

Aid and Comfort. No Person shall be convicted of Treason unless on the Testimony of two Witnesses to the same overt Act, or on Confession in open Court.

The Congress shall have Power to declare the Punishment of Treason, but no Attainder of Treason shall work Corruption of Blood, or Forfeiture except during the Life of the Person attainted.

Article IV

Section 1. Full Faith and Credit shall be given in each State to the public Acts, Records, and judicial Proceedings of every other State. And the Congress may by general Laws prescribe the Manner in which such Acts, Records, and Proceedings shall be proved, and the Effect thereof.

Section 2. The Citizens of each State shall be entitled to all Privileges and Immunities of Citizens in the several States.

A Person charged in any State with Treason, Felony, or other Crime, who shall flee from Justice, and be found in another State, shall on Demand of the executive Authority of the State from which he fled, be delivered up, to be removed to the State having Jurisdiction of the Crime.

No Person held to Service or Labour in one State, under the Laws thereof, escaping into another, shall, in Consequence of any Law or Regulation therein, be discharged from such Service or Labour, but shall be delivered up on Claim of the Party to whom such Service or Labour may be due.

Section 3. New States may be admitted by the Congress into this Union; but no new States shall be formed or erected within the Jurisdiction of any other State; nor any State be formed by the Junction of two or more States, or Parts of States, without the Consent of the Legislatures of the States concerned as well as of the Congress.

The Congress shall have Power to dispose of and make all needful Rules and Regulations respecting the Territory or other Property belonging to the United States; and nothing in this Constitution shall be so construed as to Prejudice any Claims of the United States, or of any particular State.

Section 4. The United States shall guarantee to every State in this Union a Republican Form of Government, and shall protect each of them against Invasion; and on Application of the Legislature, or of the Executive (when the Legislature cannot be convened) against domestic Violence.

Article V

The Congress, whenever two thirds of both Houses shall deem it necessary, shall propose Amendments to this Constitution, or, on the Application of the Legislatures of two thirds of the several States, shall call a Convention for proposing Amendments, which, in either Case, shall be valid to all Intents and Purposes, as Part of this Constitution, when ratified by the Legislatures of three fourths of the several States, or by Conventions in three fourths thereof, as the one or the other Mode of Ratification may be proposed by the Congress; Provided that no Amendment which may be made prior to the Year One thousand eight hundred and eight shall in any Manner affect the first and fourth Clauses in the Ninth Section of the first Article; and that no State, without its Consent, shall be deprived of its equal Suffrage in the Senate.

Article VI

All Debts contracted and Engagements entered into, before the Adoption of this Constitution, shall be as valid against the United States under this Constitution, as under the Confederation.

This Constitution, and the Laws of the United States which shall be made in Pursuance thereof; and all Treaties made, or which shall be made, under the Authority of the United States, shall be the supreme Law of the Land; and the Judges in every State shall be bound thereby, any Thing in the Constitution or Laws of any State to the Contrary not with-standing.

The Senators and Representatives before mentioned, and the Members of the several State Legislatures, and all executive and judicial Officers, both of the United States and of the several States, shall be bound by Oath or Affirmation, to support this Constitution; but no religious Test shall ever be required as a Qualification to any Office or public Trust under the United States.

Article VII

The Ratification of the Conventions of nine States, shall be sufficient for the Establishment of this Constitution between the States so ratifying the Same.

Done in Convention by the Unanimous Consent of the States present the Seventeenth Day of September in the Year of our Lord one thousand seven hundred and Eighty seven and of the Independence of the United States of America the Twelfth.

Appendix D:
Calhoun versus Webster

John C. Calhoun of South Carolina introduced the following resolutions in the United States Senate on January 22, 1833, in response to the escalating Tariff Crisis of that year – see Section Three, Position Three: Lincoln Fought to End Slavery, for a brief history of the Tariff Crisis. In these resolutions, Calhoun made a case for the Compact Theory of the Union:[1]

> *"Resolved*, That the people of the several States, composing these United States are united as parties to a constitutional compact, to which the people of each State acceded as a separate sovereign community, each binding itself by its own particular ratification; and that the union, of which the said compact is the bond, is a union between the States ratifying the same.

> *"Resolved*, That the people of the several States, thus united by the constitutional compact, in forming that instrument, and in creating a General Government to carry into effect the objects for which they were formed, delegated to that Government, for that purpose, certain definite powers, to be exercised jointly, reserving, at the same time, each State to itself, the residuary mass of powers, to be exercised by its own separate Government; and that whenever the General Government assumes the exercise of powers not delegated by the Compact, its acts are unauthorized, and are of no effect; and that the same Government is not made the final judge of the powers delegated to it, since that would make its discretion, and not the constitution, the measure of its powers; but that, as in all other cases of compact among sovereign parties, without any common judge, each has an equal right to judge for itself, as well of the infraction as of the mode and measure of redress.

> *"Resolved*, That the assertions, that the people of these United

States, taken collectively as individuals, are now, or ever have been, united on the principle of one social compact, and, as such, are now formed into one nation or people, or that they have ever been so united in any one stage of their political existence; that the people of the several States composing the Union have not, as members thereof, retained their Sovereignty, that the allegiance of their citizens has been transferred to the General Government; that they have parted with the right of punishing treason through their respective State Governments; and that they have not the right of judging in the last resort as to the extent of the powers reserved, and of the consequence, of those delegated; are not only without foundation in truth, but are contrary to the most certain and plain historical facts, and the clearest deductions of reason; and that all exercise of power on the part of the General Government, or any of its departments, claiming authority from so erroneous assumptions, must of necessity be unconstitutional, must tend, directly and inevitably to subvert the sovereignty of the States, to destroy the federal character of the Union, and to rear on its ruins a consolidated Government, without constitutional check or limitation, and which must necessarily terminate in the loss of liberty itself."

The following is a block of excerpts from Daniel Webster's reply to Calhoun's resolutions, taken from Webster's celebrated Senate speech of February 16, 1833. In these excerpts, Webster rebuts Calhoun and makes his case for a national Union of the People:[2]

The first resolution declares that the people of the several States "acceded" to the constitution, or to the constitutional compact, as it is called. This word "accede," not found either in the constitution itself, or in the ratification of it by any one of the States, has been chosen for use here, doubtless, not without a well-considered purpose.

The natural converse of accession is secession; and, therefore, when it is stated that the people of the States acceded to the Union, it may be more plausibly argued that they may secede from it. If, in adopting the constitution, nothing was done but acceding to a compact, nothing would seem necessary, to order break it up, but to secede from the same compact. But the term is wholly out of place. Accession, as a word applied to political associations, implies coming into a league, treaty, or confederacy, by one hitherto a stranger to it; and secession implies departing from such league or confederacy. The people of the United States have used no such form of expression in establishing the present Government. They do not say that they accede to a league, but they declare that they ordain and establish a constitution...

In 1789, and before this constitution was adopted, the United States had already been in a union, more or less close, for fifteen years. At least as far back as the meeting of the first Congress, in 1774, they had been, in some measure, and to some national purposes, united together. Before the confederation of 1781, they had declared independence jointly, and had carried on the war jointly, both by sea and land; and this, not as separate States, but as one people. When, therefore, they formed that confederation, and adopted its articles of perpetual union, they did not come together for the first time; and, therefore, they did not speak of the States as acceding to the confederation, although it was a league, and nothing but a league, and rested on nothing but plighted faith for its performance. Yet, even then, the States were not strangers to each other; there was a bond of union already existing between them; they were associated, united States; and the object of the confederation was to make a stronger and better bond of union. Their representatives deliberated together on these proposed articles of confederation; and, being authorized by their respective States, finally "ratified and confirmed them." Inasmuch as they were already in union, they did not speak of acceding to the new articles of confederation, but of ratifying and confirming them; and this language was not used inadvertently, because, in the same instrument, accession is used in its proper sense, when applied to Canada, which was altogether a stranger to the existing Union. "Canada," says the 11th article, "on acceding to this confederation, and joining in the measures of the United States, shall be admitted into the Union."

Having thus used the terms, *ratify* and *confirm*, even in regard to the old confederation, it would have been strange, indeed, if the people of the United States, after its formation, and when they came to establish the present constitution, had spoken of the States, or of the people of the States, as acceding to this constitution. Such language would have been ill-suited to the occasion. It would have implied an existing separation or disunion among the States, such as never existed since 1774. No such language, therefore, was used. The language actually employed is "adopt," "ratify," "ordain," "establish."

Therefore, sir, any State, before she can prove her right to dissolve the Union, must show her authority to undo what has been done, no State is at liberty to secede on the ground that she and the other States have done nothing but accede. She must show that she has a right to reverse what has been ordained, to unsettle and overthrow what has been established, to reject what the people have adopted, and to break up what they have ratified; because these are the terms which express the transactions which have actually taken place. In other words, she must show her right to make a revolution.

If, Mr. President, in drawing these resolutions, the honorable member had confined himself to the use of constitutional language, there would have been a wide and awful hiatus between his premises and his conclusions. Leaving out the two words "compact" and "accession," which are not constitutional modes of expression, and stating the matter precisely as the truth is, this first resolution would have affirmed that the people of the several States ratified this constitution, or form of government...

What the constitution says of itself, therefore, is as conclusive as what it says on any other point. Does it call itself a compact? Certainly not. It uses the word "compact" but once, and that is when it declares that the States shall enter into no Compact. Does it call itself a league, a confederacy, a subsisting Treaty between the States? Certainly not. There is not a particle of such language in all its pages. But it declares itself a constitution. What is a constitution? Certainly not a league, compact, or confederacy, but a fundamental law...

This then, sir, is declared to be a constitution. A constitution is the fundamental law of the State; and this is expressly declared to be the supreme law. It is as if the people had said. "we prescribe this fundamental law," or "this supreme law;" for they do say that they establish this constitution, and that it shall be the supreme law. They say that they ordain and establish it. Now, sir, what is the common application of these words? We do not speak of ordaining leagues and compacts. If this was intended to be a compact or league, and the States to be parties to it, why was it not so said? Why is there found no one expression in the whole instrument indicating such intent? The old confederation was expressly called a league; and into this league it was declared that the States, as States, severally entered. Why was not similar language used in the constitution, if a similar intention had existed? Why was it not said, "the States enter into this new League," "the States form this new confederation," or "the States agree to this new compact?" Or, why was it not said, in the language of the gentleman's resolution, that the people of the several States acceded to this compact in their sovereign capacities? What reason is there for supposing that the framers of the constitution rejected expressions appropriate to their own meaning, and adopted others wholly at war with that meaning?

Again, sir, the constitution speaks of that political system which is established as "the Government of the United States." Is it not doing strange violence to language to call a league or a compact between sovereign Powers a Government?...

The Constitution of the United States creates direct relations between this Government and individuals. This Government may punish individuals for treason, and all other crimes in the code, when committed against the United States. It has power, also, to tax individuals, in any mode, and to any extent; and it possesses the further power of demanding from individuals military service. Nothing certainly, can more clearly distinguish a Government from a confederation of States, than the possession of these powers...

There is no language in the whole Constitution applicable to a confederation of States. If the States be parties, as States; what are their rights, and what [are] their respective covenants and stipulations? And where are their rights, covenants, and stipulations expressed? The States engage for nothing, they promise nothing. In the articles of confederation, they did make promises, and did enter into engagements, and did plight the faith of each State for their fulfillment; but in the constitution there is nothing of that kind. The reason is, that, in the Constitution, it is the people who speak, and not the States. The people ordain the constitution, and therein address themselves to the States, and to the Legislatures of the States, in the language of injunction and prohibition...

They were asked to continue the existing compact between States; they rejected it. They rejected compact, league, and confederation, and set themselves about framing the constitution of a National Government; and they accomplished what they undertook...

Every where, the people were told that the old confederation was to be abandoned, and a new system to be tried; that a proper Government was proposed, to be founded in the name of the people, and to have a regular organization of its own. Every where, the people were told that it was to be a Government with direct powers to make laws over individuals, and to lay taxes and imposts without the consent of the States...

Such is the language, sir, addressed to the people, while they yet had the constitution under consideration. The powers conferred upon the new Government were perfectly well understood to be conferred, not by any State, or the people of any State, but by the people of the United States. Virginia is more explicit, perhaps, in this particular than any other State. Her Convention assembled to ratify the Constitution, "in the name and behalf of the people of Virginia, declare and make known, that the powers granted under the constitution, being derived from the people of the United States, may be resumed by them whenever the same shall be perverted to their injury or oppression."

Is this language which describes the formation of a compact between States, or language describing the grant of powers to a new Government, by the whole people of the United States? ...

Finally, sir, how can any man get over the words of the constitution itself? "We, the people of the United States, do ordain and establish this constitution." These words must cease to be a part of the constitution, they must be obliterated from the parchment on which they are written, before any human ingenuity or human argument can remove the popular basis on which that constitution rests, and turn the instrument into a mere compact between sovereign States.

Appendix E:

Abraham Lincoln on the Union and Secession

The following remarks are from Abraham Lincoln's first inaugural address and his speech to Congress in special session on July 4, 1861:

From Lincoln's first inaugural, March 4, 1861:

> It is seventy-two years since the first inauguration of a President under our national Constitution. During that period fifteen different and greatly distinguished citizens, have, in succession, administered the executive branch of the government. They have conducted it through many perils; and, generally, with great success. Yet, with all this scope for precedent, I now enter upon the same task for the brief constitutional term of four years, under great and peculiar difficulty. A disruption of the Federal Union heretofore only menaced, is now formidably attempted.

> I hold, that in contemplation of universal law, and of the Constitution, the Union of these States is perpetual. Perpetuity is implied, if not expressed, in the fundamental law of all national governments. It is safe to assert that no government proper, ever had a provision in its organic law for its own termination. Continue to execute all the express provisions of our national Constitution, and the Union will endure forever — it being impossible to destroy it, except by some action not provided for in the instrument itself.

> Again, if the United States be not a government proper, but an association of States in the nature of contract merely, can it, as a contract, be peaceably unmade, by less than all the parties who made it? One party to a contract may violate it — break it, so to speak; but does it not require all to lawfully rescind it?

> Descending from these general principles, we find the proposition that, in legal contemplation, the Union is perpetual, confirmed by

the history of the Union itself. The Union is much older than the Constitution. It was formed in fact, by the Articles of Association in 1774. It was matured and continued by the Declaration of Independence in 1776. It was further matured and the faith of the then thirteen States expressly plighted and engaged that it should be perpetual, by the Articles of Confederation in 1778. And finally, in 1787, one of the declared objects for ordaining and establishing the Constitution, was *"to form a more perfect union."*

But if destruction of the Union, by one, or by a part only, of the States, be lawfully possible, the Union is *less* perfect than before the Constitution, having lost the vital element of perpetuity.

It follows from these views that no State, upon its own mere motion, can lawfully get out of the Union, — that *resolves* and *ordinances* to that effect are legally void; and that acts of violence, within any State or States, against the authority of the United States, are insurrectionary or revolutionary, according to circumstances.

I therefore consider that, in view of the Constitution and the laws, the Union is unbroken; and, to the extent of my ability, I shall take care, as the Constitution itself expressly enjoins upon me, that the laws of the Union be faithfully executed in all the States. Doing this I deem to be only a simple duty on my part; and I shall perform it, so far as practicable, unless my rightful masters, the American people, shall withhold the requisite means, or, in some authoritative manner, direct the contrary. I trust this will not be regarded as a menace, but only as the declared purpose of the Union that it *will* constitutionally defend, and maintain itself.

In doing this there needs to be no bloodshed or violence; and there shall be none, unless it be forced upon the national authority. The power confided in me, will be used to hold, occupy, and possess the property, and places belonging to the government, and to collect the duties and imposts; but beyond what may be necessary for these objects, there will be no invasion—no using of force against, or among the people anywhere...

From questions of this class spring all our constitutional controversies, and we divide upon them into majorities and minorities. If the minority will not acquiesce, the majority must, or the government must cease. There is no other alternative; for continuing the government, is acquiescence on one side or the other. If a minority, in such case, will secede rather than acquiesce, they make a precedent which, in turn, will divide and ruin them; for a minority of their own will secede from them, whenever a majority refuses to be controlled by such minority. For instance, why may not any portion of a new confederacy, a year or two hence, arbitrarily secede again, precisely as portions of the present Union claim to secede from it. All who cherish disunion sentiments, are now being educated to the exact temper of doing this. Is there such perfect identity of interests among the States to compose a new Union, as to produce harmony only, and prevent renewed secession?

Plainly, the central idea of secession, is the essence of anarchy. A majority, held in restraint by constitutional checks, and limitations, and always changing easily, with deliberate changes of popular opinions and sentiments, is the only true sovereign of a free people. Whoever rejects it, does, of necessity, fly to anarchy or to despotism. Unanimity is impossible; the rule of a minority, as a permanent arrangement, is wholly inadmissible; so that, rejecting the majority principle, anarchy, or despotism in some form, is all that is left...

Physically speaking, we cannot separate. We cannot remove our respective sections from each other, nor build an impassable wall between them. A husband and wife may be divorced, and go out of the presence, and beyond the reach of each other; but the different parts of our country cannot do this. They cannot but remain face to face; and intercourse, either amicable or hostile, must continue between them. Is it possible then to make that intercourse more advantageous, or more satisfactory, *after* separation than *before*? Can aliens make treaties easier than friends can make laws? Can treaties be more faithfully enforced between aliens, than laws can among friends?...

This country, with its institutions, belongs to the people who inhabit it. Whenever they shall grow weary of the existing government, they can exercise their *constitutional* right of amending it, or their *revolutionary* right to dismember, or overthrow it. I can not be ignorant of the fact that many worthy, and patriotic citizens are desirous of having the national constitution amended. While I make no recommendation of amendments, I fully recognize the rightful authority of the people over the whole subject, to be exercised in either of the modes prescribed in the instrument itself; and I should, under existing circumstances, favor, rather than oppose, a fair opportunity being afforded the people to act upon it...

The Chief Magistrate derives all his authority from the people, and they have conferred none upon him to fix terms for the separation of the States. The people themselves can do this also if they choose; but the executive, as such, has nothing to do with it. His duty is to administer the present government, as it came to his hands, and to transmit it, unimpaired by him, to his successor...

Excerpts from Lincoln's speech to Congress in special session, July 4, 1861: [1]

Our adversaries have adopted some declarations of independence, in which, unlike the good old one, penned by Jefferson, they omit the words "all men are created equal." Why? They have adopted a temporary national constitution, in the preamble of which, unlike our good old one, signed by Washington, they omit "We, the People," and substitute "We, the deputies of the sovereign and independent States." Why? Why this deliberate pressing out of view the rights of men and the authority of the people?

And this issue embraces more than the fate of these United States. It presents to the whole family of man the question, whether a constitutional republic, or a democracy – a Government of the people by the same people – can or cannot maintain its territorial integrity against its own domestic foes. It presents the question, whether discontented individuals, too few in numbers to control administration, according to organic law, in any case, can always, upon the pretenses made in this case, or on any other pretenses, or arbitrarily, without any pretense, break up their Government, and thus practically put an end to free government upon the earth. It forces us to ask: "Is there, in all republics, this inherent and fatal weakness?" "Must a Government, of necessity, be too *strong* for the liberties of its people, or too *weak* to maintain its own existence?"

So viewing the issue, no choice was left but to call out the war power of the government, and so to resist force employed for its destruction by force for its preservation...

They [the Confederates] invented an ingenious sophism which, if conceded, was followed by perfectly logical steps, through all the incidents, to the complete destruction of the Union. The sophism itself is, that any State of the Union may, consistently with the National Constitution, and therefore *lawfully* and *peacefully*, withdraw from the Union without the consent of the Union or of any other State. The little disguise that the supposed right is to be exercised only for just cause, themselves to be the sole judge of its justice, is too thin to merit any notice...

The sophism itself [the basis upon which the Southern states seceded] derives much, perhaps the whole, of its currency from the assumption that there is some omnipotent and sacred supremacy pertaining to a State—to each State of our Federal Union. Our States have neither more nor less power than that reserved to them in the Union by the Constitution—no one of them ever having been a State out of the Union. The original ones passed into the Union even before they cast off their British colonial dependence; and the new ones each came into the Union directly for a condition of dependence, excepting Texas. And even Texas, in its temporary independence, was never designated a State. The new ones only took the designation of States on coming into the Union, while that name was first adopted for the old ones in and by the Declaration of Independence. Therein the "United Colonies" were declared to be "free and independent States;" but, even then, the object plainly was not to declare their independence from of one another, or of the Union, but directly the contrary, as their mutual pledge, and their mutual action, before, at the time, and afterwards, abundantly show. The express plighting of faith by each and all of the original thirteen in the Articles of Confederation, two years later, that the Union shall be perpetual, is most conclusive. Having never been States, either in substance or in name, outside of the Union, whence this magical omnipotence of "State rights," asserting a claim of power to lawfully destroy the Union itself?

Much is said about the "sovereignty" of the States; but the word, even, is not in the national Constitution; nor, as is believed, in any of the State constitutions. What is "sovereignty," in the political sense of the term? Would it be far wrong to define it "a political community, without a superior?" Tested by this, no one of our States, except Texas, ever was a sovereignty. And even Texas gave up the character on coming into the Union; by which act she acknowledged the Constitution of the United States and the laws and treaties of the United States made in pursuance of the Constitution to be, for her, the supreme law of the land. The States have their status in the Union, and they have no other legal status. If they break from this, they can only do so against law and by revolution. The Union, and not themselves separately, procured their independence and liberty. By conquest, or purchase, the Union gave each of them whatever of independence and liberty it has. The Union is older than any of the States, and in fact, it created them as States. Originally some dependent colonies made the Union, and, in turn, the Union threw off their old dependence for them, and made them States, such as they are. Not one of them ever had a State constitution independent of the Union. Of course, it is not forgotten that all the new States framed their constitutions before they entered the Union; nevertheless, dependent upon, and preparatory to, coming into the Union.

Unquestionably the States have the powers and rights reserved to them in and by the national Constitution; but among these, surely, are not included all conceivable powers, however mischievous or destructive; but, at most, such only as were known in the world, at the time, as governmental powers; and certainly a power to destroy the Government itself had never been known as governmental — as merely an administrative power...

What is now combated, is the position that secession is *consistent* with the Constitution – is *lawful* and *peaceful*. It is not contended that there is any express law for it; and nothing should ever be implied as law which leads to unjust or absurd consequences.

If all the States, save one, should assert the power to drive that one out of the Union, it is presumed the whole class of seceder politicians would at once deny the power, and denounce the act as the greatest outrage upon State rights. But suppose that precisely the same act, instead of being called "driving the one out" should be called "the seceding of the others from that one:" it would be exactly what the seceders claim to do; unless, indeed, they make the point that the one, because it is a minority, may rightfully do what the others, because they are a majority, may not rightfully do. These politicians are subtle and profound on the rights of minorities. They are not partial to that power which made the Constitution, and speaks from the preamble, calling itself "We, the People."

The nation purchased with money the countries out of which several of these States were formed: is it just that they shall go off without leave and without refunding? The nation paid very large sums (in the aggregate, I believe, nearly a hundred millions) to relieve Florida of its aboriginal tribes: is it just that she shall now be off without consent, or without making any return? The nation is now in debt for money applied to the benefit of these so-called seceding States in common with the rest: is it just that either the creditors shall go unpaid, or the remaining States pay the whole? A part of the present national debt was contracted to pay the old debts of Texas: is it just that she shall leave and pay no part of this herself?

Again: if one State may secede, so may another; and when all shall have seceded, none is left to pay the debts. Is this quite just to the creditors? Did we notify them of this sage view of ours when we borrowed their money? If we now recognize this doctrine by allowing the seceders to go in peace, it is difficult to see what we can do if others choose to go, or to extort terms upon which they will promise to remain.

Appendix F:

The Emancipation Proclamation

By the President of the United States of America:

A Proclamation.

Whereas, on the twenty-second day of September, in the year of our Lord one thousand eight hundred and sixty-two, a proclamation was issued by the President of the United States, containing, among other things, the following, to wit:

"That on the first day of January, in the year of our Lord one thousand eight hundred and sixty-three, all persons held as slaves within any State or designated part of a State, the people whereof shall then be in rebellion against the United States, shall be then, thenceforward, and forever free; and the Executive Government of the United States, including the military and naval authority thereof, will recognize and maintain the freedom of such persons, and will do no act or acts to repress such persons, or any of them, in any efforts they may make for their actual freedom.

"That the Executive will, on the first day of January aforesaid, by proclamation, designate the States and parts of States, if any, in which the people thereof, respectively, shall then be in rebellion against the United States; and the fact that any State, or the people thereof, shall on that day be, in good faith, represented in the Congress of the United States by members chosen thereto at elections wherein a majority of the qualified voters of such State shall have participated, shall, in the absence of strong countervailing testimony, be deemed conclusive evidence that such State, and the people thereof, are not then in rebellion against the United States."

Now, therefore I, Abraham Lincoln, President of the United States, by virtue of the power in me vested as Commander-in-Chief, of the

Army and Navy of the United States in time of actual armed rebellion against the authority and government of the United States, and as a fit and necessary war measure for suppressing said rebellion, do, on this first day of January, in the year of our Lord one thousand eight hundred and sixty-three, and in accordance with my purpose so to do publicly proclaimed for the full period of one hundred days, from the day first above mentioned, order and designate as the States and parts of States wherein the people thereof respectively, are this day in rebellion against the United States, the following, to wit:

Arkansas, Texas, Louisiana, (except the Parishes of St. Bernard, Plaquemines, Jefferson, St. John, St. Charles, St. James Ascension, Assumption, Terrebonne, Lafourche, St. Mary, St. Martin, and Orleans, including the City of New Orleans) Mississippi, Alabama, Florida, Georgia, South Carolina, North Carolina, and Virginia, (except the forty-eight counties designated as West Virginia, and also the counties of Berkley, Accomac, Northampton, Elizabeth City, York, Princess Ann, and Norfolk, including the cities of Norfolk and Portsmouth), and which excepted parts, are for the present, left precisely as if this proclamation were not issued.

And by virtue of the power, and for the purpose aforesaid, I do order and declare that all persons held as slaves within said designated States, and parts of States, are, and henceforward shall be free; and that the Executive government of the United States, including the military and naval authorities thereof, will recognize and maintain the freedom of said persons.

And I hereby enjoin upon the people so declared to be free to abstain from all violence, unless in necessary self-defence; and I recommend to them that, in all cases when allowed, they labor faithfully for reasonable wages.

And I further declare and make known, that such persons of suitable condition, will be received into the armed service of the United States to garrison forts, positions, stations, and other places, and to man vessels of all sorts in said service.

And upon this act, sincerely believed to be an act of justice, warranted by the Constitution, upon military necessity, I invoke the considerate judgment of mankind, and the gracious favor of Almighty God.

In witness whereof, I have hereunto set my hand and caused the seal of the United States to be affixed.

Done at the City of Washington, this first day of January, in the year of our Lord one thousand eight hundred and sixty three, and of the Independence of the United States of America the eighty-seventh.

By the President: ABRAHAM LINCOLN

WILLIAM H. SEWARD, Secretary of State.

Notes

Introduction

1. Jennifer Barrett: "Calling Abe Lincoln," MSNBC.com., May 27, 2004. This quote was taken from Ms. Barrett's exclusive online interview for Newsweek:
   <http://www.msnbc.com/id/5078510/site/newsweek/>

2. Joseph Curl, "Blue States Buzz over Secession," The Washington Times, November 9, 2004:
   <http://www.washingtontimes.com/national/20041109-122753-5113r.htm>

3. Rene G., "Why Prolong This Marriage: The Case for Blue State Secession," Information Clearing House, November 9, 2004:
   <http://www.informationclearinghouse.info/article7255.htm>

4. Betsy Leondar-Wright, "It's not us, it's you," The Casper Star-Tribune, November 9, 2004:
   <http://www.casperstartribune.net/articles/2004/11/09/editorial/letters/8a97f5294cac838187256f4500267b3a.txt.>

Part One:
The Compact Theory Versus the Nationalist Theory of the Union

Position One:
The Union is older than the States

1. Albert Taylor Bledsoe, *Is Davis a Traitor?* (1866, Dehlonega, GA: Crown Rights Book Company, 2001), pp. 109-110.

2. Excerpted from Jefferson's "Autobiography;" Merrill D. Peterson, ed., *Jefferson: Writings* (New York: Literary Classics of the United States, Inc., 1984), pp. 13-14.

3. Ibid, p 16.

4. Stuart Jerry Brown, *Thomas Jefferson* (New York: Washington Square Press, Inc., 1963), pp. 19-20.

5. David McCullogh, *John Adams* (New York: Simon and Schuster, 2001), p. 147.

6. Elliott's Debates, Vol. 5, pp. 219-220.

7. Peterson, ed., *Jefferson: Writings*, pp. 28-29.

8. McCullough, *John Adams*, p. 146.

9. Peterson, ed., *Jefferson: Writings*, p. 15.

10. Ibid, p. 1492.

11. From "Political Rights and Sovereignty," Elliott's Debates, Vol. I, p. 65.

12. Ibid.

13. Elliott's Debates, Vol. 5, pp.217-218.

14. Peterson, ed., *Jefferson: Writings*, p. 32.

Position Two:
Americans are One People

1. Bledsoe, *Is Davis a Traitor?* p. 108.

2. Ibid, p. 109.

3. Alexander H. Stephens, *A Constitutional View of the Late War Between the States* (1868, Harrisonburg, VA: Sprinkle Publications, 1994) I, p. 156.

4. Ibid.

5. Ibid.

6. From the Annals of Congress, 1st Congress, Senate, 2nd Session, p. 969.

7. Ibid, p. 971.

8. Ibid, p. 1017.

9. Bledsoe, *Is Davis a Traitor?* p. 14.

10. Elliott's Debates, 5, p. 158.

11. Bledsoe, *Is Davis a Traitor?* p. 13.

12. Ibid.

13. Ibid.

14. Ibid, p. 14.

15. Ibid, p. 34.

16. Jack N. Rakove, ed., *Madison: Writings* (New York: Literary Classics of the United States, Inc., 1999), p. 408.

17. Ibid, p. 440.

18. Ibid, p. 37.

19. Ibid, p. 48.

20. Ibid, pp. 69, 72.

21. Ibid, p. 137.

22. Elliott's Debates, I, p. 96.

23. Rakove, ed. *Madison: Writings*, p. 218.

24. Ibid, p. 219.

25. Peterson, ed., *Jefferson: Writings*, pp. 48, 75.

26. Ibid, p. 806.

27. Bernard Bailyn, ed., *The Debate on the Constitution*, (New York: Literary Classics of the United States, Inc., 1993), I, p. 21.

28. Ibid, p. 45.

29. Bailyn, ed., *Debate on the Constitution*, 2, p. 596.

30. Elliott's Debates, 5, p. 158.

31. Elliott's Debates, 5, p. 151.

32. Ibid, p. 214.

33. Ibid, p. 176.

34. Ibid, p. 199.

35. Ibid, p. 207.

36. Bailyn, ed., *Debate on the Constitution*, 2, pp. 596-597.

37. Ibid, p. 619.

38. Speech of Madison before the Virginia ratifying convention on June 6, 1788, as found in Rakove, ed. *Madison: Writings*, p. 362.

39. Bailyn, ed., *Debate on the Constitution*, 2, p. 641.

40. Elliott's Debates, 5, p. 140.

41. Rakove, ed. *Madison: Writings*, p. 143.

42. Ibid, pp. 311-312.

43. Ibid, p. 592.

44. Ibid, pp. 589-590.

45. Ibid, pp. 609, 611.

46. Peterson, ed., *Jefferson: Writings*, p. 449.

47. Ibid, pp. 482, 484-485.

48. Elliott's Debates, 2, p. 215.

49. Ibid, p. 267.

50. Bailyn, ed., *Debate on the Constitution*, I, pp. 789-799.

51. Bailyn, ed., *Debate on the Constitution*, 2, p. 845.

52. Bailyn, ed., *Debate on the Constitution*, I, p. 943.

53. Elliott's Debates, I, p. 224.

54. Ibid, 5, p. 157.

55. From *Life and Writings of Gouverneur Morris*, 3, p. 323, as cited in Bledsoe, *Is Davis a Traitor?* pp. 64-65.

56. Ibid, I, p. 318.

57. Ibid, 5, pp. 212-213.

58. From Thomas Jefferson's notes on the debates over the Articles of Confederation, Elliott's Debates, I, p. 77.

One Last Note About Daniel Webster

1. *Bank of Augusta v. Earle*, 38 U.S. 519 (1839)
   <http://laws.findlaw.com/us/38/519.html>

2. Ibid.

3. Stephens, *Constitutional View*, I, pp. 404-405.

Part Two:
Lincoln's Case Against Southern Secession

Position Two:
The Union is Perpetual

1. Bailyn, ed., *Debate on the Constitution*, I, pp. 3-4.

2. David Herbert Donald, *Lincoln* (New York: Simon and Schuster, 1995), p. 176

3. From Lincoln's congressional speech on the Mexican War, January 12, 1848, in Roy Basler, ed., *Abraham Lincoln: His Speeches and Writings*, (Cleveland, OH: the World Publishing Company, 1946), p. 209.

4. The Cornhill Magazine, as cited in Charles Adams, *When in the Course of Human Events: Arguing the Case for Southern Secession* (Oxford, England: Rowmand and Littlefield Publishers, Inc., 2000), p. 72.

5. Donald, *Lincoln*, pp. 268-269.

6. From "Five Men at Random," Prejudices: Third Series, 1922, pp. 175-176.

7. Basler, ed., *Abraham Lincoln: His Speeches and Writings*, p. 766.

8. Peterson, ed., *Jefferson: Writings*, pp. 1493-1494.

Position Three:
States would require permission to leave the Union

1. Elliott's Debates, 5, p. 532.

2. Ibid, p. 207.

Position Four:
There is no such thing as 'State Sovereignty'

1. Stephens, *Constitutional View*, 2, p. 22.

2. Ibid, pp. 23-24.

Position Five:
Southerners were guilty of Rebellion and Treason

1. Elliott's Debates, 5, p. 140.

2. Ibid, 2, pp. 232-233.

3. Ibid, pp. 116-117.

4. Bailyn, ed., *Debate on the Constitution*, I, p. 884.

5. From a letter by Edmund Randolph, dated October 10, 1787, in which he outlines his objections to the Constitution. Found in Ibid, p. 599.

Position Six:
The Southern States might have formed non-Republican Governments

1. Basler, ed., *Abraham Lincoln: His Speeches and Writings*, p. 599.

Position Seven:
The Southern States would have defaulted on the Debts and Obligations of the Union

1. James D. Richardson, ed., *A Compilation of the Messages and Papers of the Confederacy* (United States Publishing Company, Nashville, 1905), p. 55.

2. Jefferson Davis *The Rise and Fall of the Confederate Government* (1881, New York: Da Capo Press, Inc., 1990), I, p. 583.

Position Nine:
The South started It

1. Official Records of the War of the Rebellion, Vol. I, Series 1, Pt 1, p. 75.

2. Ibid, pp. 82-83.

3. Ibid, p. 90

4. Ibid, p. 103

5. Ibid, p. 102

6. Ibid, p. 106

7. Ibid, p. 113

8. Ibid, p. 2

9. Ibid, p. 118

10. Ibid, pp. 131-132

11. Webb Garrison, *Lincoln's Little War* (Nashville, TN: Rutledge Hill Press, 1997), p. 62.

12. Official Records, Vol. I, Series 1, Pt 1, p. 134

13. Ibid, pp. 135-136

14. Ibid, p. 140

15. Ibid, p. 191

16. Ibid

17. Ibid, p. 196

18. Ibid, p. 197

19. Ibid, p. 200

20. Donald, *Lincoln*, pp. 286-287.

21. Richard N. Current, *Lincoln and the First Shot* (New York: J.B. Lippincott Company, 1963), p. 67.

22. W.A. Swanberg, *First Blood: the Story of Fort Sumter* (Charles Scribner's Sons, New York: N.Y, 1957), p. 250.

23. Current, *Lincoln and the First Shot*, p. 74.

24. Swanberg, *First Blood*, p. 261.

25. Garrison, *Lincoln's Little War*, p. 62.

26. Davis, *Rise and Fall of the Confederate Government*, I, p. 220.

27. George Winston Smith and Charles Judah, *Life in the North During the Civil War: A Source History* (The University of New Mexico Press, 1966), p. 6.

28. James McPherson, *Battle Cry of Freedom: The Civil War Era* (Oxford University Press, New York, 1988), p. 197.

29. Smith and Judah, *Life in the North During the Civil War*, p. 9.

30. Current, *Lincoln and the First Shot*, pp. 80-81.

31. Allan Nevins, *War for the Union* (New York: Kronecky & Kronecky, 1960), I, p. 55.

32. Official Records, Vol I, Sec I, Pt I, p. 294.

33. Davis, *Rise and Fall of the Confederate Government*, I, pp. 252, 254.

34. Official Records, Vol I, Series I, Pt I, p. 583.

35. Ibid, p. 232.

36. Ibid, p. 233.

37. Official Records, Vol I, Series I, Pt I, p. 263.

38. Swanberg, *First Blood*, p. 271.

39. Shelby Foote, *The Civil War: A Narrative, From Sumter to Perryville* (New York, Random House, 1958), p. 46.

40. Current, *Lincoln and the First Shot*, p.125.

41. Davis, *Rise and Fall of the Confederate Government*, I, 584-585.

42. Official Records, Vol I, Series I, Pt I, p. 294.

43. Davis, *Rise and Fall of the Confederate Government*, I, pp. 587-588.

44. Garrison, *Lincoln's Little War*, p. 58.

45. Davis, *Rise and Fall of the Confederate Government*, I, pp. 590-591.

46. Ibid, p. 237.

47. Ibid

48. Stephen Oats, *Abraham Lincoln: The Man Behind the Myths* (New York: Harper Collins Publishers, Inc. 1984), p.

49. Donald, *Lincoln*, p. 293.

50. Ibid.

51. Ibid.

52. Foote, *The Civil War: A Narrative, From Sumter to Perryville*, p. 44.

53. McPherson, *Battle Cry*, p. 215.

54. Hudson Strode, *Jefferson Davis: Confederate President* (Harcourt, Brace and Co., New York: NY, 1959), p. 39.

55. William and Bruce Catton, *Two Roads to Sumter: Abe Lincoln, Jeff Davis and the March to Civil War* (reprint, Phoenix Press, London, 1988), p. 278.

56. Donald, *Lincoln*, pp. 293-294.

57. Robert W. Johannsen, *Stephen A. Douglas* (New York: Oxford University Press, 1973), p. 835.

58. Donald, *Lincoln*, p. 268.

59. Avery Craven, *The Coming of the Civil War* (the University of Chicago Press, 1942), p. 432.

60. Michael Burnlingame, ed., *Lincoln Observed: Civil War Dispatches of Noah Brooks* (Baltimore, MD: The John Hopkins University Press, 1998), p. 178.

61. Nevins, *War for the Union*, I, p. 49.

62. Garrison, *Lincoln's Little War*, p. 83.

63. Davis, *Rise and Fall of the Confederate Government*, I, p. 247.

64. Donald, *Lincoln*, p. 238.

65. Stephens, *A Constitutional View of the Late War Between the States*, II, pp. 35-36.

Part Three:
The Modern Case Against Secession

Position One:
Secession is un-American

1. Charles Bracelen Flood, *Lee: The Last Years* (New York: Houghton-Mifflin Company, 1981), p. 202. *Note...Mrs. Lee's belongings were eventually returned to the family in 1903 by President William McKinley. Robert E. Lee Jr. noted this in his book, *The Recollections and Letters of Robert E. Lee*, (Smithmark, 1995 ed.), p. 338.

2. Hans L. Trefousse, *Thaddeus Stevens, Nineteenth Century Egalitarian* (Raleigh: The University of North Carolina Press, 1997), pp. 112, 125.

3. Charles Royster, ed., *Sherman: Memoirs,* (New York: Literary Classics of the United States, Inc., 1990), p. 705.

4. Ibid, pp. 363-367.

5. Burlingame, *Lincoln Observed,* p. 585.

6. Lee Kennett, *Marching Through Georgia* (New York: Harper Collins Publishers, Inc., 1995), pp. 236, 238.

7. Burke Davis, *Sherman's March* (New York: Random House, Inc., 1980), p. 152.

8. Henry Hitchcock, *Marching with Sherman: Passages from the Letters and Campaign Diaries of Henry Hitchcock, Major and Assistant Adjutant General of Volunteers, November 1864-May 1865,* ed. M. A. Dewolfe Howe (Lincoln, NE: University of Nebraska Press, 1995) p. 77, Questia, 29 Mar. 2006
    <http://www.questia.com/PM.qst?a=o&d=1152423>

9. Davis, *Sherman's March,* p. 37.

10. Royster, ed., *Sherman: Memoirs,* p. 719.

11. Hitchcock, *Marching with Sherman,* p. 125.

12. Davis, *Sherman's March,* p. 41.

13. Royster, ed., *Sherman: Memoirs,* p. 700.

14. Ibid. p. 690.

15. Sherman proudly displayed this letter of commendation in Ibid, p. 707.

16. Official Records, Vol I, Series 43, Pt 2, p. 202.

17. Official Records, Vol I, Series 40, Pt 3, p. 223.

18. Stephen V. Ash, *When the Yankees Came: Conflict and Chaos in the Occupied South, 1861-1865.* (Chapel Hill, NC: The University of North Carolina Press, 1995), p. 58.

19. Raphael Semmes, *Memoirs of Service Afloat During the War Between the States* (1868, Baton Rouge: Louisiana State University Press, 1996), p. 614.

20. Royster, ed., *Sherman: Memoirs,* pp. 363-367.

21. Burlingame, *Lincoln Observed,* pp. 367-368.

22. Oats, *Lincoln, The Man Behind the Myths*, pp. 135-136.

23. Don Feder, "NATO would have favored Confederacy," The Boston Herald, April 19, 1999.
<http://www.bostonherald.com/bostonherald/colm/feder04191999.htm>

24. Oats, *Lincoln, The Man Behind the Myths*, pp. 92-93.

25. Ibid, p. 17.

26. General Order No. 73 was found in William J. Jones, *Personal Reminiscences of General Robert E. Lee* (reprint, Richmond, VA: United States Historical Society Press, 1989), p. 188.

Position Two:

The Constitution and the Laws were suspended under Lincoln

1. From Lincoln's "Lyceum Address," January 27, 1838, in Basler, ed., *Abraham Lincoln: His Speeches and Writings*, pp. 80-81.

2. Annals of Congress, 2nd Congress, 1st Session.

3. Daniel Webster, quoted in Stephens, *Constitutional View*, II, pp. 405-406.

4. Congressional Globe, 37th Congress, 4th (special) Session, p. 1458.

5. Senate Journals, 37th Congress, Special Session, March 26, 1861, pp. 428-429.

6. Congressional Globe, 37th Congress, 2nd Session, p. 1458.

7. Richard N. Current, *Old Thad Stevens: A Story of Ambition* (Madison, WI: The University of Wisconsin Press, 1943), pp. 146-147.

8. Basler, ed., *Abraham Lincoln: His Speeches and Writings*. p. 600.

9. Michael Burnlingame, ed., *Lincoln Observed*, p. 209.

10. Congressional Globe, 37th Congress, 2nd Session, p. 1458.

11. Basler, ed., *Abraham Lincoln: His Speeches and Writings*. p. 600-601.

12. Ex Parte Merryman

13. Ibid.

14. Ibid.

15. Ibid.

16. Jeffrey Rogers Hummel, *Emancipating Slaves, Enslaving Free Men: A History of the American Civil War* (Chicago: Open Court Publishing Company, 1996), p. 142; also see Adams, *When in the Course of Human Events*, p. 46.

17. Adams, *When in the Course of Human Events*, p. 44.

18. Quoted in Nevins, *War for the Union*, 4, p. 130.

19. Stephens, *Constitutional View*, 2, p. 409.

20. Simon Cameron is quoted in Ibid, p. 413.

21. Hummel, *Emancipating Slaves, Enslaving Free Men*, pp. 142-143.

22. Ibid, p. 146.

23. Allan Nevins, *War for the Union* (New York: Kronecky & Kronecky, 1960), I, p. 129.

24. Burnlingame, ed., *Lincoln Observed*, 131.

25. Oats, *Lincoln, The Man Behind the Myths*, p. 125.

26. Hummel, *Emancipating Slaves, Enslaving Free Men*, pp. 349, 359

27. Frederic Bastiat, *The Law* (1850, New York: The Foundation for Economic Education, Inc., 1990), p. 24.

28. Chief Justice Rehnquist made these remarks at the 100th anniversary celebration of the Norfolk and Portsmouth Bar Association on May 3, 2001. These excerpts from his speech were taken from the full transcript on the United States Supreme Court's website: <http://www.supremecourtus.gov/publicinfo/speeches/sp_05-03-00.html>

29. Tom Curry, "For his foes, Ashcroft became symbol of lost liberties," MSNBC.com, November 9, 2004: <http://www.msnbc.msn.com/id/6447305/>

30. Ibid.

31. Garrison, *Lincoln's Little War*, p. 136.

32. Basler, ed., *Abraham Lincoln: His Speeches and Writings*. pp. 608-609

Position Three:

Lincoln fought to end Slavery

1. Peterson, ed., *Jefferson: Writings*, p. 1434.

2. Joseph J. Ellis, *Founding Brothers* (New York: Random House, 2000), p. 112.

3. Rakove, ed. *Madison: Writings*, p. 56.

4. James Monroe's letter to Patrick Henry is quoted in Davis, *Rise and Fall of the Confederate Government*, I, p. 60.

5. Ibid, p. 60

6. Ibid.

7. Ibid, p. 63.

8. Rakove, ed., *Madison: Writings*, pp. 771-772.

9. Athearn, *The American Heritage New Illustrated History of the United States*, 5, p. 376.

10. Rakove, ed., *Madison: Writings*, pp. 771.

11. Peterson, ed., *Jefferson: Writings*, p. 1434.

12. Ibid.

13. Ibid, pp. 1448-1449.

14. Athearn, *New Illustrated History of the United States*, 5, p. 400.

15. *Acts and resolutions passed by the Legislature of Massachusetts in the year 1844*, p. 319, as cited by the Honorable Joseph Wheeler (AL) in a speech to Congress, July 31, 1894, and recorded by the Richmond, Virginia *Dispatch*.

16. Summary of Senate vote on extending the Missouri Compromise line to the Pacific as cited in Ibid, I, p. 10.

17. The Congressional Globe, Senate, 31st Congress, 1st Session, March 4, 1850.

18. Ibid, March 7, 1850.

19. Ibid.

20. From an excerpt of Lincoln's letter to Alexander Stephens, as found in the manuscript copy inserted between pages 266 and 267 of Stephens' *Constitutional View*, 2, Sprinkle Publications edition.

21. Adams, *When in the Course of Human Events*, p. 139.

22. Basler, ed., *Abraham Lincoln: His Speeches and Writings*, p. 443.

23. *Lincoln: Selected Speeches and Writings* (New York: First Vintage Books, Library of America edition, 1989), p. 173.

24. Basler, ed., Abraham Lincoln: *His Speeches and Writings*, p. 444-445.

25. Lincoln: *Selected Speeches and Writings*, pp. 178-179.

26. Howard Zinn, *A People's History of the United States, 1492-Present* (New York: Harper-Collins Publishers, Inc., 1995), p. 203.

27. Africans in America, "Judgment Day: 1831-1865," Part I, Antebellum Slavery, "Eric Foner on the Abolitionist Movement," (WGBH Educational Foundation, WGBH Interactive for PBS Online, 1999). <http://www.pbs.org/wgbh/aia/part4/4i2974.html>

28. Africans in America, "Judgment Day: 1831-1865," Part III, Fugitive Slaves and Northern Racism, Modern Voices, "Margaret Washington on Northern Racism," (WGBH Educational Foundation, WGBH Interactive for PBS Online, 1999). <http://www.pbs.org/wgbh/aia/part4/4i2987.html>

29. Oswald Villard, *John Brown: 1800-1859, A Biography Fifty Years Later* (1910, Gloucester, MA: Peter Smith, 1965), p. 476.

30. The Congressional Globe, 31st Congress, 1st Session, March 7, 1850.

31. Davis, *Rise and Fall of the Confederate Government*, I, p. 304.

32. Basler, ed., *Abraham Lincoln: His Speeches and Writings*, p. 612.

33. Ibid, p. 766.

34. There are numerous sources where this famous letter has been published. For one, refer to ibid, p. 652.

35. Oats, *Lincoln, The Man Behind the Myths*, p. 61.

36. Nevins, *War for the Union*, 2, p. 235.

37. Ibid, p. 262.

38. Mary S. and William Drake, McFeely, eds., *Grant: Memoirs and Selected Letters*, (New York: Literary Classics of the United States, Inc., 1990) p. 494.

39. Ibid, p. 748.

40. Royster, ed., *Sherman: Memoirs*, p. 366.

41. Ibid, pp. 600-601.

42. Semmes, *Memoirs of Service Afloat*, p. 20.

43. Jefferson Davis, *Rise and Fall of the Confederate Government*, I, p. 200.

44. J. William Jones, *Personal Reminiscences of General Robert E. Lee* (reprint, Richmond, VA: United States Historical Society Press, 1989), pp. 422-423.

45. Ibid, p. 423.

46. Lee, *Recollections and Letters*, p. 151.

47. Jones, *Personal Reminiscences of General Robert E. Lee*, pp. 213-214.

48. Quoted in Rod Gragg, "The Quotable Robert E. Lee," Southern Partisan, 4th Qtr, 1989, p. 30.

49. Paul Casdorph, *Lee and Jackson* (New York: Bantam Dell Doubleday Publishing Group Inc., 1992), p. 248.

50. Charles P. Roland, *Albert Sydney Johnston, Soldier of Three Republics* (Austin, TX: University of Texas Press, 1964), pp. 275-276.

51. Varina H. Davis, *Jefferson Davis, A Memoir By His Wife* (New York: Belford Company Publishers, 1890), I, p. 167.

52. Jones, *Personal Reminiscences of General Robert E. Lee*, pp. 189-190.

53. From Sherman's record of his correspondence with General Hood following the Atlanta campaign, 1864. Royster, ed., *Sherman: Memoirs*, p. 596.

54. Varina Davis, *Jefferson Davis*, I, p. 216.

55. The responses of the various governors to Lincoln's call for troops as well as the secession ordinances of the last four states to leave the Union are all available in the Official Records of the War of the Rebellion, Series I, Volume I, Part I.

56. James McPherson, from his introduction to Jefferson Davis' *Rise and Fall of the Confederate Government*, Da Capo Press, 1990 edition, p. iv.

57. James McPherson, *What They Fought For, 1861-1865* (Baton Rouge: Louisiana State University Press, 1994), pp. 12, 35.

58. Zinn, *A People's History of the United States*, p. 187.

59. Stephens, *Constitutional View*, 2, pp. 85-86.

Position Four:

The United States & Confederate States could not have peacefully Co-existed

1. Timothy Pickering's letter to George Cabot is quoted in Richard Hoftadter, ed., *Great Issues in American History, Vol I, 1765-1865* (New York, NY: Random House, 1958), p. 224.

Position Five:

The United States is too important in World Affairs to permit Secession

1. Smith and Judah, *Life in the North During the Civil War*, p. 4.

2. Garrison, *Lincoln's Little War*, p. 208.

3. Mark Strauss, "Let's Ditch Dixie: The Case for Northern Secession," Slate.msn.com, March 13, 2001.

Position Six:

The Founders opposed Secession and hoped for Consolidation

1. Rakove, ed. *Madison: Writings*, p. 863.

2. Elliott's Debates, I, p. 306.

3. Peterson, ed., *Jefferson: Writings*, p. 1044.

4. Ibid, p. 883.

5. From a speech by John Quincy Adams, April 30, 1839, at the 50th anniversary celebration of George Washington's inauguration, cited by Joseph Wheeler in the United States House of Representatives, July 13, 1894.

6. Ibid, pp. 449, 454.

7. Peterson, ed., *Jefferson: Writings*, p. 484.

8. Rakove, ed. *Madison: Writings*, p. 860.

9. Ibid, p. 862.

10. Ibid, p. 589.

11. Ibid, p. 363.

12. Ibid, p. 804.

13. Peterson, ed., *Jefferson: Writings*, p. 1472.

Position Seven:
Secession is a Question for the Supreme Court

1. Athearn, *The American Heritage New Illustrated History of the United States*, 5, p. 371.

2. Rakove, ed., *Madison: Writings*, p. 734.

3. Peterson, ed., *Jefferson: Writings*, p. 802.

4. Ibid, p. 1474.

5. Ibid, p. 1476.

6. Al Gore's quote is taken from the transcript of a March 14, 2000 interview with PBS's "NewsHour" host Jim Lehrer: <http://www.pbs.org/newshour/election2000/candidates/gore_3-14c.html>

7. Joel Dyer, *Harvest of Rage: Why Oklahoma City is Only the Beginning*, (Boulder, Colorado: Westview Press, 1997), pp. 159-160.

8. State of Texas v. White, 74 U.S. 700 (1868) <http://caselaw.lp.findlaw.com/scripts/getcase.pl?court=US&vol=74&invol=700>

Part Four:
Lincoln's Legacy and Modern Secession Movements

A Contest Years in the Making

1. Ellis, *Founding Brothers*, p. 16.

2. Stuart Gerry Brown, *Thomas Jefferson*, p. 63.

The Perplexing Lincoln Legacy

1. Cynthia Tucker, "Americans increasingly unwilling to surrender civil liberties," The Baltimore Sun, July 5, 2004.

2. Ibid.

3. The Washington Post online, January 16, 2006. <http://www.washingtonpost.com/wpdyn/content/article/200 6/01/16/AR2006011600779.html>

A Changing Country, a Growing Backlash

1. Jerome D. Tucille, "Dear Liberal Friend," November 17, 2004, Used with Mr. Tucille's permission: <http://www.tuccille.com/scribble/fullauto/auto68.htm>

2. "Court allows 'dirty bomb' suspect to be held," MSNBC.com, September 9, 2005. <http://www.msnbc.msn.com/id/9268598>

3. Patrick J. Buchanan, *The Death of the West* (New York: St. Martin's Press, 2002), pp. 2-3.

4. Congressman Ron Paul's quote was found on the congressman's site: "Ron Paul's Texas Straight Talk": <http://www.house.gov/paul/tst/tst2004/tst090604.htm> Congressman Paul is a noted supporter of strict constitutional interpretation.

5. Dan Popkey, "Chenoweth-Hage right to challenge pat-downs," The Idaho Statesman, October 10, 2004.

6. *Hamdi et al. v. Rumsfeld, Secretary of Defense*, No. 03-6696. Argued April 28, 2004, Decided June 28, 2004. <http://laws.findlaw.com/us/000/03-6696.html>

7. Ibid.

8. Joint Resolution 19, The Congressional Record, 103rd Congress, Senate, Vol. 139.

9. Joel Dyer, *Harvest of Rage*, p. 4.

10. Ibid, p. 7.

Appendix D:
Calhoun Versus Webster

1. The Congressional Register of Debates, Senate, 22nd Congress, 2nd Session, January 22, 1833, pp. 191-192.

2. The Congressional Register of Debates, Senate, 22nd Congress, 2nd Session, February 16, 1833, pp. 553-570.

Appendix E:

Lincoln on the Union and Secession

1.   Basler, ed., *Abraham Lincoln: His Speeches and Writings,* pp. 598-609.